Theory of Value Structure

Theory of Value Structure

From Values to Decisions

Erich H. Rast

LEXINGTON BOOKS

Lanham • Boulder • New York • London

Published by Lexington Books
An imprint of The Rowman & Littlefield Publishing Group, Inc.
4501 Forbes Boulevard, Suite 200, Lanham, Maryland 20706
www.rowman.com

86-90 Paul Street, London EC2A 4NE

British Library Cataloguing in Publication Information Available

Library of Congress Cataloging-in-Publication Data

Names: Rast, Erich H., author.
Title: Theory of value structure : from values to decisions / Erich H. Rast.
Description: Lanham : Lexington Books, [2022] | Includes bibliographical references and index.
Identifiers: LCCN 2021057416 (print) | LCCN 2021057417 (ebook) | ISBN 9781793616944 (cloth) | ISBN 9781793616951 (ebook)
Subjects: LCSH: Values.
Classification: LCC BD232 .R253 2022 (print) | LCC BD232 (ebook) | DDC 170—dc23/eng/202201191
LC record available at https://lccn.loc.gov/2021057416
LC ebook record available at https://lccn.loc.gov/2021057417

Contents

To my parents Herbert and Luise Rast,

who made this book possible.

Preface

The Theory of Value Structure in metaethics is primarily concerned with abstract and structural aspects of values. Although it borrows concepts and some of the technical apparatus from economics and decision-making, this subdiscipline of ethics differs in perspective from the standard modeling in economics. Economists take preferences to represent consumer choices and have also tried to derive preferences from real or hypothetical choices. Preferences in this sense barely play a role in formal axiology. For the axiologist, value comparisons of individual persons may exemplify value structure and intuitions of individual persons may serve to justify more general value judgments, but values are generally considered to transcend an individual's preferences and choices. Talking about preference relations in this area is thus merely a case of using vocabulary established by other disciplines and should not be taken too literally. To give an example, many value pluralists would subscribe to the view that it can be rational for someone to prefer X over Y in a given situation while supporting the more general and impersonal position that Y is better than X. For instance, it is not necessarily irrational for a smoker to believe that it is better not to smoke and nevertheless prefer to have a cigarette right now. Conflicts between personal preferences, which may even be weaker than what ethicists have sometimes called prudential values, and values in general are a special instance of value conflicts, and it is often acknowledged in value theory that conflicts between values can arise and may not always be resolvable. The theory of value structure is broader in scope than the theory of preferences and rational choice. It aims at laying out, in an abstract fashion, the structure behind the value predicates we use to evaluate things and not just the structure of personal preferences.

Despite these differences, much of the formal work in the modeling of preferences and decision-making is highly relevant for the theory of value structure. I decided to write this book when I realized that methods from decision-making and formal approaches to value structure could be useful for more general work in ethics and practical reasoning. At the same time, this book also addresses philosophically interesting aspects of values that are often neglected in the literature on decision-making and in economic models. My hope is that this book contributes to uniting these diverse areas further and may also be helpful for researchers from neighboring disciplines like computer science and linguistics to get an overview of the structural requirements of values. At the same time, the book is also opinionated; I defend a particular theory of "better than" in the second part of it. Since excessive hand-waving must be avoided and the book is supposed to be self-contained, some technical definitions and a certain amount of precision in introducing concepts is unavoidable. Some readers may find parts of the book too formal while others may miss proofs and axiomatizations. To these people I can only say that it is impossible to please everyone. I have done my best to find a balance between readability and precision that is fruitful as a basis for further discussion.

The book is divided into two parts. In the first part, the standard modeling of preferences is applied to values and various nonstandard changes and extensions are discussed. This part provides the basis for being able to address more elaborate questions about value structure. The second part addresses the key philosophical problems of the theory of value structure such as parity and Spectrum arguments, using the instruments and concepts introduced in the first part. It is therefore not advisable to jump directly to the second part. In any case, please bear in mind that expected utility theory cannot be assumed anywhere in this book, as it is considered the outcome of certain philosophical convictions rather than a starting point.

Acknowledgments

This book would not have been possible without the help and support of many people. Work on this book was funded by national funds through the Portuguese Foundation for Science and Technology (FCT) under the personal grant SRFH/BPD/84612/2012, the Norma Transitória grant DL 57/

2016/CP1453/CT0002, and the projects UIDB/00183/2020 and PTDC/MHC-FIL/0521/2014. I am very grateful to FCT for their continued support of my research. I would also like to thank Pedro Abreu, Per Algander, Erik Carlson, Susana Cadilha, Bianca Cepollaro, Sean English, Poppy Mankowitz, Dima Mohammed, Wlodek Rabinowicz, Javier Gonzales de Prado Salas, members of the ArgLab Colloquium, the project "Values in Argumentative Discourse," and the Eplab Reading Group in Ethics and Political Philosophy at the Nova Institute of Philosophy of the Universidade Nova de Lisboa, as well as the members of the Uppsala Higher Seminar in Ethics at Uppsala University for useful comments about various aspects of this book that I have presented in talks over the years. A big thanks also goes to Jana Hodges-Kluck from Lexington for her professional support of this project and to an anonymous reviewer who has made various suggestions for improvement from which this book has benefited. Finally, I would like to thank my parents and my partner for the continuing support they have provided for my intellectual endeavors.

Part I

Preliminaries

Chapter 1

Basic Monist Value Structure

This investigation begins by looking at value comparisons according to one aspect, criterion, or attribute only. As we will see in later chapters, these are mere building blocks and not adequate for representing value comparisons in general. However, they provide a good starting point for discussion and the basis for more complex and adequate value representations.

1.1 Introduction

It is a fact of everyday life that we are not indifferent about things and states of affairs around us. Instead, we regularly monitor and classify our environment based on our personal value systems. Such systems can, of course, be investigated from a variety of perspectives, for example, from the perspective of value psychology, sociology, and normative ethics. This book focuses on the structure of values, sometimes called axiology, and how to represent values formally. Much work in this field has been conducted in economics and decision-making, and to a lesser extent also in mathematical psychology, behavioral economics, and metaethics. This rich tradition creates a certain philosophical tension throughout this book: On the one hand, tools from economics and decision-making are used for modeling value structure. On the other hand, the conceptual underpinnings, the reasons for adopting a specific representation of value structure, may differ vastly from those assumed by economists. Axiologists commonly reject two assumptions that economists often make.

According to the Preference Satisfaction Principle, "[o]ne thing A is better for a person than another thing B if and only if the person prefers A to B" (Broome, 1999, p. 3). However, as Broome puts it, "…the preference-satisfaction theory is obviously false, and no one really believes it." (ibid.: p. 4). Even idealized versions of the principle are highly contentious, and I will not endorse them in what follows. Only if we take the principle as describing a tendency of what humans strive for does it seem plausible. In the absence of akrasia and confusion, when we are not addicted, forced by external circumstances, or otherwise impaired, mentally healthy humans strive to opt for what they think is best for them at a given time.

A related view in economics is known as the Revealed Preference Thesis and ranges back to Pareto's and Samuelson's work.[1] It states that a consumer's preferences may be observed and reconstructed from the consumer's choices. Just like in the case of the preference satisfaction view, there is some grain of truth to this thesis, and Samuelson started a large program in economics to deliver the underpinnings for this empirical footing of microeconomics. Because of the nearness of values to preferences, it is thus tempting to define values similarly by their choice-guiding nature. However, the assumption turned out to be methodologically problematic for preferences in economics and ethicists do not generally accept it for values. In what follows, I will not assume such a principle for values. The choice-guiding nature of values is important, but it is not their sole defining characteristic.

A third preliminary remark concerns the agent-relativity of values or lack thereof. When two agents disagree about a value-laden issue, this may indicate a form of misunderstanding or difference of opinion about factual matters, or it may indicate that they endorse different values. However, disagreement about values does not indicate that these are subjective and also does not indicate that they are agent-relative. A value may be agent-relative and objective. For example, it may be better for me to take a particular medicament but not for others. A value may be agent-relative and subjective. For example, collecting stamps may contribute to the well-being of someone who enjoys this kind of activity, and as long as it does not substantially harm that person—like, for example, an addiction might do—it cannot be argued reasonably that there are objective reasons against it. Whether one enjoys activities such as collecting stamps, forging medieval swords, and paragliding are purely subjective matters. According to some metaethical positions, a value might also be agent-neutral and subjective. For example, a subjectivist might claim that it is better to help someone in need than to ignore that person's bad fate, but that the reason for this is a subjective, though generally shared feeling of empathy among normal humans.[2] Finally, a value absolutist would classify the same value as being agent-neutral and objective. In each of these cases, however, the value will elicit a particular structure and whatever we say about this structure is orthogonal to these philosophical distinctions. Unless noted otherwise, value structure should be understood as being neutral about the above distinctions and other metaethical stances such as value expressivism versus value subjectivism versus value absolutism.

But what *is* a value? It is better not to attempt to provide an exhaustive analytic definition of the term, which is notoriously vague and hard to capture precisely. Instead, we may refer to our practices and actual language use. We have an intuitive grasp of what it means to evaluate things and states of affairs, and we use a rich vocabulary of value predicates such as "healthy," "brave," "cheap," and "good" to express value judgments in our daily evaluative practices. If they are not meant as mere expressions of opinions or personal preferences, which is rarely the case, then these judgments can be understood as partially constituting an aspect of the structure of an underlying value according to what the respective person who makes the judgment believes. For example, if John thinks it is better to live in a representative than in a direct democracy, this judgment partly determines the structure of the value of living in different societies according to what John believes. Whether John's views about societies are right, and how to justify them, is a matter of normative ethics.

Individual judgments may also vary about structural requirements of values, yet the comparative nature of values is fairly uncontested in metaethics and can be taken as a partial defining characteristic; it gives rise to value structure. In one form or another, the linguistic expression of a value must allow for some kind of ordering by comparing items such as states of affairs, things, persons, and activities with each other. For example, the mentioned classificatory concepts have corresponding comparative forms "healthier than," "braver than," "cheaper than," and "better than" for making comparisons.

As is usual in the literature on value structure, the thin paradigmatic value comparative "better than" will be the main subject of inquiry, and we will assume from now on that other value comparisons elicit similar structural requirements. The fact that we are primarily concerned with value comparisons in what follows does not imply that the investigation is empirical, though. Philosophical claims about value structure are generally normative, and whenever individual judgments are given as examples in what follows, these are supposed to represent more general viewpoints about the underlying values. These judgments could only be *mere* expressions of personal opinion if the underlying values are subjective and agent-relative, but no such assumption will be made in general in what follows. My general take in this book is that individual value judgments are usually stated to inform or persuade others of general value comparisons and that it is commonly assumed that if an interlocutor does not agree with an explicit value comparison, then they are mistaken or wrong. To determine whether they really are mistaken and what exactly the underlying value may be is a second step, and the business of a vast variety of further disciplines such as normative ethics, aesthetics, economics, medicine, engineering, and so forth. The purpose of a metaethical inquiry of value structure is primarily to investigate and carve out the options for modeling the structures of values and "better than" comparisons and justify them philosophically.

This investigation starts in this and the following chapter with monist values in a qualitative setting. A monist value is one that only has one dimension, but there are several ways of understanding this characterization. First, a monist value may be taken as a notion of overall betterness in a certain respect. This conception is at play when one state of affairs is judged better than another, all things considered. These values result from aggregating various aspects into an overall comparison, which is problematic from a philosophical point of view. How do we know that there always is such a neatly determinable aggregate value? Second, a monist value may be taken as a value that only has one dimension or aspect to it. Corresponding value predicates are unidimensional, although one might argue that not many evaluative predicates are unidimensional in this sense. Perhaps only taste predicates like "salty" belong to this category and it is questionable whether these are evaluative.[3] Nevertheless, even if actual value predicates turn out to be richer, the unidimensional setting provides a good starting point. In this view, individual dimensions are parts of a value which are aggregated into a larger value. Although not uncontroversial, this is the stance taken throughout this book. To make the investigation general enough, we should also start by considering a qualitative model first. This means that ordinal value comparisons are taken as a basis rather than intensities or levels of value. Quantitative conceptions of value such as cardinal utilities are deferred to Chapter 3 and later. The reason for this order of exposition is that value intensities and levels need to represent the underlying ordinal comparisons expressed by the respective comparative of a value predicate such as "better than," and it is an additional step to ensure by means of a representation theorem that these ordinal comparisons are faithfully represented by a corresponding quantitative notion such as a cardinal utility function.

1.2 Comparative Forms

In the English language, many value predicates are adjectives that allow for a comparative form. One may build the comparative "healthier" and the superlative "healthiest" from the positive form "healthy." The same holds for the paradigmatic expression of overall value: "good," "better," "best." Other value-laden adjectives such as "wrong" do not allow for such comparative forms, or these are considered contrived or incorrect use of language. To many English speakers, "wronger" sounds wrong, or, perhaps, like a joke not to be taken literally. Other examples are open to more interpretation. For example, "excellent" has a superlative flavor to it that makes the comparative "more excellent" sound odd, but speakers may have conflicting opinions about the issue.[4]

In the theory of value structure it is generally assumed that values allow for comparisons, which are expressed by comparative forms of value predicates under normal conditions. These comparative forms then serve as a base case from which the positive and superlative readings are derived. There have also been attempts to define the comparative and superlative forms in terms of the positive form of a value predicate, for example to define "better than" and "best" in terms of "good." This makes sense from a linguistic point of view, as the positive form is often the base syntactic form and the other forms are morphosyntactically derived from it.[5] For example, "healthier" is morphologically derived from "healthy" and not vice versa. However, this derivation direction is more complicated from a logical point of view and does not do justice to the essentially comparative nature of values. Therefore, in this book the comparison structure of monist value is taken as a basis from which corresponding classificatory concepts can be derived.

A terminological matter needs to be settled before going on. If comparisons give values their structure, then it is natural to ask what they compare. This is a significant problem of analytic value philosophy because evaluative language turns out to be highly polymorphic at a closer look. For instance, in the right context, almost anything can be compared by "better than": states of affairs, abstract concepts, goods, principles, rules, social systems, methods of resource distribution, policies, virtues and character traits, etc. States of affairs (viz., possible worlds) and situations are among the most general entities under comparison, which is why they often serve as a basis in preference logic and deontic logic. However, translating other types of comparison objects into corresponding talk about states of affairs may be difficult; there are many problems with reducing everything to states of affairs such as the question of how to deal with possibly varying domains of objects and resources at states of affairs and more generally the question of how these are individuated with respect to the value predicate under consideration. To avoid some of these difficulties for the time being, I will remain agnostic about these issues and talk very neutrally about items, and sometimes also about alternatives when choices are considered. In particular examples the ontic categories of items will be apparent from the context. However, we will return to the question of what items can be at several occasions in this book, as it is relevant to the problem of how to compare items across value domains. States of affairs will also play a role later, in Chapter 10 on risk, where they will serve as outcomes of possible actions and bundle items that are evaluated.

1.3 Representation by Preorders

This section starts with a brief overview of binary relations to keep this book self-contained. These are an obvious representation choice because the comparative form of a value predicate compares at least two items with each other, and comparing two items with each other is a special case of relating one to the other. Extensionally, a binary relation R can be defined as a set of ordered pairs of elements from a first set A and a second set B. For example, the pairs $\langle$Anna, red$\rangle$, $\langle$Bob, blue$\rangle$, $\langle$Charly, blue$\rangle$, $\langle$Anna, green$\rangle$

could represent Anna, Bob, and Charly's favorite colors. In that example, the first set is {Anna, Bob, Charly}, but it could also be a larger set of persons, and the second set might be the set of all colors with simple English names. Notice that Anna has two favorite colors, red and green, and therefore the set of pairs making up the relation does not represent a function from individuals to colors.

Since the Cartesian product $A \times B$ is defined as $A \times B = \{\langle a, b\rangle \mid a \in A, b \in B\}$, any binary relation between items in A and items in B is a subset of $A \times B$. This is why in the formal literature one often finds the notation $\langle a, b\rangle \in R$ instead of the simpler $R(a, b)$, where the angle brackets construct ordered pairs. For simplicity, it may be convenient to combine the two sets into one domain, and in that case it is customary to speak of a binary relation over that domain, a short way of stating $R \subseteq (D \times D)$.[6] For instance, a binary relation over the set {Anna, Bob, Charly} is a subset of the Cartesian product $A \times A = \{\langle x, y\rangle \mid x, y \in A\}$. It is a good exercise to write down all nine ordered pairs of this Cartesian product and write down a few exemplary binary relations over the set such as "x likes y," "x knows y," "x works together with y," "x is identical to y," and "x is a better swimmer than y." Since this section only deals with binary relations, we may omit the attribute "binary" in what follows; the concepts introduced below can be extended to n-ary relations by considering only two of their argument places at a time. As another convenient shortcut, we may write $a \not R b$ when it is not the case that aRb.

Let us now check which common properties hold for the proposed representation of the comparison structure of value predicates. A relation is reflexive whenever aRa holds for all a in the domain D. Conversely, it is irreflexive if aRa does not hold for any $a \in D$, or, in other words, if $a \not R a$ for all $a \in D$. Notice that not being reflexive is not the same as being irreflexive: Irreflexivity is not the mere absence of reflexivity, but a stronger condition, and similar points can be made about other properties of relations and their negative counterparts that will be introduced below.[7] Intuitively, value comparisons of comparatives like "better than" and "healthier" are irreflexive. For instance, John cannot be healthier than himself and Mary cannot be better at playing the lute than herself at the same time. Their health and lute playing performances can worsen or improve, of course. If improvements over time would need to be taken into account in these examples, we would have to introduce time explicitly, for instance by defining a function from points in time to potentially different binary relations that represent the respective value at that time. By the same token, the dependence on particular agents can be taken as a function from these agents to binary relations. However, it is generally a good idea to avoid such contextual factors unless they play a crucial part in the theorizing. Right now, the focus is on the properties of the abstract comparisons behind a value and additional factors would only muddy our investigation of these properties.

A relation is symmetric if and only if from aRb it follows that bRa. Although it would be nice if love was symmetric, this is not the case. From the fact that John loves Mary it cannot generally be inferred that Mary loves John. A classical textbook example of a symmetric relation is rather "being a relative of." If John is a relative of Mary, then Mary is also a relative of John. This principle always holds. In contrast to this, love is sometimes but not always mutual. What about value comparisons? They are not symmetric, as long as they are meant in a strict sense. If one knife is better than another, then the other cannot be better than the first. Knife a might be better than b in one aspect, and b might be better than a in another aspect, but these types of complex value judgments are not monist and we will not address them before Chapter 4. One striking feature of the monist reading of "better than" is that it is not only not symmetric but in fact asymmetric: A relation is asymmetric if from aRb it follows that $b\not{R}a$ for all $a, b \in D$, which is precisely what the monist reading of "better than" in the knife example implies. Generally speaking, if a is better than b *in one particular aspect*, then b cannot be better than a at the same time in the very same aspect. We may call this a "strict betterness relation" to keep it apart from the relation of "weak betterness" that may be paraphrased as "better than or equally good." There is a similar property often confused with asymmetry that needs to be mentioned. A relation is antisymmetric if from aRb and bRa it follows that $a = b$. This condition is slightly weaker than asymmetry because it remains compatible with reflexivity. A reflexive relation can be antisymmetric, but not asymmetric, whereas an asymmetric relation is always irreflexive. To complete the picture, duly note that a relation may be neither symmetric nor antisymmetric. A textbook example is "a is the brother of b."

A hotly debated property attributed to value comparisons is transitivity. A relation is transitive if from aRb and bRc it follows that aRc. At first sight, value comparisons have this property. If orange juice is healthier than whiskey, and water is healthier than orange juice, than water is also healthier than whiskey. If sergeant Millikan was braver than private Walker in battle, and specialist Black was even braver than Millikan, then Black was surely braver than Walker. If democracy is better than tyranny and oligarchic kleptocracy is better than democracy, then the latter is also better than tyranny.[8] There is a strong "intuitive pull" towards a transitive reading of betterness and other, more specific value comparisons. However, Larry Temkin has argued that value comparisons might not be transitive, and his theses have cast doubt on the common practice of merely assuming transitivity. I will argue in Chapter 8 that apparent failures of transitivity of "better than" comparisons result from conflicts between different aspects of values or between different values in a complex value comparison setting and that the transitivity of overall betterness can be preserved in a multidimensional model with lexicographic comparisons of value aspects. For the time being, it suffices to note that the transitivity of value comparisons is an option to consider, and also routinely postulated in economics and decision-making.

So far, we have only considered strict comparisons between two items, when one item is better, healthier, braver, nicer, etc. than another item. Such a strict comparison is often denoted by the letter P for strict preference and sometimes also written '$\succ$' and, slightly misleading, with the symbol '$>$'. However, we also often judge two items equally good, equally healthy, matching in bravery, etc. This relation is written as I, '$\sim$', or even '='. In the language of preferences this relation is often called indifference but in axiology it stands for "equally good." Used as a representation of a specific value predicate, its paraphrase should always be clear from the respective base predicate, like in the above examples. What properties does this relation have?

For a start, it is reflexive. An item is equally good as itself, a specific apple is as healthy as this very same apple, and a particular hammer is as useful as itself. These formulations sound a bit odd and that is no coincidence; the oddity comes from the fact that we rarely have a reason, outside the realm of abstract mathematics, to relate an item to itself. It is a sort of technical condition. For "equally good" it need not be stipulated separately, because this relation is also clearly symmetric, and reflexivity follows from symmetry. To say that a is as good as b is the same as to say that b is as good as a, and it is more natural to just state that a and b are equally good. At least at first sight transitivity also seems to hold. By way of example, suppose Mary is deliberating how to spend Saturday afternoon and she figures that going to the cinema is as good as staying at home and reading a novel, and that reading a novel is just as good to her in the given situation as going shopping downtown. In that case, going to the cinema is also equally good as going shopping as a way for her to spend the afternoon (according to her), and she will likely be indifferent between the options.

However, not all ways of understanding phrases like "equally good" or "as good as" are compatible with a reading as indifference. Although value judgments express value attributions, the attribution itself may not have anything to do with the attitudes of the judge. In many contexts it would be misleading to insinuate that the fact that two items are equally good has anything to do with an attitude of the agent who judges them in this way. From the point of view of abstract value structure, it might follow from the fact that two items are equally good that a rational agent is indifferent between them, but the converse does not hold in general. An agent may be indifferent between two alternatives for action without considering them equally good; for instance, the evaluative differences might not matter in a particular choice situation. Moreover, examples of attributions of equal value that are not transitive have been discussed extensively in the literature since the 1950s. For the time being, we take the transitivity of I as one option for a representation of value comparisons by "equally good" and note that I is also reflexive and symmetric.

Taken together, P and I constitute what is more or less the standard view of preferences, and insofar as preferences reflect value structure they can also be used as a starting point in formal value theory. An irreflexive, asymmetric and transitive relation is also called a strict ordering, and a reflexive, symmetric and transitive relation is called an equivalence relation. They constitute the strict part and the symmetric part of the weak betterness relation. In this view, strict preferences and, correspondingly, strict value comparisons are imposing a strict ordering on the items between which they hold. Equipreference, indifference, and "equally good" state that two items are equally preferable, that an agent is indifferent between them, and that they are equally good respectively.

Given all of the above, a preorder representation is basically just a way to combine the relations of strict betterness and equal goodness into one convenient base relation of weak betterness. A preorder is a reflexive and transitive binary relation. It is often denoted by the letter R, by the symbol '$\succeq$' or '$\geq$', and called weak preference relation in the literature on preferences. It can be read as "equipreferable or more preferable than" or, when it is applied to value predicates, as "as good as or better," "as brave or braver," and so forth. As the reading suggests, it expresses a disjunction of the other two relations. If it is used as a basis, the other two relations can be derived by the following definitions:

$$aPb \text{ if and only if } aRb \text{ and } b\not{R}a \quad \text{(Df.P)}$$

$$aIb \text{ if and only if } aRb \text{ and } bRa \quad \text{(Df.I)}$$

When they are defined this way, P is called the strict part and I is called the symmetric part of the characteristic relation R. Correspondingly, a preorder relation may be recovered from strict preferences and equipreference as follows:

$$aRb \text{ if and only if } aPb \text{ or } aIb \quad \text{(Df.R)}$$

These correspondences mean that it makes no difference whether P together with I or R alone is taken as a basis, but there is one potential problem to watch out for. So far, I have silently presumed that all relations are complete. A relation R is complete (or, total) with respect to a domain D if it is the case that aRb or bRa holds for all $a, b \in D$. However, suppose the weak preference relation is complete with respect to a given domain of items. If we define it in terms of a strict part and an equivalence relation, completeness of the defined weak relation does not follow. To give an example, suppose that there are four items under consideration, aPc, aPd, bPc, and bPd, and additionally cId holds. Figure 1.1a depicts these relations, where an arrow marks strict preference and an arc without arrow marks equipreference. This case leaves the relation between a and b open. In contrast to this, if R is a complete relation over the domain $\{a, b, c, d\}$, then it follows from definitions Df.P and Df.I that any two items are either in a relation of strict preference or equipreference to each other, i.e., that either xPy or yPx or xIy (the case yIx following from symmetry). To ensure completeness of relation R with respect to some

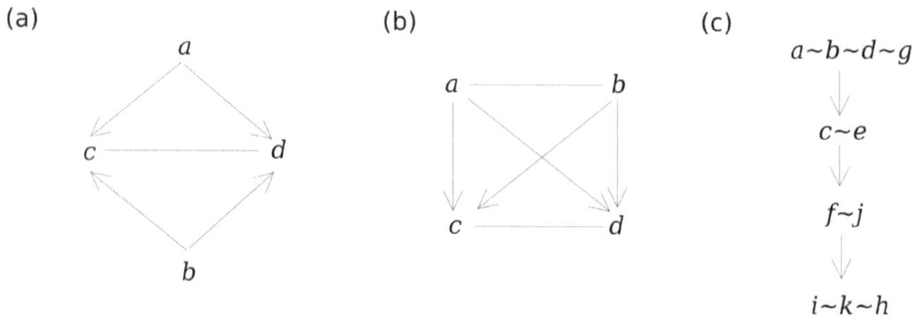

Figure 1.1: Examples of (a) incomplete preferences, (b) complete preferences, and (c) the layering of equivalence classes of a complete preorder.

domain D, a requirement needs to be added to Definition Df.R that states that P and I, taken together, are defined for all items in D. We then obtain an ordering like in Figure 1.1b in which the strict preference relation orders all equivalence classes, although some of them may only contain one element. Such complete preorders can be simplified into hierarchies of equipreference classes as in the example in Figure 1.1c.

We have already seen the most important properties of the preorder representation but a few additional ones need to be mentioned. If the preorder is complete, all items are comparable. Neither hesitation to commit to a value judgment nor any forms of noncomparability or incommensurability between items can be expressed in this framework, so this a fairly strong condition. For this reason, preorder-based representations without completeness will be discussed in the next section. Completeness has technical advantages, though, as it also allows for strict betterness or preference to be taken as a basis. Equal goodness is then defined as aIb if and only if $a \not P b$ and $b \not P a$. It is easy to see that this trick only works when the corresponding relation R is complete, since otherwise $a \not P b$ and $b \not P a$ might also mean that a and b are not comparable at all. Further worth noting is that if the weak order relation is complete, then the asymmetry of the strict part follows. In light of definitions Df.P and Df.I, completeness means that either aPb or bPa or aIb. So if aPb is the case, then $b \not P a$ must also be the case, since otherwise by the two definitions taken together aIb would hold.

Another important point is the relation between acyclicity and transitivity. What is a cycle? A relation R has a cycle if there is a sequence of distinct items $a_1, a_2, \ldots, a_n$ such that $a_1Ra_2, a_2Ra_3, \ldots, a_{n-1}Ra_n$ and a_nRa_1 holds. It is clear where the name comes from; a cycle occurs when such a relation is depicted as a directed graph with arrows as edges. Correspondingly, a relation is cyclic if its graph contains one or more cycles, and a relation is acyclic if its graph does not contain any cycle. In this way of talking, an arrow that leads from an item to itself does not count as a cycle; instead, it is usually called a loop. These are usually harmless and the loops of reflexive relations are often left out in graph representations. In contrast to this, cycles can create real problems. The most notorious problem concerns decision-making on the basis of value judgments. Suppose you want to make a decision and after careful deliberation narrow down the set of possible actions to three alternatives a, b, and c, but your overall valuations are aPb, bPc and cPa. It does not matter whether P represents strict preferences or betterness, all things considered. The obvious problem with the cycle is that there is no best or most preferred alternative. No matter which alternative you choose, there is always one that you prefer—or should prefer, if the underlying relation has a normative reading—or that you judge better than the chosen one. This situation is very different from aRb, bRc, and cRa, which simply means that you may rationally pick whichever alternative you like. Picking the first or last item, or picking a random item are equally rational in this case.[9] Such a choice cannot be rational when a better alternative is available, though. We will discuss further below under which circumstances cycles become problematic, but let us note for the moment that a cycle in a strict betterness relation can be malicious when value-based choices are concerned.

Sometimes cycle-prohibitions are conflated with transitivity, although this is not entirely correct. A transitive relation may contain cycles. Figure 1.2 illustrates the case with three items. However, the cycle in combination with transitivity collapses the cyclic part of the relation into a symmetric part. We may prove this by induction. Consider a cycle a_1Ra_2, a_2Ra_3, $\ldots$, $a_{n-1}Ra_n$, a_nRa_1. Let us call this a cycle of length n, except when $n = 1$, which is a loop. If $n = 2$ then the cycle is a_1Ra_2, a_2Ra_1, which is symmetric. Suppose $n \geq 3$. Then from a_1Ra_2 and a_2Ra_3 we get a_1Ra_3 by transitivity and thus a cycle a_1Ra_3, a_3Ra_4, $\ldots$, $a_{n-1}Ra_n$, a_nRa_1 of length $n - 1$. Repeated application of transitivity shrinks the length of the cycle by 1 each time, until $n = 2$ (qed). If the cycle is a full cycle like in the figure, it thus follows that the whole relation becomes an equivalence

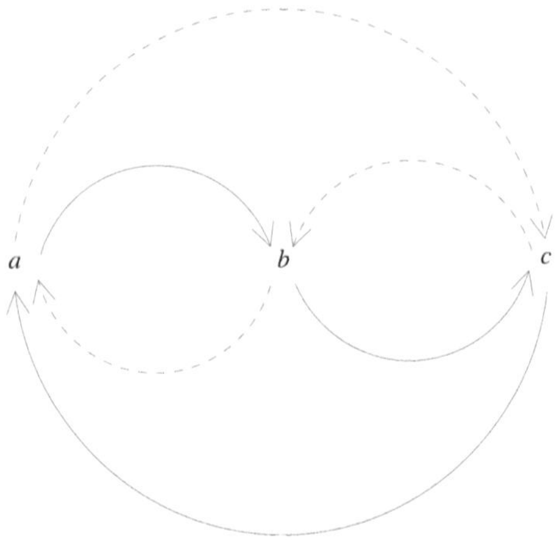

Figure 1.2: A transitive relation with full cycle (loops are left out).

relation without any strict preferences. On the other hand, if we look at strict preferences, the combination of irreflexivity and transitivity excludes cycles. To see this, note that in the figure loops are left out that follow from transitivity, too. For example, from aRb and bRa it follows by transitivity that aRa, violating irreflexivity. The asymmetry of strict preference is also violated, of course.

Let us take a look at the other way around. Does acyclicity ensure transitivity? Again, the answer is No. The relation aRb, aRc is acyclic but not transitive, for instance, and it is easy to come up with more counterexamples.

To summarize, we have seen that strict preferences are acyclic due to their asymmetry and transitivity, and it is not hard to show that a weaker combination of antisymmetry and transitivity is also cycle-free if we follow the convention that loops do not count. The cycle prohibition of strict preferences and strict betterness has been criticized at times, and transitivity plus asymmetry is an even stronger condition than acyclicity, so an argument for acyclicity is not automatically an argument for the transitivity of preferences. Nevertheless, both the transitivity of equal goodness and the transitivity of strict betterness have a strong intuitive appeal. If a is better than b and b is better than c, then it seems clear that a is also better than c. Let us call this Preorder Model, the first model of value comparisons to consider, and defer a more detailed discussion of the pros and cons of this standard account for later.

Model 1 (Complete Preorder Model). *Let D be the domain of items for which a value predicate allows judgments. The structure of monist value comparisons is represented by either (1) a complete reflexive and transitive relation (total preorder) R over D, or (2) by an equivalence relation I for value equality and an asymmetric and transitive relation P for strict value comparisons over subsets of D, where $P \cap I = \emptyset$, such that for all $a, b \in D$ either aPb or bPa or aIb.*

If P and I are taken as a basis on their own, the last condition is needed to ensure completeness. Note that asymmetry implies irreflexivity, so it does not have to be stated as an additional condition.

Because of its prevalence in economics and decision-making, I will also call this model the "standard model."

1.4 Incommensurability and Partial Orderings

One of the most pertinent problems of the standard model is totality or completeness, which is the topic of this section. Recall what the completeness condition states. It says that the base relations are defined everywhere over a given domain. As laid out above, this means that either aPb or bPa or aIb must be the case for any two items $a, b \in D$. Why is this a problem?

First, the condition seems to require an agent who has internalized a value to be able to come up with a decisive value judgment about any two items. However, it is worth noting that there is no technical reason for this interpretation since the definition of completeness hinges on a particular domain and does not restrict the choice of a domain. Nothing keeps us from making D smaller than the range of items to which a value predicate can be applied. The problem is that a Complete Preorder Model does not provide any mechanism for expressing the case when an agent would like to or has to suspend judgment. If this case is allowed, then the model is not adequate for value judgments because it does not adequately capture the modeling requirements. In other words, we want the domain to represent all items that may play a role when an agent considers applications of a given value predicate, or, in the case of preferences in decision-making, all alternatives that the agent takes into account. Insofar as value judgments are indicative of more abstract value structure, we may take suspension of judgments as an indicator for a gap in the value structure itself. If so, then it seems that we need to account for gaps in general. So suppose that gaps are allowed and hence the underlying preorder relation is not complete but a partial relation over the domain D. This domain then represents all items for which a comparison is considered prima facie, even if they are incomparable at a closer sight. We will use the following definition:

$$aNb \text{ if and only if neither } aRb \text{ nor } bRa \text{ is defined.} \qquad \text{(Df.N)}$$

If R is otherwise a preorder like described in the last section, then this definition yields the second type of candidate model for representing value comparison structures:

Model 2 (Partial Preorder Model). *Let D be the domain of items for a value predicate. The structure of monist value comparisons is represented by (1a) a partial reflexive and transitive relation (preorder) R over D,* or, *(1b) a partial equivalence relation for value equality I and a partial, asymmetric and transitive relation P for strict value comparisons over D, where $P \cap I = \emptyset$, and (2a) a relation N defined as in Definition Df.N, or alternatively (2b) defined as aNb if and only if neither aIb nor aPb nor bPa.*

Before discussing this approach's formal implications, it is worth considering some possible readings and interpretations of this new case, for it can be understood in different ways that are not necessarily compatible with each other. First, aNb might represent a case of suspension of judgment by an agent in a given situation of making a value judgment rather than a principal gap in value structure. The revised model does not reflect this very well because it does not contain agent indices. However, it would not be hard to add them. Add a finite group G of agents, each of whom is equipped with a partial preorder relation R_x and the corresponding defined relations P_x, I_x and N_x. Once a model is augmented in this way, it makes sense to regard aN_xb a case of suspension of judgment by agent x and leave out the index when only one agent is under consideration. In this view, aNb expresses that an agent does not want to commit to a definite judgment about the respective value relation between a and b in some particular comparison situation. This type of suspension of judgment may, but does not need to indicate a stronger form of value incommensurability. We may call it weak, agent-relative incomparability. As a typical example, imagine you are asked to judge which of two of your favorite novels is better than the other, and you simply cannot decide between them, nor do you want to state that they are exactly equally good. This situation is very common, and it is perfectly reasonable to decline making a judgment in such a case.

Another good reason for suspending judgment is when not enough information is available. Suppose you are asked to decide about two proposals for building an airport outside the city, but no environmental studies are available yet. Since the environmental impact of these constructions is an important factor, it makes sense to suspend final, overall judgment even under the assumption that you have a perfectly fine and valid method of coming to an overall assessment based on the various aspects of the proposals. The information is incomplete; hence, you do not wish to prematurely commit to an assessment. The example differs from the previous one—the previous one is characterized by an indisposition to commit to a judgment, whereas the airport example is characterized by a lack of information needed to come to an overall assessment. However, they both have in common that the suspension of judgment may be revoked later. You can make up your mind about your personal preferences and you may come to a final verdict about the airport once the environmental studies are delivered.

The cases mentioned so far remain compatible with the view that the underlying value structure is complete, as long as we distinguish between this structure and the individual judgments of agents. A stronger form of value incomparability occurs whenever two items turn out to be incomparable tout court at a closer look or in hindsight. Again, two cases must be distinguished.

First, suppose there was at least some prima facie reason for taking the items to be comparable, or otherwise the items would be trivially not comparable. In the words of Chang (2015), substantive incomparability has to be distinguished from merely formal incomparability: If one or two items do not fall under what she calls a covering consideration, which is some respect such as health, well-being, or happiness under which the items are compared, then they fail to be comparable for merely formal reasons. (She calls this noncomparability.) It is clear that there can be trivial cases of formal incomparability. For example, an idea cannot be better for cutting meat than a particular knife. Even a skeptic about the idea of a covering value will have to concede that there are formal failures of comparability, which are usually trivial and, as Chang puts it, philosophically uninteresting.

Second, strong substantive value incomparability occurs when two items that were initially thought to be comparable by a value predicate turn out to be principally incomparable at a closer look. While it is controversial whether such cases actually exist, moral dilemmas and certain types of long-term ethical decisions might provide good examples. Sartre (1946) discusses the case of a French resistance fighter who cannot decide between his duty to fight against the oppressive Nazi regime and his duty to stay with his sick mother. Another type of examples is discussed by Raz (1986) and concerns overall comparisons between different ways of life. Suppose you are equally inclined towards two career paths but for vastly different reasons. Should you become a professional clarinet player or a lawyer? The two ways of life that might result from this choice might be so different that they are principally incomparable.[10] The idea is in both of the examples that the items under consideration are not fully comparable according to one form of overall betterness, not just because an agent is reluctant to make a judgments but because there is a principal conflict between supporting reasons or (sub-)values. These cases seem to primarily occur as a side effect of complex value comparisons, hence might only affect aggregative value relations which are discussed in Chapter 5. For the time being, let us take note that aNb can represent such cases.

Do the properties of N that follow from Definition Df.N capture the properties that we would like to attribute to one of the above readings of incomparability? What are those properties? From the definition, it follows that if aRa is not defined, then aNa holds. This follows directly, since stating that aRa is not defined implies $\langle a, a\rangle \notin R$ which is the case if and only if aNa. So for the elements for which N is defined, it is reflexive. Incomparability of this sort is also symmetric. To see this, assume aNb, which holds by Definition Df.N if and only if $\langle a, b\rangle \notin R$ and $\langle b, a\rangle \notin R$ which by the very same definition is the case if and only if bNa. The relation is not transitive, though, as a counterexample illustrates. Suppose that aNb and bNc. This holds when $\langle a, b\rangle, \langle b, a\rangle \notin R$ and $\langle b, c\rangle, \langle c, b\rangle \notin R$.

Now assume that also $\langle a, c \rangle \in R$ is the case. No property of R is violated but aRc holds, and so also $a\cancel{N}c$, whereas from transitivity aNc would follow. Thus, N is not transitive.

Are these properties desirable? The case for symmetry is obvious. If a is not comparable with b then b is not comparable with a either. What about the lack of transitivity then? For weak incomparability this property makes sense. Someone may suspend judgment about two items a and b, and about b and c, for example, because these are very near to each other, and still remain reluctant to call them equally good. Perhaps the agent also suspects that there is not enough information to decide a from b and b from c respectively in terms of their value-related properties, but with more information available a decision could be made. In a situation in which a final verdict is not needed, not required, the agent might thus suspend judgment in both cases. Nevertheless, it seems plausible that it may be possible to come to a definite assessment of the value relation between a and c in such a case. Suppose, for example, that aPb and bPc became clear after additional information had been obtained. A little bit less information might suffice to justify aPc, whereas it might not suffice to justify "smaller" comparisons between a and b or b and c. To give a concrete example, suppose someone asks you to evaluate two novels that differ in genre, perhaps a is autobiographic fiction whereas b is a detective story, and they are equally entertaining to you. However, you are not a style expert and not quite sure about their artistic qualities, so you would like to abstain from a judgment. Now suppose there is a novel c, another detective story like b, and this time you have a nagging suspicion that b should be called "better than" c, because it is more original and the plot is constructed in a much more elaborate way, but you rarely read detective stories and c appears to be written a bit better than b, and so you want to abstain from a final judgment. It is perfectly conceivable in this scenario to come to the conclusion that a is overall better than c. This type of example is parallel to those that have been put forward to support the thesis that equipreference is not transitive, and there is also a connection to Chang's notion of parity to be explored later. For the time being, this and similar examples make it plausible that weak incomparability need not be transitive.

What holds for weak incomparability might not apply to strong incomparability. The argument goes as follows. Suppose there are reasons why a and b can in principle not be compared with each other with respect to some monist value predicate such as overall "better than," and b and c can principally not be compared either. In this case, it seems hard to make it plausible that a and c can be compared. The adverb "principally" excludes lack of information and knowledge about the items and indicates that the incomparability obtains for principle reasons such as category mistakes or other violations of underlying rules at the level of value structure rather than individual value judgments. If there are such reasons, and therefore strong incomparability makes sense, then it seems that those reasons should also speak against comparing a with c in a meaningful way by the same underlying value predicate.

However, this line of reasoning is not conclusive. If a has property P and b has property $\neg P$, and because of this a rule is violated, then in principle c may have property P again, which may make a and c comparable. Perhaps a and c are of the right kind, whereas b is not, and then we get exactly such a case. As mentioned earlier, there must be a reason to include b into the domain of items in the first place, or else the whole series of comparisons would illustrate mere formal incomparability. Perhaps there are such reasons in practice. Suppose a and c are books and b is a painting and the reason for including the latter is that someone asks you to. You could then argue that books and paintings cannot be compared with each other, to the effect that aNb and bNc hold, while at the same time aPc may clearly hold. So transitivity is not warranted for strong incomparability either, although in any particular case three items may turn out to be strongly incomparable, of course.

We may still ask about the consequences of assuming that incomparability is transitive. A relation R is negatively transitive if from $a\not R b$ and $b\not R c$ it follows that $a\not R c$. As it turns out, if N is transitive, then weak preference is negatively transitive. To see this, note that transitivity of N by Definition Df.N means that from $\langle a,b\rangle, \langle b,a\rangle \notin R$ and $\langle b,c\rangle, \langle c,b\rangle \notin R$ it follows that $\langle a,c\rangle, \langle c,a\rangle \notin R$ as well, from which negative transitivity follows. This consideration also works the other way round: Even if it is not transitive, incomparability is negatively transitive, provided that it is defined as above and R is transitive. For suppose that $a\not N b$ and $b\not N c$. This can only be the case if aRb and bRc, hence by transitivity aRc and therefore by Definition Df.N $a\not N c$ must also be the case.

Finally, it is worth noting that Definition Df.N may need to be adjusted if other types of value relations are assumed in addition to those that have been discussed so far. Chang (2002, 2005, 2012) has argued for the existence of a value relation called parity. This relation is the topic of Chapter 7 and also discussed in Chapter 9. Before we address it in more detail, bear in mind that the above definitions must be adapted accordingly if parity or any other nontraditional value relations are added.[11] It can even make sense to introduce incomparability as a primitive relation with the above properties. For example, suppose we would like to refine the partial preorder model to allow for distinguishing between formal and substantive incomparability. One way to achieve this is by introducing a domain D' that is larger than the base domain D, defining a preorder relation R and a relation of substantive incomparability N over D, requiring $R \cap N = \emptyset$, and then defining formal incomparability F as aFb if and only if neither aRb nor aNb holds for any $a, b \in D'$.

Chapter 2

Relaxing Requirements

It is possible to further generalize the monist value representations of the previous chapter by relaxing some of their requirements. This chapter is dedicated to laying out some of the most common generalizations and how they might impact philosophical views about value structure.

2.1 Nontransitive Value Equality and Equipreference

As Vincke and Pirlot (1997, Ch. 2) lay out, economists like Georgescu-Roegen (1936) and Armstrong (1939) recognized early on that actual persons sometimes fail to have transitive equipreferences. This phenomenon has also been studied extensively by mathematical psychologists such as Tversky (1969). A theory to deal with such cases based on semiorders was first developed by Luce (1956), and we shall take a look at this approach for the representation of monist value comparisons in this section.

Let us start with Luce's example. It summarizes very neatly why equipreference interpreted as indifference may fail to be transitive, and similar arguments can be used for expressions like "equally good" and "as good as." Suppose you like your coffee black with sugar, and suppose a_0 is a cup of coffee without any sugar. Now let a_1 contain one grain of sugar. Surely, you cannot distinguish a_0 from a_1 and so you might state that you are indifferent between them, i.e., that $a_0 I a_1$ holds. Suppose a_2 contains two grains of sugar, a_3 three, and so forth. Then there will be some cup of coffee a_k that you can distinguish from a_0 even if you are unable to distinguish a_{k-1} from a_k. So written down with "I" interpreted as indifference relation, we obtain a chain of judgments $a_0 I a_1$, $a_1 I a_2$, ..., $a_{k-1} I a_k$, but $a_0 \not{I} a_k$. If you generally prefer your coffee with sugar, then you might even state explicitly that $a_k P a_0$. Maybe you would also judge for some $m < k$ that $a_o \not{I} a_m$ in hindsight, but that does not matter to the argument, since only the fact that $k \geq 2$ counts and we could set $k = m$. What counts is that this is a clear-cut failure of transitivity. Successive application of transitivity shortens the jumps to $a_0 I a_2$, $a_2 I a_4$, and again to $a_0 I a_4$, etc., for all places in between a_0 and a_k, until $a_0 I a_k$ is reached. Hence, I is not a proper equivalence relation in this case.

Luce's example is a Sorites Puzzle, as they are known from many debates in philosophy, and one might also consider it a case of vagueness. Like we are unable to distinguish, say, small changes in color, and therefore the boundary between orange and red is vague in the epistemic sense elaborated by Williamson (1994), we are unable to distinguish small differences of the amount of sugar in a cup of coffee, even though we can easily discern larger differences. Thus, "being sweet coffee" is a vague predicate. However, this connection with vagueness is not very illuminating because there are many forms of vagueness. We are interested in a specific form that arises from a failure to notice small differences. In the example, the vagueness depends on the comparison context. Large differences are distinguishable, whereas small differences are not. This fact leads to a specific type of transitivity failure. So let us put vagueness aside as an issue that might detract more than it may help.

When quantities can be measured, then the phenomenon may be understood by the existence of a threshold of indiscernibility. Suppose $g(a)$ represents the number of grains of sugar in the coffee. Then the failure of transitivity can be understood by introducing a threshold q such that aPb holds whenever $g(a) > g(b) + q$ and aIb holds whenever $|g(a) - g(b)| \leq q$. Figure 2.1 illustrates one way of understanding the coffee example from this perspective. Choosing $q = 8$ and $g(a) =$ *the number of sugar grains*, it can be seen that $g(a_9) > g(a_0) + q$ and thus $a_9 P a_0$, whereas there is indifference between all other cups.

If no interval is contained in another interval, which is the case in Figure 2.1, then the intervals are representable by a semiorder.[1] To define a semiorder directly in terms of relations rather than using real-valued func-

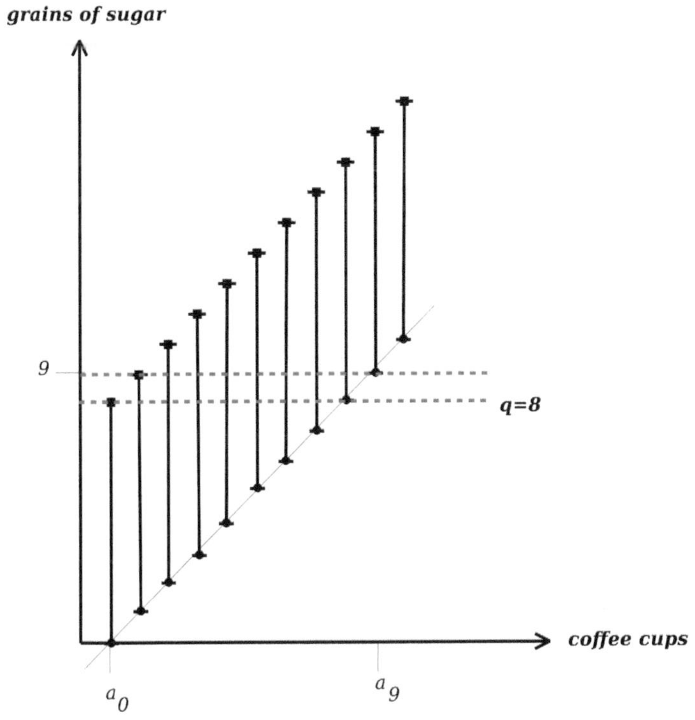

Figure 2.1: Grains of sugar in coffee; example based on Luce (1956).

tions, a strict P and a symmetric part I are often used, and the semiorder is their union $R = P \cup I$. The following axioms from Jacquet-Lagrèze (1975, p. 89) characterize a semiorder:

S1. Either aPb, bPa or aIb holds for all $a, b \in D$.

S2. aIa for all $a \in D$.

S3. If aPb, bIc and cPd, then aPd.

S4. If aPb, bPc and bId, then not both aId and cId hold.

A similar definition makes use of the properties of semitransitivity and Ferrers property. A binary relation R over domain D is semitransitive if for all $a, b, c, d \in D$ from aRb, bRc and $d\not{R}c$ it follows that aRd. Figure

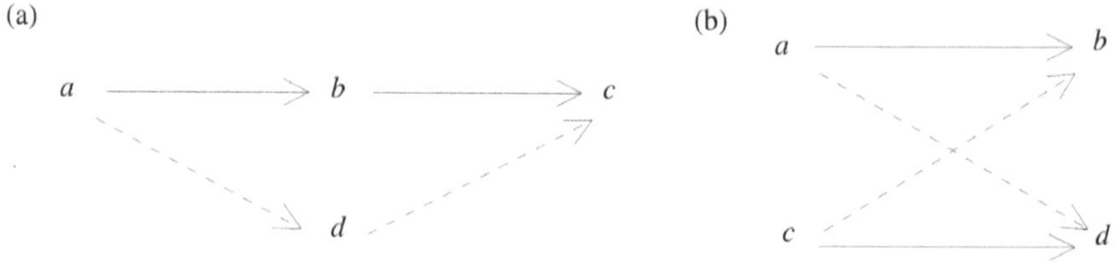

Figure 2.2: Illustration of (a) semitransitivity, and (b) the Ferrers property.

2.2a illustrates this property, where one or both of the dashed arrows may be the case. The idea behind the definition is that at least one of the links aRd or dRc must obtain; so if $d \not R c$, then the other one must hold. Another way of stating the condition is as follows: A relation R over D is semitransitive if for all $a, b, c, d \in D$ from aRb and bRc it follows that aRd or dRc. The second condition we need is called "Ferrers property." A relation R over domain D is a Ferrers relation (has the Ferrers property) if for all $a, b, c, d \in D$ from aRb, $c \not R b$ and cRd it follows that aRd. This is illustrated in Figure 2.2b. Again, the condition might be stated with an explicit disjunction: A relation R over D is Ferrers if for all a, b, c, d from aRb and cRd it follows that aRb or cRd.

Given these new properties, we can proceed with the definition. A semiorder is a reflexive semitransitive relation with the Ferrers property.[2] If R is a complete semiorder over some domain D, and I is defined as aIb if and only if aRb and bRa, then I will be symmetric, but transitivity might fail as the interval example calls for. If the semitransitivity condition is dropped, we get a so-called interval order which can additionally represent the case when one interval is nested in another. Interval orders have been studied extensively by Fishburn (1970a, 1985).

It is fair to say that the properties of semiorders are not obvious at first sight, but what is going on can to some extent be read off the above conditions. These ensure that P is transitive while allowing failure of transitivity in I. To see the first point, assume that aPb and bPc holds. We have to show aPc. From the irreflexivity condition (i) we know that $b \not P b$, and hence from the definition of I we get bIb. So we have aPb, bIb and bPc, which is an instance of (ii), and therefore we can conclude aPc. As for the second point, we already know that from the transitivity of P it only follows that I is negatively transitive. However, in order to establish transitivity from negative transitivity I would also need to be asymmetric, which is clearly not the case. Other proofs, particularly those establishing the above correspondence to intervals, are elaborated by Roberts (1979, pp. 257–272), Roubens and Vincke (1985, Ch. 3), and Vincke and Pirlot (1997, Ch. 3). The following definition summarizes the approach:

Model 3 (Semiorder Model). *For a domain D of items for which a given value predicates allows judgments, a semiorder-based model represents the predicates' comparison structure by a semiorder relation $R \subseteq D \times D$. This gives rise to transitive strict betterness and nontransitive equal goodness (viz., equipreference, indifference).*

What are the philosophical merits of this monist value representation? First of all, according to the above definitions incomparability is not allowed. The consequences of relaxing this requirement will be discussed in the next section, so let us assume for the time being that R is complete over the domain D as in the above axiom S1, and consider the reasons one might have for assuming nontransitive equal goodness. Is the failure of transitivity of "equally good" a result of measuring inadequacies or suspensions of judgment, or the result of more fundamental troubles? Parallel to the terminology of the previous chapter, we might call the former kind of transitivity failure weak and the latter strong, but this label does not seem to be very revealing in this case. The problem is how to understand the adjective "fundamental" in this context.

Suppose a weak failure merely indicates a lack of knowledge in borderline cases. For example, we cannot easily distinguish two cups of coffee which only differ in one grain of sugar, and this may be understood as epistemic vagueness of the predicate "sweet."[3] There can hardly be any doubt that there are weak agent-relative cases in this sense. The interval structure that semiorders represent suggests that these arise whenever small differences are indistinguishable, but larger differences are noticed, and whenever the corresponding preferences are elicited under the influence of a constant measurement error. This does not only happen in seemingly innocuous cases of perception and subjective value judgments like Luce's coffee example, for it is easy to construct similar cases for judgments of overall betterness that do not merely reflect someone's personal taste or arise from limitations of our perceptual system. Consider, for instance, resource allocations in society from an overall egalitarian perspective. Small differences in the resource allocations of states of society a and b and c are unavoidable and may lead to a case when a compared with b in isolation from c is just as good as b, and b compared with c in isolation from a is just as good as c. Nevertheless, there may be good reasons to think that a is better than c in such a case, or vice versa. Such thresholds are often unavoidable in overall assessments when the items under comparison are only roughly estimated and roughly compared with each other, and it is easy to come up with chains of comparisons that lead to nontransitive equality judgments. However, in these kinds of examples we can, in principle, measure more precisely and obtain a more detailed picture of how the resources have been allocated to resolve the apparent lack of transitivity.

To establish a strong failure of transitivity we need an example of nontransitive equal goodness that does not result from a lack of knowledge or difficulties with distinguishing items from one another. So the question is: Can transitivity fail, for principal reasons, when one item is considered as good as another item under a particular aspect? The answer is Yes. On the one hand, not being able to distinguish two items with respect to a particular aspect of a value can be the result of principal limitations. For instance, take the instrumental goodness of knives and sharpness as the aspect under consideration that would somehow enter into an assessment of their overall goodness for a certain purpose.[4] Two equally sharp knives might be considered equally good with respect to their sharpness, although there is reason to assume that their sharpness will not be exactly identical. The supposed transitivity of equal goodness with respect to sharpness might fail in such a scenario, and it would not make much sense to claim that any two knives can be ordered strictly by their sharpness—there may be limits to the concept of sharpness, which is itself vague and context dependent. As another example, suppose someone asks you to judge the quality of life in certain neighborhoods of a town. Even when being limited to only one aspect, nontransitive indifferences can come up in the comparison. Take, for instance, the distance of your home to the next supermarket as one such aspect. This distance only enters that particular aspect of goodness as a soft constraint or vague predicate. For instance, a difference of one meter between two such distances does not count. If that is so, then "equally good with respect to the distance to the next supermarket" may very well become nontransitive.

These examples suggest that vague predicates or rules with soft boundaries may be a component of a form of goodness, thus potentially counting as a monist form of a more specific form of goodness that only concerns a particular aspect like the above one, and that it need not be possible to make such predicates precise without changing the concept they express. Hence, the nontransitivity of equal value that arises because of them is principal. The nontransitivity of equal value is fundamental whenever one or more predicates that enter the respective aspect of goodness are fundamentally vague, where "fundamentally vague" is meant in the sense that a value predicate is not just vague because an agent lacks knowledge at a particular occasion of its use, but that any attempt to eliminate the vagueness in question might implicitly change the predicate's meaning in a way that might affect the kind of goodness under consideration. We have strong nontransitivity of equal value when a vague value predicate cannot be made more precise without thereby distorting the kind of betterness for which it is constitutive.

A problem is worth mentioning. If "equally good" is represented in the above way by a semiorder, then this relation is no longer Euclidean. A relation R is Euclidean if and only if for all a, b, c in its domain if aRb and aRc, then bRc. It can be proved that any symmetric and transitive relation is Euclidean. Vice versa, any symmetric Euclidean relation is also transitive. So the problem is that since I in the present case is no longer transitive, it is also not Euclidean, and allows for the case aIb, aIc and bPc. In contrast to the mere failure of transitivity of I, this seems to lead to really odd consequences. It allows an agent to consider a and b equally good and a and c equally good, and still consider b better than c (or vice versa). On the one hand, this is just another side of the same coin, a technical aspect of giving up the transitivity of I. If we add a condition that states that I must be Euclidean, we get the result that I is also transitive, and thus R becomes a preorder. On the other hand, what might seem like a reasonable statement about the (lack of) transitivity of I, may become hard to swallow when it is spelled out in terms of the lack of Euclideanness of I.

To summarize, there is as much evidence for the nontransitivity of equal goodness as there is for equipreference. This evidence may justify choosing a semiorder model as a representation of a given kind of betterness. In at least some of those examples the failure of transitivity is fundamental, as it is tied to fundamentally vague predicates whose meaning cannot be stratified into a precise concept without missing the point. The problem is that the nonstrict part of a semiorder is also not Euclidean, and it seems hard to come up with an intuitively compelling example for this property of semiorders.

2.2 Partial Semiorders

For completeness, let us explicitly introduce the partial variant of the previous model:

Model 4 (Partial Semiorder Model). *For a domain D of items for which a given value predicates allows judgments, a partial semiorder model represents the predicates' comparison structure by a semiorder R over a subset $D' \subset D$ and a corresponding equipreference relation I defined as aIb if and only if aRb and bRa for $a, b \in D'$. Incomparability is defined as aNb if and only if $a, b \in D \setminus D'$.*

Roubens and Vincke (1985, pp. 61–64) investigate partial semiorders and similar structures in a slightly different setting than the one assumed here. What we need to bear in mind for the application to value structure is that a failure of the transitivity of equal goodness can itself sometimes be regarded as an example of incomparability, if in case of $aIbIc$ and aPc the items have some feature that cannot be determined precisely enough in individual comparisons of a, b and b, c. In contrast to full incomparability, however, the items in question are just as good to each other, even though there may be small differences between them.

2.3 Weak Eligibility

There are further, less common deviations from the standard model. As mentioned in Section 1.3 of Chapter 1, a transitive and asymmetric strict preference relation is also acyclic. What about allowing cyclic preferences or value comparisons, though? As one might expect, these can be obtained by dropping the transitivity requirement, making P an asymmetric relation only. Then aPb and bPc become compatible with cPa, and so we might get a cycle. Larger cycles may also occur since iterated applications of transitivity are no longer ensured either. The smallest cycle is of the form aPb and bPa and can occur even when aPa is prohibited.

One might think that a cyclic value structure cannot be adequate when a value is supposed to guide decisions directly. The argument for this position is as follows. Take "better than" as a generic value predicate and ignore any complications that may arise from its aggregative nature for the time being. Suppose a is better than b, and b is better than c, but also c is better than a. In this case, none of the three candidates can be chosen based on this understanding of "better than," if making a decision requires one to fetch the best item among the available candidates. Hence, the underlying value is not choice guiding. Since this argument can be made in general, it is concluded that value relations need to be at least acyclic for decision-making, which under normal conditions, when strict betterness is asymmetric, boils down to making "better than" transitive.

However, this argument is flawed, as the following counterexample demonstrates. John wants to buy a new phone and has narrowed down the choices to four candidates labeled a to d. He thinks phone a is better than b, b is better than c, c is better than d, and d is better than b. Clearly, his judgments of betterness in this situation are cyclic. This does not keep him from making an informed decision, though; of course, he chooses a, since it is the best alternative.

This example illustrates that a general cycle prohibition is not a necessary condition for making a decision. Intuitively, only top cycles have to be prohibited, i.e., cycles of the strict betterness relation that contain no item for which there is a better item outside of the cycle. Since in the above example a is not part of the cycle and better than any item in the cycle, it can be recommended by the respective value predicate. The cycle below this top item does not block the decision-making process. Although seemingly clear from an intuitive point of view, it is not easy to define "top cycles" correctly. Consider the simplest cycle aPb and bPa. Which element is the top element? Instead of thinking about a relation without a cycle and then adding a link that creates the top cycle, it is conceptually clearer to use weak eligibility from Hansson (2001, p. 24). An item a is weakly eligible iff. for all items b it holds that $b\not{P}a$. Given that, we may say that a preference or strict betterness relation P over a given domain is weakly eligible whenever at least one item in the domain is weakly eligible.

Weak eligibility excludes the kind of cycles we are interested in but allows cycles that occur lower in the ordering. In addition to weak eligibility, Hansson requires a property he calls "top-transitivity of weak eligibility": If a is weakly eligible for a value relation P over a given domain D, and aIb holds as well, then b must also be weakly eligible with respect to P and D.[5] This condition is needed to maintain the intuition that I should express some kind of equivalence of value.[6]

A top-transitive weak eligibility relation is then a weak eligibility relation which also fulfills the top-transitivity of weak eligibility. We obtain the following model:

Model 5 (Weak Eligibility Model with Transitive Equal Goodness). *For a domain D of items to which a given value predicates is applicable, a top-cycle free transitive equipreference model represents the predicates' comparison structure by an asymmetric top-transitive weak-eligibility relation P and a reflexive and transitive relation I, where $P \cap I = \emptyset$. Incomparability is defined as aNb if and only if $a\not{P}b$, $b\not{P}a$ and $a\not{I}b$.*

This leaves it open whether the two relations exhaust the space of possibilities. We may speak of a complete top-cycle free model with transitive equal goodness when N is empty, and partial top-cycle free model with transitive equal goodness if N is non-empty.

2.4 Strong Eligibility

Hansson also considers strong eligibility, which generally seems to fare better with certain anomalous situations of choice. Consider a choice situation in which no item can be compared with any other item. Then, according to the definition of weak eligibility, all of them are weakly eligible. Hence, all of them are recommended for choice by the underlying value. This recommendation is perhaps not more counter-intuitive than cycles in the first place. If lack of knowledge is the cause of incomparability, for instance, then choosing one item in an arbitrary way may be justified. For example, if you have to choose between three sorts of tea you have never tasted before, which cost the same, and about which you've never heard anything, it seems alright to pick one of them randomly—or by any other method you might come up with—and experiment to gather more information. The rationale for this behavior is essentially the same as for deciding between items that are deemed equally good.

However, weak eligibility also makes less convincing recommendations. Suppose that in the small cycle model aPb, bPc and cPb there is also an item d that is incomparable with all other items. Then according to the definition of weak eligibility, both a and d are weakly eligible. Again, this might be acceptable, for example if the incomparability is the result of a lack of knowledge, and a choice of the unknown d is considered on a par with the safe choice a. However, it might also sometimes be unacceptable, for example when d is incomparable to the other items for more fundamental reasons. Strong eligibility avoids both recommendations. An item a is strongly eligible if and only if for all b it is the case that aRb. Or equivalently, a is strongly eligible if and only if for all items b either aPb or aIb holds. As before, a relation over a given domain is strongly eligible, if at least one item is strongly eligible with respect to the relation and the domain, and a Strong Eligibility Model is defined as in Model 5 by substituting weak with strong eligibility. Whenever N is empty, the two types of models coincide.

In case all items are incomparable, strong eligibility recommends none of them. Likewise, in the second example, d is no longer recommended because only a is strongly eligible.

2.5 What Consistency Requirements Are Needed?

From a philosophical point of view, it is persistently hard to conclusively justify one type of model or another. As we have seen in Section 1.4 of Chapter 1, it is hard to clearly distinguish between eliminable and fundamental value incomparability. By the same token, it is far from clear how many constraints are needed for a rational monist value representation.

Some popular arguments for the standard model have already been debunked. First, the transitivity of equipreference and "equally good" seems to be a fairly strong rationality principle in practice, because we often lack a reliable, extensive measurement method for determining the value of items within one dimension of a value predicate. If we do not have such a method or it is imprecise, then cases of failure of the transitivity of "equally good" can occur. Even simple physical properties measurable with a yardstick or other conventional devices may give rise to measurement errors that lead to an nontransitive form of value equality. Furthermore, I have argued based on Hansson (2001), that the transitivity of the strict comparison form of a value predicate such as strict preferences, strict betterness, healthier than, and so forth, cannot be justified by choice-guidance *alone*. Depending on whether incomparable items are present or not, either weak or strong eligibility suffices for rational decision-making in particular choice situations.

Does that mean that we should choose the path of least resistance and assume eligibility models for all values? There are various arguments against this minimalist conception of value structure. Hansson (2001) himself provides an argument that is based on the dynamics of value relations. What happens if more or fewer items are considered, i.e., when the underlying domain D is extended or shrunk? If the domain is extended, then weak eligibility will only continue to hold if no new top cycle is introduced. By the same token, it is clear that shrinking the domain may cause weak eligibility to fail—just consider the example of the last section when a is removed and only the cyclic comparisons bPc and cPb remain. As a remedy, one might require eligibility to hold restrictably for a given value relation: A relation R over domain D has a property P restrictably whenever R also is P when it has been restricted to a smaller domain $D' \subseteq D$. Applying this condition, R is restrictably weakly eligible in domain D if and only if it is weakly eligible in D and also any restriction of R to a domain $D' \subseteq D$ is weakly eligible in D'. As it turns out, any relation that is weakly eligible and satisfies this condition will be acyclic. Moreover, any top-transitive strongly eligible relation with a corresponding restrictability condition will be complete and transitive.[7] Hence, fairly strong rationality conditions are recovered once weak and strong eligibility are required to hold restrictably for a value relation. With restrictable strong eligibility we even return to the standard model.

The argument based on restrictability is not very strong, though. It is not surprising that requiring weak eligibility to also hold in smaller domains amounts to imposing a cycle prohibition. Weak eligibility excludes top cycles, so if the domain is shrunk by the top elements and top cycles in the new domain are again prohibited, and this line of reasoning continues, then all cycles are prohibited in the end, of course. Restrictability seems to suggest that value relations are always choice-guiding, no matter what set of items they are applied to, and it is doubtful whether this is a viable conception of value relations. Instead, a value relation may be taken as an ordering of items with respect to some variety of goodness or aspect thereof, and agents only need to check whether it yields enough information to make a rational decision based on this value when they apply the value relation in a *specific* choice situation. From this point of view, top-transitive eligibility within a given domain is a minimal condition for being able to make a rational decision based on a monist value relation, and when this condition is not fulfilled, then a decision cannot be made rationally using that relation in that specific choice situation. In this view, values do not have to be organized in a way that always allows agents to make a rational decision based on them. This idea is not new: Agents may also fail to make a choice-guiding decision in a partial preorder model.

Another type of argument are money pumps or Dutch book arguments. These have been devised to establish the transitivity, or at least acyclicity, of strict preferences. Going back to Ramsey (1931), de Finetti (1931), de Finetti (1937), and Davidson et al. (1955), the central idea of a money pump is that agents who use cyclic strict value relations for decision-making would lose money if they were to sell and buy items. For example, suppose John values aPb, bPc, cPa over three collectors items, say, rare vinyl records a, b, and c, and he possesses c, which is worth \$20. Since bPc, he should be willing to trade in c in order to get b for \$20 plus some amount of money, say, \$5. So he gets b for \$25, and since aPb, he should be willing to trade in b to get a for \$25 plus some amount of money. Let this be \$5 again for simplicity. He then possesses a for a worth of \$30, and since cPa he should be willing to trade in a to get c for \$30 plus some small amount of money such as \$5, and so he gets c again and has already lost \$15. However, the cycle does not stop at that point, defenders of money pumps claim. John believes that b is better than c, so the cycle continues until John has lost all of his money and some lucky second-hand record merchant has made a fortune. This behavior is irrational, and since John only uses the underlying value relation to guide his decisions, this relation seems to be irrational, too. This is a money pump of the first kind, since it is based on a value relation's strict part.[8]

It is also possible to come up with money pumps of the second kind, i.e., money pumps for a nontransitive weak part of a value relation like in a semiorder model. Suppose aIb, bIc, and aPc. Suppose the agent has c.

Since aPc, the agent should be willing to give up c in favor of a for some amount such as \$10. Due to aIb it would seem rational for the agent to accept a deal to give up a for b for some smaller amount than the initial one, say, \$2, and again because of bIc to make a deal to swap b for c and getting another \$2 in return. As a result, the agent has lost \$6, and the cycle can continue.[9]

Top transitive strong eligibility ensures that there are one or more best items, and so a money pump is not applicable to the strict part. Nevertheless, a money pump will be applicable whenever only items lower in the ordering are up for sale, and in this sense money pump arguments can serve as an illustration of restrictability. One might go even further and argue that it is irrational to have a "better than" cycle anywhere in the value ordering, because if the agent in question was offered a choice to sell and buy items from anywhere in the domain, then they would become irrational if the items belong to a cycle. Again, this is an argument for the restrictability property of eligibility, combined with the money pump as a positive argument for the irrationality of cycles. Cycles are irrational because agents with cyclic preferences would be susceptible to infinite losses if they were offered a choice to buy and sell items at prices that match their value ordering. Money pumps of the second kind may be used against semiorder models.

Before going on with criticism, a few remarks shall rule out some common misperceptions about money pumps. First, nothing in money pump arguments hinges on monetary value. We can reformulate any money pump argument with something else than money that has some exchange value for the two agents. The above example does not change substantially if you replace the five dollar difference between two adjacent items with a bag of peanuts. Money pumps only rely on the idea that an agent who judges that a is better than b in some decisive respect will be willing to trade in b in favor of a and some additional cost that indicates that aPb holds. In utility theory this requirement states that $u(a) > u(b)$ for a utility function $u(\cdot)$ that faithfully represents the value relation presumed by a particular agent, and that there is an associated positive value k that both agents are willing to trade for switching from b to a. The exact representation conditions for utilities will be addressed in the next chapter, but it is worth noting that this k does not need to be the utility difference $u(a) - u(b)$ and that the above type of money pump argument does not presume cardinal utilities either. It merely requires the existence of additional items that have an adequate positive value for both the seller and the buyer. The second issue to mention is that in Ramsey's original paper and much of the subsequent work, money pumps were discussed in the context of decision-making under risk, whereas we have discussed them in the context of decision-making under full certainty. It is important to keep the two things apart, since in decision-making under risk many other factors such as risk-attitude and the evaluation of subjective probabilities might interfere, which do not play a role in decision-making under certainty. Money pumps like the above ones may be more plausible than those based on bets, and not all arguments against the latter will be persuasive against the former.[10]

Are money pumps decisive as an argument? As authors like Schick (1986), Hansson (2001), and Hajek (2009) point out, money pumps make fairly strong assumptions. They assume that there is something of positive value to trade for and that an agent will always be willing to trade in a less-valued for a higher-valued item. Particularly the second assumption may be too strong. Why can an agent not simply detect the cycle and stop trading or refuse to trade in the first place because of the cycle? There seems to be no reason why such a requirement could not be added for *trades*. In this view, the money pump merely shows that you ought not make arbitrary trades if your evaluations are cyclic, but instead check for the absence of such cycles before trading. As Schick (1986) and many others have suggested, in a money pump scenario a rational agent should have a capacity to take a step back and look at the situation as a whole rather than sticking only with pairwise comparisons of individual items. For example, John might tell himself: "What if I buy b, a, and c again? Then I would end up losing $15, so I may just as well stick with c." This breaks the cycle by giving priority to the smallest loss compatible with his evaluation. The crucial question is this: Should John revise his views about the underlying value relation to make it acyclic based on such a consideration, or does it suffice if he breaks the cycle in some way in any concrete choice situation? The second position minimally amounts to imposing top transitive eligibility in any concrete choice situation—or mere eligibility in the case of semiorder representations—whereas the first position results in additionally imposing restrictability of eligibility and thus makes the strict value relation acyclic (viz., transitive if strong eligibility is assumed). I agree with the above authors and many others that money pumps do not conclusively show the first position, since values need not be choice-guiding at all, and even if one requires them to be choice-guiding in particular situations of choice, top transitive eligibility of a value relation over a given domain of items in a concrete choice situation suffices to enable the decision maker to come to a rational decision in that specific choice situation.

There is an argument for stronger rationality postulates. Unfortunately, it is not very powerful for defeating skeptics, but that does not make it inconclusive. One might argue that transitivity is part of the meaning of the comparative form of certain or all value predicates. That is Broome's position in *Weighing Lives* when he writes:

> A comparative relation is necessarily transitive. This is an analytic feature of the operator 'more... than': the meaning of 'more... than' is transitive. [...] Some authors write as though the transitivity of betterness is an issue in ethics. It is not; it is an issue in semantics. (Broome, 2004, pp. 51–52)

However, in Chapter 8 so-called Spectrum Cases by L. Temkin and S. Rachels against the transitivity of "better than" will be discussed against which the semantic argument appears particularly weak. While Broome's position is a valid standpoint, it would be desirable to have a theory of "better than" that does not rely on our semantic intuitions but instead is based on independent philosophical arguments about value structure. The theory in Chapter 9 will be of this sort. It is based on the idea that examples of cyclic evaluations always arise from mixed criteria which should be represented by more than one value relation. When the above example is spelled out, at one point or another a second aspect of betterness different from R slips in, maybe without anyone noticing, that turns the problem into a value aggregation problem. The thesis is that any particular strict value relation can be transitive at least for all comparable items, but that the transitivity of any aggregate value relation is harder to warrant. In the end, the theory of betterness of Chapter 9 will even retain the transitivity of aggregated overall "better than" while remaining compatible with Temkin's and Rachels's arguments, but at the price of making lexicographic comparisons that involve thresholds. For the time being, we may note that there is no decisive criterion for or against rationality postulates that go beyond weak and strong eligibility, and that there seems to be room for stronger or weaker rationality constraints on value relations even when a purely normative perspective is assumed.

Chapter 3

Utility Functions

In this chapter, I address a question that has kept decision theorists and experts in measurement theory busy during the 20th century: Is there a numeric representation that adequately represents a given base value relation? The answers to this question are less straightforward than one might think once the domain becomes uncountably infinite. In order to avoid these technicalities, we will assume finite domains in what follows unless noted otherwise.

3.1 A Historical Remark

Before going into more detail, a brief historical overview is necessary to provide some context. For the standard model and slight variations thereof, numerical representations have been provided through utility functions that sometimes provide amounts in a fictitious unit "util" standing for abstract value. The mathematical concept of utility has its roots in economics. It came up when economists attempted to formally capture the corresponding philosophical concept of utility from early versions of utilitarianism like Bentham (1789) and Mill (1906) by the end of the 18th and during the early 19th centuries. The concept of utility of early utilitarians like John Stuart Mill was not formally developed. They explained it in terms of different sorts of pleasure and pain. During the 19th century, economists like Gossen (1854) and Marshall (1890) detached the notion to some extent from its philosophical background and formalized it using the full apparatus of calculus for continuous functions. In this tradition, utilities did not express underlying preference relations or other relations of value structure. Consequently, early conceptions of utility made fairly strong assumptions about the comparability of items under consideration, about both interpersonal and intrapersonal comparability of utilities for different values and agents, and the existence of a measurable scale given by "utils."

The situation changed at the beginning of the 20th century thanks to the work of Pareto (1900, 1906) and Samuelson (1938, 1947), among others. By that time, utility was considered a sort of subjective but still intersubjectively comparable response of individual agents that could be measured like a physical property. Pareto was dissatisfied with this unfounded assumption. He started to develop the theory of ordinal utilities in which classes of utility functions represent an agent's preferences, i.e., qualitative comparisons like the ones we have discussed in the previous chapters. Samuelson extended this new foundation of microeconomics by elaborating the methods for empirically grounding utilities in observed preferences, thereby seeking the empirical foundations for the revealed preferences thesis mentioned in Chapter 1, according to which agents' preferences are revealed by their choices.

For the current project of representing value structure in general, empirical methods of preference elicitation are less critical, because we are interested in the structure of values from a normative point of view rather than in agents' individual preferences. Obviously, such a conception of value structure is way more general than whatever underlying values consumer choices may reflect. What is important, however, is to bear in mind that utility is neither mathematically nor philosophically a uniform concept. It started out as as a way of talking about pleasure and pain.[1] It was then elaborated by utilitarian economists in the form of cardinal utility functions under the strong assumptions that the value of any item for a consumer can be expressed directly in terms of a utility function. Economists did not investigate utility functions as representations of underlying relations before the beginning of the 20th century.

Another point worth noting is that much of the development after Pareto was also driven by theories of decision-making under risk such as Ramsey (1931), von Neumann and Morgenstern (1944), and Savage (1951, 1954). In much of the literature on value-based rational decision-making aspects of values are intertwined with aspects of risk and uncertainty. Adding probabilities right from the start can simplify the mathematics of representing value under risk. Since in this volume the topic of risk is deferred to Chapter 10, the following brief overview of numeric representations of value structure may look quite different from the sometimes intriguingly simple-looking axiomatic foundations of decision-making under risk.

For the present purpose, it is unavoidable to keep the two issues apart, although they historically came in a package, since our representations of value structure need not be choice-guiding at all. Nevertheless, from the point of view of measurement theory such as Krantz et al. (1990) and Roberts (1979), it is easier and mathematically more elegant to consider the elicitation of preferences jointly with the probabilities of events and possible consequences of actions. Colloquially speaking, this is so, because defining arbitrary mixtures of probabilities and valuations in lotteries guarantees that the space of alternatives is large enough to accommodate all possible comparisons. The problem with adopting this view for axiology is that it is based on the idea of empirically measuring value and corresponding subjective probabilities. In contrast, we currently investigate the rationality constraints and normative principles of the structure of values. The purpose of axiology is *not* to measure revealed preferences and subjective probabilities; it is to lay out underlying structural principles of the comparisons made by "better than" and other comparatives of value predicates from a normative perspective. Whenever we use numbers to represent these comparisons, the method must satisfy the respective conditions from measurement theory for scale types and corresponding representation theorems. However, in the present view the choice of the underlying model is not derived from observed preferences but instead from more general normative considerations, although common "intuitions" about examples and thought experiments may also play a role. It is vital to keep this difference in mind in this and the following chapters.

3.2 Representation of the Standard Model

Suppose R is a complete preorder relation over a domain of items D with at least two elements. Now let $u(\cdot)$ be a utility function that maps all domain members to the real numbers, i.e., it is a function $u : D \mapsto \mathbb{R}$.

In which sense can this numeric representation be said to represent the relation faithfully? An obvious answer is that it must fulfill the following representation condition for all $a, b \in D$:

$$u(a) \geq u(b) \Leftrightarrow aRb \tag{3.1}$$

Such a utility function can always be constructed when the domain D is finite. In other words, a utility function $u(\cdot)$ that satisfies the Representation Condition 3.1 is guaranteed to exist in the mathematical sense whenever D is finite.[2] Since there are finitely many items in D, there must be a non-empty set of bottom elements $D_1 \subseteq D$ such that there is no $b \in D$ for which $a_i Pb$ for any bottom element $a_i \in D_1$. We may call this set the lowest level of the value ordering and set $u(a_i) = 1$ for all $a_i \in D_1$. Then we can define a notion of immediate dominance: An item a immediately dominates an item b if and only if aPb and there is no $c \in D$ such that aPc, cPb and $c\not I b$. The next level, level 2 in our ad hoc numbering scheme, is then the set of items D_2 that immediately dominate the bottom elements, and we set $u(a_i) = 2$ for all $a_i \in D_2$. This process continues until it reaches the topmost items; it is guaranteed to finish at one or more top items, because D is finite.[3] To normalize the utility function to the interval $[0, 1]$ when there are n levels, we can use the fact that $\sum_{k=1}^{n} k = \frac{1}{2}n(n+1)$ and divide all utility values by this factor.

We cannot use the same construction when the domain is countably infinite, because then each level might contain infinitely many items of equal value. However, there are other ways. I will outline a proof paraphrased from Roberts (1979, pp. 109–111), adopted to our preorder representation. Since the domain is countable, we can enumerate the items in it as $a_1, a_2, \ldots$ and define a function $M(i, j)$ that is 1 if $a_i R a_j$ and 0 otherwise. Note that if $a_i I a_j$, then $M(i, j) = M(j, i)$ because I is symmetric, but if $a_i P a_j$, then $M(i, j) = 1$ and $M(j, i) = 0$ because P is asymmetric. Based on M, we define the utility function as follows:

$$u(a_i) = \sum_{j=1}^{\infty} \frac{1}{2^j} M(i, j) \tag{3.2}$$

This equation converges to a finite value, because

$$\sum_{i=1}^{\infty} \frac{1}{2^i} \tag{3.3}$$

converges to 1 from below and $M(i, j)$ is only 1 or 0. To check that Formula 3.2 fulfills the Representation Condition 3.1, it must be shown that $u(a) = u(b)$ whenever aIb, that $u(a) > u(b)$ whenever aPb, and that the transitivity of R also holds for the utility function. These details follow from the construction of Formula 3.2.

The ability to enumerate items in the domain is needed for this kind of proof. There is a famous counterexample to the idea that the same construction could be used for an uncountable domain. It uses basic theorems of number theory that we have to presuppose here, since proving them would go beyond the scope of this volume. An ordering is defined over pairs of real numbers as follows: $(x_1, y_1)P(x_2, y_2)$ if and only if $x_1 > x_2$, or $x_1 = x_2$ and $y_1 > y_2$. This ordering is called lexicographic, because it works in the same way as when strings of characters are ordered. You sort by the first letter, then by the second letter, and so forth. The proof that there is no utility function for this relation is indirect by reductio ad absurdum. Suppose there is a $u(\cdot)$ that represents P. Since it represents P, from $(x_1, 1)P(x_1, 0)$ it follows that $u(x_1, 1) > u(x_1, 0)$. It is known that between any two distinct real numbers there is a rational number, i.e., a number that can be represented as a fraction of two integers. The set of rational numbers is usually written $\mathbb{Q}$. Now suppose there was a function $r : \mathbb{R} \to \mathbb{Q}$ such that the following holds:

$$u(x_1, 1) > r(x_1) > u(x_1, 0) \tag{3.4}$$

Based on the assumptions so far, there should be such a function. However, this cannot be the case. Choose two arbitrary $x, y \in \mathbb{R}$ and assume $x > y$. Then by Condition 3.4 it follows that $r(x) > u(x, 0)$, and furthermore $u(x, 0) > u(y, 1)$, since $x > y$, and $u(y, 1) > r(y)$ because of Condition 3.4. Since x and y are arbitrary real numbers, it follows that $r(\cdot)$ maps any two real numbers x, y to two distinct rational numbers $r(x)$ and $r(y)$. Hence, $r(\cdot)$ would be an injective mapping of the real numbers to the rationals. We know that such a mapping cannot exist, because the rational numbers are countable and the real numbers are uncountable. So we get a contradiction and can conclude that there is no utility function for this lexicographic ordering P of pairs in $\mathbb{R} \times \mathbb{R}$. Since it is easy to see that P is complete, transitive and antisymmetric, this means that the Representation Condition 3.1 is not fulfilled for arbitrary uncountable domains.

The value relation needs to be restricted for a given uncountable domain in order to ensure that it can be represented in the sense of Condition 3.1. A preorder R over domain D is Jaffray order-separable if there is a countable subset $C \subset D$ such that for each $a, b \in D$ for which aPb there are two $x, y \in C$ such that $aRxPyRb$ holds. It can be shown that a utility function for a preorder R satisfies the Representation Condition 3.1 in an uncountable domain D if and only if R is Jaffray order-separable in D.[4] Debreu (1954) proved that such a utility function is also continuous. More information about these rather technical conditions and their variations can be found in compendiums like Hammond (1998).

3.3 Representations for All Models

The other models discussed so far have been investigated by decision theorists and all except for eligibility models have some utility representations. However, these representations tend to be less intuitive and more complicated than the standard model and I will not address them in detail. For completeness, I list the respective representation conditions for strict value and equal value relations over finite domains with only a few remarks in what follows.

Starting with complete relations that do not allow one to express incomparability or withholding of judgments, we know from the last section that the relations derived from total preorders satisfy the following conditions:

Representation 1 (Complete Preorder Representation, Debreu 1954).

$$aPb \Leftrightarrow u(a) > u(b) \tag{3.5}$$
$$aIb \Leftrightarrow u(a) = u(b) \tag{3.6}$$

One thing worth noting about these correspondences is that for eliciting preferences or opinions about values from actual human agents, $u(a) = u(b)$ and aIb are not on a par. Suppose you ask people to give direct scores using real numbers. They may be less willing to attribute exactly the same number to them than if you ask them to compare the items and judge whether one of them is better than the other or both are equally good, and likewise for other value predicates. This is one of the reasons why direct scoring is bad methodology and should be avoided.[5] The comparisons expressed by the utility relation should be derived from a prior qualitative ordering rather than vice versa.

Representation 2 (Complete Semiorder Representation, Scott and Suppes 1958).

$$aPb \Leftrightarrow u(a) > u(b) + \delta \quad (3.7)$$
$$aIb \Leftrightarrow |u(a) - u(b)| \leq \delta, \quad (3.8)$$

where δ is a positive real number.

As laid out in Section 2.1 of the previous chapter, δ defines an interval. If the utilities of two items partially overlap in this interval, then these items are of equal value; if on the other hand the lower bound of the interval associated with $u(a)$ is higher than the higher bound of the interval associated with $u(b)$, i.e., if $u(a) > u(b) + \delta$, then a is strictly better than b. (See Figure 2.1 on page 27 for illustration.) The value δ can also be interpreted as an uncertainty threshold.[6] Under that interpretation (3.8) is not postulated but instead if $|u(a) - u(b)| < \delta$, aNb is concluded and the strict order is partial.

If intervals may be embedded into each other, then an interval order can represent them according to the following conditions:

Representation 3 (Complete Interval Order Representation, Fishburn 1970a).

$$aPb \Leftrightarrow u(a) > u(b) + q(b) \quad (3.9)$$
$$aIb \Leftrightarrow |u(a) - u(b)| \leq q(b), \quad (3.10)$$

where $q(b)$ is a non-negative function from the domain of items to real numbers.

Finally, distinct unary utility functions cannot represent weak eligibility models, since a unary utility function automatically makes strict preference transitive. Even for Condition 3.9, the weakest utility representation so far, P can only be transitive. This follows immediately from the right-hand side of Condition 3.9, since from $u(a) > u(b)+q(b)$ and $u(b) > u(c)+q(c)$ it follows that $u(a) > u(c) + q(c)$, but from the nontransitive case aPb,

bPc and $a\not{P}c$ we would obtain $u(a) \leq u(c) + q(c)$, which contradicts the previous implication.

Instead of using a unary utility function, weak eligibility models with cyclic strict preferences can be represented to some extent by a combined, two-place utility function:

Representation 4 (Dyadic Utility Representation).

$$aPb \Leftrightarrow f(a,b) > 0 \tag{3.11}$$

$$aIb \Leftrightarrow f(a,b) = 0 \tag{3.12}$$

where f is a function $f : D \times D \rightarrow \mathbb{R}$ that can be negative.

It is sometimes possible to decompose f into a difference structure $u(a) - u(b)$ expressible by a unary utility function, but not in general. One way of converting such a function into a traditional utility representation is to determine the largest cycles at each level below the weakly eligible elements, if there are such cycles, and treat all items within that cycle as if they were equipreferred or equally good. For example, suppose the strict value comparisons are as depicted in Figure 3.1a and note that an arrow x to y and from y to x for any two items x, y does *not* symbolize equal value like in the standard model in this case but a direct cycle between two items. The largest cycle is bPd, dPb, and so we derive the new standard model in Figure 3.1b in which $aPbIcIdPe$ holds.[7] This has a utility representation that assigns $u(e) = 1$, $u(a) = 3$, and $u(x) = 2$ to all other arguments $x \in \{b, c, d\}$. As I mentioned earlier, the usefulness of such a reduction is questionable, though. After all, the cyclic part contains information about an agent's possibly irrational strict preferences, including two cycles, or, from the perspective of abstract value structure, the information that there really is an evaluative cycle (for whatever philosophical reasons one might presume). This information is lost by the reduction. One might argue that if such a reduction makes sense, then the standard model's stronger rationality postulates should have been imposed right from the start.

Let us now turn to the partial variants of the models. What does aNb mean for a utility function? Since it is implemented as the case when the base relation R is not defined, or when neither a comparison by P nor by I is possible when strict betterness and equal goodness are taken as a basis, it seems that the utility function cannot be defined in this case either.

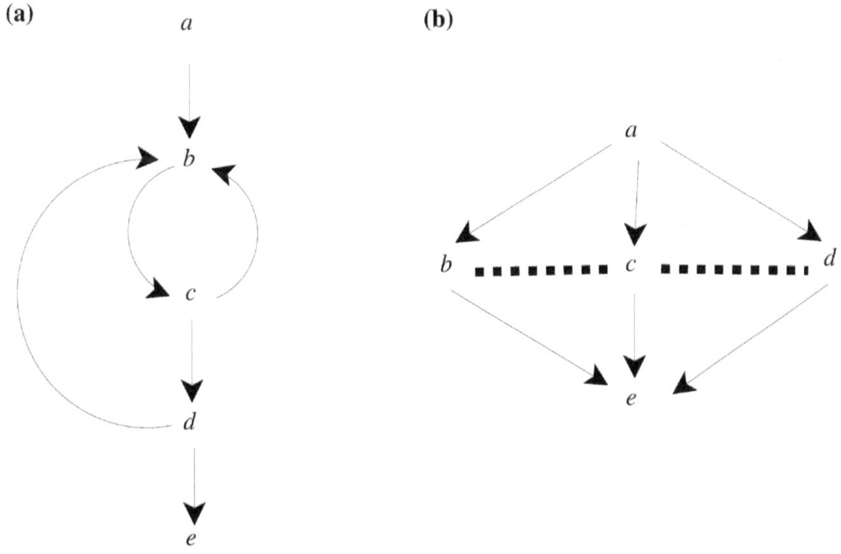

Figure 3.1: (a) Weak eligibility model with cyclic preferences and (b) its reduction to a standard model. Arrows symbolize strict preferences and dotted lines equipreference.

We have to define it over the union of the domains for which I and P are defined respectively. Therefore, the representation condition becomes a conditional instead of a biconditional. For example, for a partial preorder model it becomes

$$aRb \Rightarrow u(a) \geq u(b). \tag{3.13}$$

The same applies to the other representation conditions. The biconditional is replaced by a conditional. Consequently, we are left with a sort of meaning postulate rather than a representation condition. The utility function does not contain enough information to recover the partial relation because the partial relation is partial with respect to a larger domain. This is only a problem if we attempt to take the utility representation as the sole basis for a representation of overall preference or betterness. Some utilitarians like Harsanyi (1977, Ch. 1–5) make this assumption. However, the problem can be fixed by looking at a larger domain than the one over which the utility functions are defined, i.e., by making the utility functions "partial" and introducing some explicit way of talking about the case when they are not defined. In that case, two items a and b are incomparable, if the utility $u(.)$ is not defined for a, b, or both.

3.4 Ordinal Versus Cardinal Utilities

It is part of the folklore in economics that the representation theorem of the standard model is accompanied by a uniqueness theorem that characterizes the equivalence class of functions representing a given complete preorder relation. It states that if $u(\cdot)$ is a utility function representing a complete preorder R according to the Representation Condition 3.1 on page 46, then for any strictly increasing positive function f the utility function u' defined as $u'(x) = f(u(x))$ also represents R and satisfies the Representation Condition 3.1, where a function f is strictly increasing if and only if for all x, y such that $x > y$ it follows that $f(x) > f(y)$. So there are in fact infinitely many utility functions that represent a complete preorder, but they are unique up to strictly increasing transformations: It does not matter how much we bend or stretch such a utility function, it will still represent the underlying qualitative ordering. If this invariance under strictly increasing transformation holds, then u is an ordinal utility function. Such a utility function is nothing else than an alternative way of formulating a standard model. The actual numbers do not matter, since any other numbers transformed by a strictly increasing function would also do. If a utility function is ordinal in the sense of *only* encoding ordinal information, then a utility comparison may only take into account the relative rankings of items that coincide with the underlying ordering. Of course, this limitation has serious implications for value aggregation and comparison methods, and we will return to this issue in Chapter 4.

The idea of cardinal utility functions goes back to Nicolas Bernoulli, who proposed a logarithmic utility function to solve the then-popular St. Petersburg Paradox in a letter to Pierre Raymond de Montmort in September 1713. Later the solution was published by his brother Daniel Bernoulli (Bernoulli, 1738). Generally speaking, cardinal information is additional information about intensities and utility differences, and hence in the context of the present discussion concerns value intensities. Following Stevens (1946), scale types need to be distinguished by the transformations that allow meaningful translations between two utility functions.[8] On a ratio scale, the utility information is preserved only between two utility functions $u(\cdot)$ and $u'(\cdot)$ if $u(x) = \alpha u'(x)$ for some real number $\alpha > 0$. The condition is rather strict. It ensures that ratios are preserved and remain comparable and that the 0-point of the scale is not arbitrary, i.e., that $u(x) = 0 \Leftrightarrow u'(x) = 0$. Height, weight, and age are on ratio scales. On an interval scale, the utility information is preserved by any positive linear transformation, i.e., $u'(x)$ represents the same interval scale as $u(x)$ iff. $u'(x) = \alpha u(x) + \beta$ for real number $\alpha > 0$. This means that difference comparisons like $u(a) - u(b) > u(c) - u(d)$ remain meaningful, but the 0-point is given by convention and has no absolute meaning. Temperature in Celsius and temperature in Fahrenheit are on an interval scale. In contrast, temperature in Kelvin is on a ratio scale because the 0 is meaningful according to this temperature measure; it represents absolute zero temperature and is not given by mere convention.[9] Utilities on interval and ratio scales are usually called cardinal utilities. Another cardinal utility scale is the nominal scale. It does not play any important role in our context, because it is defined by identity. A utility function $u'(.)$ simply represents the same function $u(.)$ on the nominal scale iff. $u'(x) = u(x)$ for all x. This is the scale on which counting is based.

Do value predicates express cardinal information? To answer this question, let us first consider some arguments against cardinality that are ultimately not decisive. First, technical difficulties that may arise if we combine nonstandard models with cardinal information need not speak against cardinal utility. For example, the fact that noncomparability turns representation theorems into conditionals does not disqualify cardinal utilities in general, for one may argue that utility differences and intensities are meaningful whenever two items *can* be compared, even though they do not make sense when two items cannot be compared. Moreover, it would be technically possible to introduce "numeric degrees of noncomparability" with meaningful differences and make them represent an additional relation of noncomparability. However, cardinal information in semiorder models must respect the fact that these already represent intervals. Since according to Condition 3.8 on page 49 overlapping intervals are equipreferable or equally good, utility differences that are smaller than the interval size δ ought not lead to evaluative differences. For example, if $|u(a) - u(b)| < \delta$, then a comparison like $u(a) - u(b) < u(c) - u(d)$

might not make sense, because a and b are already equipreferable, of equal value, or, depending on the interpretation of I, even indistinguishable from each other. So we have to be careful only to take into account differences above the threshold. When the differences are larger than δ, it seems that difference comparisons become possible again, and so cardinal information can be contained in the utility representation of semiorders, too. Generally speaking, how to elicit and represent cardinal information in nonstandard models should be regarded as a technical problem. One might argue that if cardinal information is present in a value, then the value model better be able to accommodate it, instead of doing the opposite and determining the properties of a value with corresponding value predicate based on a premeditated model.[10]

Second, from the fact that extensively measurable quantities such as length rest on a ratio scale, the converse cannot be concluded. It is feasible for some preferences plus utility intensities or differences to give rise to a ratio or an interval scale without being measurable in the same way as length or temperature in degree Celsius. For extensive measurement, something akin to a ruler and some concatenation operation is needed that corresponds to the addition of two lengths.[11] For example, "taller than" is based on physical length and therefore falls under the theory of extensive measurement. Lengths can be added, subtracted, and freely translated from one measurement scale to another. However, it is possible to empirically detect or normatively prescribe the presence of an underlying ratio scale without determining easily any associated operations like addition, using a ruler, and so forth. Once one leaves the confines of purely empirical measurement and normative considerations enter, it may be possible to identify a particular scale type based on more general arguments about the rationality and normativity of a given value. The perspective of measurement theory is misleading in this context, since it rests on the idea of measuring individual value judgments in empirical value psychology, as for example was the goal of Samuelson's Revealed Preference Theory. However, there is no way to normatively justify why a given value predicate *should* elicit a certain underlying structure on the basis of empirical measurements of value judgments alone. At some point, normative considerations must come into play.

This point is crucial for an assessment of the interpersonal comparability of utilities or lack thereof. If a value predicate had a ratio scale like length and fulfilled the requirements for extensive measurement, then utilities would be freely comparable across agents out-of-the-box, so to say. However, most value predicates are not based on such objectively measurable physical dimensions. Even if they seem to have such dimensions, such as the time to finish a project or the monetary cost of a course of action, the same quantity of a dimension like monetary costs may be evaluated differently by different agents and one and the same agent may evaluate increasing quantities of the dimension in a nonlinear fashion. When present, both distortions indicate that in the end such dimensions are prima facie evaluated subjectively—unless one is willing to defend a particular philosophical theory why they should be objective. Because of this potential subjectivity and agent-relativity of values, comparisons of evaluations by different agents are inherently more problematic than the measurement of a physical property, irrespectively of the scale type exhibited or attributed to the predicate for other, perhaps normative reasons. A rational evaluation of items should be based on their physical properties at one point or another but being grounded in physical properties does not imply that the underlying value can simply be measured. It may be subjective or it may be principally agent-relative in another way. Conversely, a valid and sound argument against an interpersonal scale may not generally work as an argument against cardinality, since assuming a common scale among agents is a way stronger thesis than merely assuming a ratio or interval scale.

Some arguments seem to speak for the presence of cardinal value expressed by certain value predicates but are not decisive either. One may argue that we frequently use phrases like "This X is much better than that X," and that the intensifier "much" indicates, as the name suggests, an intensity that requires at least an interval scale.[12] However, this is doubtful. An interval scale requires comparisons of differences between four items to be meaningful, but in a phrase like "This plan is much better than the one you previously proposed" no such comparisons are made. It is in fact tremendously difficult to come up with a convincing example of a difference comparison made with "better than," because this would force us to talk about and compare different "amounts of betterness" or use similar contorted language. We do not say that the amount of betterness of a minus the amount of betterness of b is greater than the amount of betterness of c minus the amount of betterness of d. What "a is much

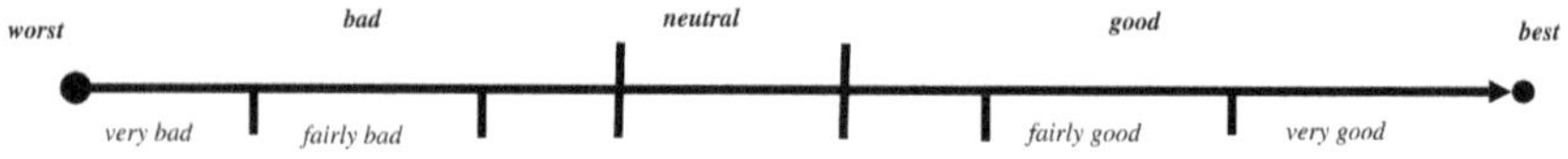

Figure 3.2: Goodness scale with examples of modifiers.

better than b" rather seems to mean is that the distance in terms of relative ranks between a and b is large relative to some contextually-provided standard. As long as only ranks are used, this remains compatible with ordinal utilities or using base relations alone.

A similar reply can be given to arguments for ratio scales based on ratio modifiers like "twice" in "twice as good." Purely rank-based explanations of such modifiers can be given. What "twice as good" then means, is "roughly twice in relative rank." For instance, if $aPbPcPdPePf$, then c is twice is good as e, because the ordinal rank of c is 4 and that of e is 2. Speaking for this analysis is the fact that ratio modifiers like "1.17 times better than" appear to be unacceptable or at least contrived.[13] It might be necessary to make the relative distances used for expressions like "much" and "a little bit" invariant with respect to the size of the domain, but this normalization is easy to achieve in a purely qualitative, ordinal framework, too, by properly dividing distances by the size of the domain or similar adjustments. Likewise, "very good" and similar modifiers do not pose a particular problem to ordinal value representations. Ignoring context for a moment to simplify, expressions like "good," "fairly good," "very good," and "best" provide an ordering that is represented on the "better than" axis in Figure 3.2.[14] The respective starting points need not be any utility values but can instead be exemplary, designated items in the ordering.

The point of these considerations is not that value adjectives reside on ordinal scales only, the point is rather that linguistic examples do not decide the issue since purely rank-based explanations of the respective modifiers can also be provided. Bearing that in mind, it is not easy to dismiss cardinal information when an underlying domain is extensively measurable. Many types of attributes are extensively measurable and are common enough for economists to use them as a basis, and they also seek to quantify other value dimensions when they are not based on physically measurable properties. Suppose a value dimension is clearly measurable by extensive measurement. Then the respective quantity itself gives rise to meaningful difference comparisons, just like we can say that John is ten inches taller than Mary whereas Bob is only five inches taller than Jack. For example, the hardness of a material is measurable on the Rockwell scale. So insofar as the material plays a role in how good it is for constructing or using some artifact, this attribute enters the overall goodness of the material. We can make meaningful comparisons between different amounts of hardness of different kinds of materials. The evaluative aspect "hardness" is thus cardinal out of the box. Unless this cardinality is somehow lost, an evaluation of the attribute will also be cardinal. How could it be lost? We may decide that cardinal information should not play any role, for example, for making interpersonal comparisons of utility functions. However, there may be no good reason to assume that an attribute that can be measured directly on a cardinal scale does not give rise to a cardinal utility function.

Money is a paradigmatic example. First, the amount of money one has is a simple quantity. Second, by the Principle of Diminishing Marginal Utility, the more money an agent has, the less subjective worth it will have for that agent. If this is so, then the utility function is concave, which implies at least an interval scale.[15] So whenever monetary cost is at play, the corresponding utility function will encode cardinal information in addition to an underlying preference ordering. Economists often make other assumptions, such as "more is better," which means the utility function is monotonically increasing with the amount of the attribute under consideration. Such assumptions must be critically evaluated in the context of philosophical value theory. Prima facie, whenever an extensively measurable quantity constitutes a value domain, this suggests cardinal utility—a value theorist cannot presume, without further argument, that information about the amount of something can be discarded and should not play any role.

To summarize the discussion, additional cardinal information seems to sometimes enter a value representation by a utility function and sometimes not. When the underlying domain of items is extensively measurable, then it is reasonable to assume that the corresponding monist value, or value dimension in case of a complex value, also contains cardinal information. An additional argument is needed to support the thesis that the respective value dimension does not give rise to cardinal utility. When an underlying domain of items is not extensively measurable and instead based on mere rankings right from the start, as one might expect for many aesthetic and moral value predicates, then it is reasonable to assume that the corresponding utility function is ordinal in the absence of further evidence to the contrary. An additional argument is needed to support the thesis that the respective value dimension also contains cardinal information. This poses an immense conceptual challenge because there does not seem to be any sound way to combine cardinal and ordinal value dimensions without losing some cardinal information. I will return to this problem in Chapter 5 and Chapter 9.

Chapter 4

The Complexity of Value

We are now ready to deal with the various ways in which values become complex and require more complex representations than the ones introduced so far. Many value predicates have a positive and a superlative in addition to a comparative form. In a setting based on value comparisons, these forms need to be derived from the comparative form of a gradable value predicate. Another topic of this chapter is satisficing, the case when an item is "good enough" for a certain purpose.

4.1 Positive, Comparative, Superlative

We have already seen positive and superlative forms of value predicates in Chapter 1 and Section 3.4 of the previous chapter. These will now be addressed in more detail. The positive form can be derived from the comparative by a designated element that serves as a starting point. Consider "good" as the positive form of "better than" and assume a fixed context in which a particular reading like "good for a kitchen knife" is prevalent and uncontroversial. Not every item compared by "better than" may be good in the standard model. Instead, as Figure 3.2 on page 56 suggests, some of them are worst, some are bad, some may be neutral, some may be good, and some are best. In between may be additional, more fine-grained distinctions such as "very good" and "good enough." If the domain of items is finite and there are enough items to compare, then there may be one or more good items such that an item that is worse than them no longer counts as good but instead either as bad or neutral. By the same token, any better items than those first good items will remain good.

Analogous distinctions can be made in the other direction for "bad." The only problem is that in this case the direction is reversed, so the grammatical term "positive form" is a bit misleading. We may instead use the term "simple form" to denote any non-superlative predicates for value and disvalue based on a given comparative form. For example, "bad" is a simple disvalue predicate derived from "worse than" and "good" a simple value predicate derived from "better than." The attribute "simple" does not imply that these predicates are not further analyzable. Sources of context-dependence are ignored in what follows.

Based on this terminology, the following definitions capture the properties discussed so far.

Definition 1 (Lower and Upper Boundary). *Let C be the comparative form of a value predicate with underlying comparison relations P and I over domain D. With respect to a simple value predicate G derived from C, the lower boundary of G is the set of elements $L(G) \subseteq D$ such that for all $a_i \in L(G)$: $G(a_i)$ and there is no $b \in D$ such that $a_i P b$ and $G(b)$. Correspondingly, with respect to a simple disvalue predicate B derived from C, the upper boundary of B is the set of elements $U(B) \subseteq D$ such that for all $a_i \in U(B)$: $B(a_i)$ and there is no $b \in D$ such that $b P a_i$ and $B(b)$.*

Definition 2 (Upwards and Downwards Monotonicity). *A simple value predicate G with underlying strict preferences P over domain D is upwards monotonous if and only if for all a in the lower boundary of G and all b such that bPa, it is the case that $G(b)$. A simple value predicate B with underlying strict preferences P over domain D is downwards monotonous if and only if for all a in the upper boundary of B and all b such that aPb, it is the case that $B(b)$.*

Hansson (2001) and other authors call the upwards monotonicity of "good" positivity and the downwards monotonicity of "bad" negativity.

Definition 3 (Maximal and Minimal Items). *For a given comparative form C of a value predicate with underlying comparison relations R, P and I over domain D, the P-maximal items $C_\top(D)$ in D are all strongly eligible items* *and the P-minimal items $C_\bot(D)$ are those for which there is no less valued item:*

$$C_\top(D) = \{x \mid \forall y \in D : xPy \text{ or } xIy\} \tag{4.1}$$
$$C_\bot(D) = \{x \mid \forall y \in D : yPx \text{ or } xIy\} \tag{4.2}$$

These are standard definitions that are used in many other applications of order theory, too. The existence of maximal and minimal items is only guaranteed if the domain is non-empty and finite. If the domain is infinite, there could be infinite ascending and descending chains of comparisons without any maximal or minimal items. To ensure that a strict ordering P has a set of maximal and minimal items respectively in an infinite domain, corresponding well-ordering conditions need to be stipulated. These restate the above definitions as conditions on the ordering and the domain, that R, or, correspondingly, the union of P and I, has sets of maximal and minimal elements in the domain, i.e., $C_\top(A) \neq \emptyset$ and $C_\bot(A) \neq \emptyset$ for any non-empty subset $A \subseteq D$.

Definition 4 (Positive and Superlative Forms). *For the comparative C of a monadic value predicate with underlying strict ordering P and equipreference I, the maximal items constitute the truth-conditions for the value superlative and the minimal items constitute the truth-conditions for the disvalue superlative. The corresponding simple value form (positive form) is an upwards monotonic simple value predicate G with lower boundary $L(G)$. The corresponding simple disvalue form is a downwards monotonic monadic disvalue predicate B with upper boundary $U(B)$, and additionally it must hold that for all x, y: If $x \in L(G)$ and $y \in U(B)$, then xPy. The possibly empty set of value neutral items is $N = \{x \mid xPy \text{ and } zPx \text{ for all } y \in U(B) \text{ and } z \in L(G)\}$.*

For example, let "better than" be the comparative. Its simple value form is "good" and its simple disvalue form is "bad." The corresponding value superlative is, of course, "best" and the disvalue superlative is "worst."

The monotonicity properties of value and disvalue predicates might seem odd from the perspective of everyday language use. It may seem odd to state of the best items that they are good and of the worst items that they are bad, but the reasons for this oddity are pragmatic. By their underlying orderings, value predicates trigger scalar implicatures along the value and disvalue axes. If someone asserts that x is good, then this implicates that x is not best, and if someone asserts that x is bad, then this implicates that x is not the worst. By the same token, it can be a violation of the Gricean maxim of quality to only state that x is bad when x is in fact among the worst and that x is good if x is in fact among the best items under consideration.

Opinions are divided about whether every item that can be compared with some respect of "better than" is either good or bad. Following Chisholm and Sosa (1966), many axiologists agree that items under consideration may also be neutral with respect to a particular understanding of "better than" in a given context of using the predicate. In that case, the set of value neutral items is not empty.

4.2 Good in Terms of Better Than

There is a vast literature on defining "good" in terms of "better than" when the latter holds not between arbitrary items, but between propositions that can be negated.[1] According to a suggestion of Brogan (1919), the simple value predicate G for "good" is defined as $Ga \Leftrightarrow aP\neg a$, which can be read as "that a is the case is good if and only if it is better for a to be the case than it is for a not to be the case," and the predicate B for "bad" is defined as $Ba \Leftrightarrow \neg aPa$. According to Chisholm and Sosa (1966) this definition is inadequate, because it implies that the negation of a good proposition is always bad. In their opinion, this is not always the case; there are also neutral cases. They therefore define "good" in a way such that Ga is true if a is better than some proposition b that is equipreferred to its negation. Correspondingly, the predicate B for "bad" is true of those propositions that are worse than some proposition that is equipreferred to its negation:

$$Ga \Leftrightarrow \exists b[aPb \wedge bI\neg b] \tag{4.3}$$

$$Ba \Leftrightarrow \exists b[bPa \wedge bI\neg b] \tag{4.4}$$

Hansson (2018a) calls Chisholm and Sosa's conceptions "indifference-related good and bad." Hansson (1990) instead proposes the more general definitions of what he calls "canonical good and bad":

$$Ga \Leftrightarrow \forall b[bR^*a \rightarrow bP\neg b] \tag{4.5}$$
$$Ba \Leftrightarrow \forall b[aR^*b \rightarrow \neg bPb] \tag{4.6}$$

Hereby, aR^*b holds if and only if aRb or there is a sequence $c_1, \ldots, c_n$ such that $aRc_1, c_2Rc_3, \ldots, c_nRb$.

Several other ways of obtaining "good" and "bad" in terms of "better than" are laid out by van Dalen (1974, pp. 173–175). Van Dalen discusses a system with neutral items like the one proposed here, and how to include these in a preference logic based on the principle that $v_iI\neg v_i$ holds for all neutral propositions v_i. In what follows, let v without the index stand for any neutral item. In van Dalen's system with neutral items neutrality, "good," "bad," and "better than" are related to each other by the following principles from van Dalen (1974, pp. 173–174) in addition to the principles governing the underlying ordering relation:

$$Ga \wedge bPa \rightarrow Gb \tag{4.7}$$
$$Ba \wedge aPb \rightarrow Bb \tag{4.8}$$
$$Ga \wedge Bb \rightarrow aPb \tag{4.9}$$
$$Ga \rightarrow \neg Ba \tag{4.10}$$
$$Ba \rightarrow \neg Ga \tag{4.11}$$
$$vI\neg v \tag{4.12}$$
$$aPv \rightarrow Ga \tag{4.13}$$
$$vPa \rightarrow Ba \tag{4.14}$$

4.7 represents the upwards monotonicity (positivity) of "good" and 4.8 the downwards monotonicity (negativity) of "bad" with respect to "better than." 4.9 expresses the directional ordering of "good" and "bad" with respect to "better than." 4.10 and 4.11 together represent what Hansson (1990) calls duplicity, that Ga and Ba cannot be true at the same time with respect to the same value ordering. 4.12 encodes the idea that a neutral proposition is as good as its negation; together with 4.13 and 4.14 it ensures that the good propositions are above the neutral ones and the bad propositions are below them. These principles are not minimal axioms, as for example, 4.10, 4.11, and 4.9 follow from 4.12, 4.13, and 4.14 together.

Since I do not wish to presume that items can be negated and instead items are supposed to represent arbitrary, mutually exclusive alternatives, I will not go into more details about proposition-based approaches and instead refer the reader to Hansson (1990, 2001, 2018a).

4.3 Satisficing

A special form of value predicates is often paraphrased with "enough." Something may be "good enough," "healthy enough," "smart enough," "polite enough," and even "bad enough" (to deserve punishment, for example). In decision-making, "good enough" can be taken as the basis of a satisficing account. The idea behind satisficing goes back to work by Simon (1956). Human agents are resource-bounded and do not have the time and other resources to look at all possibilities exhaustively in a decision situation; instead, they may make a shortcut and choose an item that is merely good enough instead of trying to determine the best.

What is the meaning of "good enough?" Contextualists like Recanati (2004, 2010) have emphasized in the Philosophy of Language that "enough" is context-sensitive. As Recanati's hotly-debated example "Steel is strong enough" illustrates, what counts as enough of something depends on purposes, goals, and other factors that the speaker may have in mind at one occasion or another. What counts as "good enough" in a decision situation must also hinge on such additional factors. A course of action is good enough relative to some contextually-provided assessment criteria, which must be rationally justifiable if the decision is supposed to count as a rational choice. Once such criteria have been determined, the structural constraint expressed by "good enough" on the goodness scale does not substantially differ from those of other predicates on the scale. What is good enough is above the lower boundary of what is good but may lie below what is best, and it inherits upwards monotonicity from goodness simpliciter. If a is good enough for some purpose, and b is better than a, then b must also be good enough for that purpose.[2] Once the contextual threshold for "enough" has been determined, "good enough" merely replaces "best" by reinterpreting what is best as whatever item lies at or above that threshold. Hence, from the point of view of value structure, a satisficing account of goodness does not offer anything radically different for choice-guidance. The only difference to choosing the best items is that items that are good enough need not be considered equally good at a closer look. However, they still form an equivalence class by being good enough.

To make better sense of satisficing it should therefore be regarded as a type of resource-boundedness that already plays a substantial role when agents select items in a given choice situation and changes the whole assessment procedure. Instead of collecting items on the whole betterness scale and trying to find, say, courses of action that are optimal in every respect, the agent uses shortcuts from the very beginning and stops looking at any kind of improvements that could be made to courses of action that are already good enough. This saves resources while still allowing the agent to come to an acceptable decision, although perhaps not an optimal one. Satisficing does not pertain to value itself in this view, but rather concerns heuristics one might use to save time and efforts when making choices based on values.

4.4 How Context-Sensitive Are Values?

There are numerous ways in which "better than" comparisons and comparisons by comparatives of other value adjectives may be considered context-sensitive. Just as an item can be good enough for a particular purpose, an item can also be good for a particular purpose and not good for another purpose. Likewise, a can be better than b for some purpose and b better than a for another purpose. As von Wright (1963) lays out, there are also many different sorts of goodness. An apple may be good in the medical sense, which according to von Wright is a special form of instrumental goodness. The same apple may be bad in the hedonic sense for someone who really hates apples.

Moreover, we may distinguish between being good or better simpliciter and being good or better for some benefactor. For example, going by plane may be good for some individual but bad for the environment. Something can also be good according to someone and not good according to someone else. For example, ice cream may be good for John according to John, but not good for him according to his doctor. Finally, "good" can be used attributively and predicatively. In an attributive use the goodness is always expressed with respect to some entities, as in being a good painter or being a good speaker. In contrast, a predicative use of "good" does not need to involve such a respect; it can also be unconditional. For example, it is used unconditionally in the following sentence, as long as we assume that there are no hidden contextual factors at play: "Friendship is good."[3]

Geach (1956) famously argued against Moore (1903) that the unconditional, predicative uses of "good" are meaningless, or at the very best shortcuts and imprecise ways of talking about being good in certain respects or being good as falling under some class of items or activities. In this view, to say that someone is good as a painter is another way of saying that this person is a good painter. Often, a purpose also needs to be added to make sense of the phrase, for example in "a good knife for cutting meat" and "a good knife for carving wood." If these complements are missing, one may argue that they need to be contextually provided. While the debate can hardly be taken as having been decided for one side or another, we can say that the grammatical distinction between predicative and attributive uses is a bit misleading. As the previous examples show, it is not the predicative or attributive position of the adjective that counts. Instead, the debate is really about whether the underlying betterness comparisons can be made according to one decisive, overall monist betterness comparison or not, and whether such a comparison can be considered context-invariant. The core of the controversy is whether something can be good simpliciter.

Can it? I do not see how, and agree with Geach that it is hard to make sense of completely unconditional predicative uses of "good." As Chang (2012) puts it, in practice a value comparison is always made under some covering considerations. These may be purposes for evaluating or may be overarching "covering values." For instance, eating more salad and less steak is good under the covering value of medical goodness, good for the purpose of leading a healthy life. The same activity can be bad from a hedonic perspective for someone who hates salad and loves steak. As a perhaps more interesting example, consider the decisions of a company. These can be good from an economic perspective, even considering the economy of a country as a whole, yet at the same time bad for the majority of a society's citizens if the economic benefits are outweighed by disvalues such as environmental pollution. The position according to which there can be an overall unconditional value assessment amounts to stating that all imaginable aspects of a value comparison can be aggregated into one overall, all things considered assessment. This seems questionable to me. First, there may always be certain aspects that we have not imagined. Second, such an overall assessment is not possible when there is a principal and insolvable conflict between different aspects of "better than." This is the case in Sartre's resistance fighter example from Section 1.4 of Chapter 1, for instance. A genuine value pluralist position allows for such moral dilemmas, and these may occasionally prevent aggregation into an overall value.

Generally speaking, from a multidimensional value pluralist perspective, an unconditional predicative monist value comparison is the result of an aggregation process that combines different aspects of a value comparison into an overall verdict. However, in case of a moral dilemma such an aggregation may fail, and even if it succeeds, different evaluations of the aspects involved may lead to a different outcome and the overall result hinges on the choice of the aspects taken into consideration. Even if unconditional predicative uses of "good" are sometimes justifiable for making some abstract philosophical value comparisons, it seems to me that in our evaluative practices covering values and value aspects are always at play. This is especially relevant for the choice-guiding nature of values in decision-making, since every action has a certain cost.[4] So, for example, if we say that friendship is good, this is unconditional only in a very abstract sense. In practice, any decision regarding friendship will have to take into account a multitude of factors.

Having settled this problem, admittedly in a cursory way, the question is how to deal with the context-dependencies mentioned above in such a setting. To answer this, let me start with an observation: One of the cases listed above does not exemplify a context-sensitivity of the value predicate. Saying that a is better than b according to X is a way of making the value assessment relative to X's testimony or beliefs. Without claiming that it is exactly the same, a rough approximation could be given by the paraphrase "X believes that a is better than b." Another interpretation is "According to what X has told me, a is better than b." Expressions like "according to" and "believes that" relativize the statement to the testimony or beliefs of an agent. They act as intensional operators that embed the evaluative clause. In the embedded clause, there is no context-dependence in addition to that of "a is better than b." So we can put these cases aside.

The remaining examples boil down to restricting available value aspects in the proposed multidimensional setting to a smaller set of admissible value aspects. For determining what is good for someone only those aspects of evaluation are taken into account that contribute value or disvalue to the benefactor. For determining what is good under the covering value of medical goodness only value aspects that concern health are taken into consideration. For determining what is good for an entrepreneur only value aspects that contribute value or disvalue to entrepreneurs are taken into account. Formally, a covering consideration is thus a filter that yields a subset of available value aspects. However, it does not seem to make sense to model this context-dependence formally in great detail because it does not follow general, normatively justifiable rules. From a normative perspective, what items are considered and what value aspects are taken as being relevant for an evaluation are choices that need to be justified. These justifications do not follow a mechanism and they depend on a large number of normative factors outside the realm of axiology. Think about the various purposes for evaluating and various constraints such as maximum costs, procedural rules and social norms applying in the evaluation situation, the selection of admissible evidence and applicability of laws in legal contexts, and criteria concerning the division of power in group decision-making, just to name a few factors. All of these factors might influence the decision as to which value aspects are relevant in a given evaluative situation. There is no single nontrivial mechanism that could adequately model all these contributing factors.[5]

Consequently, I will not attempt to model these contextual factors in what follows and instead only assume that they somehow influence which items and value aspects are chosen in a given evaluative context. These value aspects are the topic of the next chapter.

Chapter 5

Multidimensional Value

As I mentioned in Chapter 1, an item is rarely (if at all) better or worse than another item simpliciter. In our daily value comparisons we take into account various factors that contribute to these assessments and regard the items under different aspects of "better than." That is, value predicates are multidimensional. This multidimensionality has been modeled in decision theory using multiple value relations with corresponding utility functions, which are then aggregated into an overall assessment. Such representations and the corresponding Problem of Value Aggregation are the topic of this chapter.

5.1 Introduction

A value predicate is multidimensional whenever it orders items under various aspects. These aspects need not necessarily be part of the truth-conditional meaning of the predicate under consideration, whether they do so or not hinges on a variety of linguistic factors, the presumed conception of semantics, and whatever one thinks about the semantics/pragmatics interface. Instead of locating dimensions in the meaning of a value predicate, it is more fruitful to consider them constituting part of proper justifications of comparisons made by the predicate's comparative form. This approach leaves the question open whether the multiple dimensions are part of the meaning, generated or determinable by pragmatic mechanisms, or only part of sound value-based justifications. There cannot be much doubt that many, if not all, value predicates are multidimensional in this reasonably weak sense of the word.

For example, consider the usefulness of a kitchen knife as an instrument in the kitchen. A good kitchen knife must be sharp, but that alone does not suffice. It should also have a good handle, so it does not slip out of the hand of its user or the grip loosens after some time, should be made from high-quality steel that does not rust, should be durable, it should be possible to re-sharpen it without destroying the blade, and so forth. Maybe it should even look good to delight the chef. Suppose a knife is sharp but has a lousy handle that bends easily. Then it is not a good kitchen knife. In turn, suppose that a knife has an excellent handle but consists of bad steel that rusts and breaks easily. Then it is also not a good kitchen knife. One might believe that the best kitchen knife is the one for which all those properties are optimal: It is made of the best steel, has the best possible handle, is sharpest, has the best design, etc. However, even if this knife might count as the best knife in general, it might still not be the best knife in a situation of choice when you want to buy a new kitchen knife because there are also costs to consider. Maybe a multibillionaire could hire the world's best material scientists to develop the best kitchen knife ever, but this would hardly be the best choice for ordinary people who like cooking. Moreover, sometimes improving one dimension may also go hand-in-hand with worsening another dimension. For example, maybe making the knife sharper makes the blade less sturdy, and vice versa. Maybe material science tells us that it is impossible to create a knife with a blade that is both the sturdiest and sharpest possible.

Considerations like these have led decision theorists like Keeney and Raiffa (1976) and Keeney (1996) to acknowledge that there are always value trade-offs. Different value dimensions must be weighed or ranked against each other. It is important to stress that we do not just need trade-offs because of the costs. Different aspects of a value are often not jointly optimizable, since they "pull into different directions," as in the knife example. Another typical example is designing a car. Some lovely designs are undesirable from an aerodynamic point of view, and, vice versa, optimal aerodynamics can make the design dull and indistinguishable from those of other brands.

These types of incompatibilities between different value dimensions, different values, and values and disvalues occur everywhere in the evaluative realm. They are not just confined to subjective personal values and what is sometimes called "prudential values." Trade-offs are always necessary and require some form of weighing or ranking. Since this a somewhat controversial claim (although it really shouldn't be), let us look at two examples of morally relevant trade-offs.

The first example concerns public policymaking and statistical deaths. These are death tolls that may in principle be made smaller or larger depending on which policy is adopted, but can only be measured in total, are usually not wholly preventable, and the single cases are also not predictable. For example, yearly victims of traffic accidents, airplane accidents, and diseases like cancer will occur as statistical deaths in public health and safety statistics. The number of statistical deaths within a period clearly constitutes a disvalue, something bad that has to be minimized. However, any measure to minimize the number of statistical deaths will cost money, which could be used elsewhere. Although laypeople sometimes propose this, the idea of disregarding costs to reduce statistical deaths at any cost is untenable. Taxes would rise indefinitely and other crucial domains like infrastructure would get zero funding, making the citizens' long and healthy lives a miserable grind to maintain the economy needed to keep up the health and environmental control system. Even without taking costs into account, minimizing statistical deaths is usually not feasible. For example, one can undoubtedly minimize traffic accidents by prohibiting cars. However, then the economy would break down and there might also be an issue with other value dimensions like the worth of individual freedom.

As a second example, suppose a farmer in a rural community diverts water from the river that passes through the village onto his fields. Clearly, irrigation for his fields are good for his work, hence also good for the farmer. At the same time, if the farmer diverts too much water from the river, potentially turning it into a trickle, this may be bad for other inhabitants of the village, and through possible sanctions and because he cares about his contemporaries, this effect would also create a disvalue for himself. It is easy to imagine a scenario in which the right amount of water to take is an equilibrium that trades one attribute "water for my fields" against another attribute "water for the rest of the village" in dependence of the respective values and disvalues of the amounts of water attributed to the fields and other villagers. Note that this example does not depend on whether the farmer acts primarily for selfish or altruistic reasons or a mixture of both. If the farmer is essentially egoistic, it may still be in his interest to avoid sanctions and sell the crop to other villagers. If the farmer is essentially altruistic, it may still be in his interest to water his fields so others can benefit from his crop. A value trade-off is also not necessarily related to the benefactor. If the fields belong to the village as a whole and volunteers attend to them in turns, the question still arises how much water should be diverted to the fields if the resource is overall limited and water is also needed elsewhere. In another scenario there might not be any village at all, but the same farmer might run a mill for his own benefits a little bit farther downstream.

Value trade-offs are unavoidable in both examples, and the reason is not, as one might think at first glance, that they are based on measurable quantities like the amount of water or the number of deaths by traffic accidents. These quantities do not represent an assessment of their goodness and badness, they instead enter this assessment as an input that is evaluated based on the respective conception of goodness and badness. This evaluation is not necessarily linear and may involve other factors as well. For example, there might be a threshold for the amount of water that reaches the village: Any amount above that threshold is acceptable and anything below the threshold completely unacceptable. Or, the judgment could be more gradual and involve a subjective factor like "impact of the amount of water on the overall quality of life"—having barely enough water might be within the range of admissible possibilities, but lead to a lower quality of life, for instance. As mentioned in Section 3.4 of Chapter 3, the value of physically measurable quantities need not correspond to their amount. With cardinal utilities it can be bent, stretched, and distorted in various ways. Even in a purely ordinal setting there need not be any direct linear relation between the amount of the physically measurable property and its evaluation. For example, a flow of n gallons of water per hour might be good for the fields, $2n$ might be better, $3n$ might be just as good as $2n$, and $4n$ or higher might be worse than n, and so the ordering is $3n \sim 2n \succ n \succ 4n \sim 5n \sim 6n \sim \ldots$, which is a cycle-free value structure of the standard model.

The above examples illustrate three points. First, values are complex because they almost always involve multiple dimensions. Second, trade-offs between different value aspects are often unavoidable. Third, at some point a multidimensional value predicate may be used to express an overall value judgment, which means that attributes of its underlying dimensions such as "amount of water," "cost of a course of action," or "estimated statistical deaths per year" need to be evaluated and somehow aggregated into an overall value. These three issues need to be addressed not just by any theory of rational decision-making based on values, but also by any rational value theory that involves multiple value aspects.

The first point will not be questioned any further in what follows. It seems obvious enough that our evaluative practices are always—or, at least, most of the time—based on multidimensional value comparisons. The second point is more complicated. I will argue in the second part of this book that more than a mere weighing is needed to do justice to "better than" comparisons from a normative perspective, and the details will have to wait until we have seen the corresponding philosophical puzzles. The remainder of this chapter deals with some of the traditional ways of dealing with the third issue, the problem of aggregating value aspects in various dimensions into an overall value.

Before going on, some terminology has to be fixed, though. A value dimension represents the range of property moments that are evaluated. Dimensions need to be based on properties of the items under consideration. In contrast, a value aspect represents the evaluation of particular items in a dimension. The two are not mapped onto each other one-on-one. The same dimension can support several value aspects. In decision theory, aspects are also sometimes called "features," "criteria," or "attributes." These are often associated with n-dimensional vector spaces of real numbers, however, and so I prefer to use the term "aspect" to avoid potential misunderstandings. To illustrate the difference between value aspects and dimensions, consider someone who is thinking about applying for a job and needs to evaluate different offers.[1] Different jobs (items) come with different salaries. The underlying dimension is how much money you get in the respective job. The value aspect is the value you attribute to the respective salary. Different jobs also yield different levels of a sense of recognition and fulfillment. The underlying dimension consists of the actual events or activities in a job that would satisfy you. The relevant value aspect is based on comparing these activities and thus evaluating them relative to each other with respect to the fulfillment they provide. From the point of view of evaluation, only value aspects count. However, from time to time we will also have to talk about the underlying dimensions.

5.2 Additive Value Aggregation

Let us consider the standard model for the time being and think of different ways in which value aspects might be aggregated into an overall assessment. As we have seen in Section 3.2 of Chapter 3, the standard model has full-fledged utility representations in the finite and countable case and additional conditions for uncountable domains. As is well-known, this correspondence is used in economics and decision theory to aggregate the value relations that represent preferences into an overall assessment. Suppose $R_1, R_2, R_3, \ldots, R_n$ are preorder relations that represent different aspects of the comparative form of a value predicate like "better than" in a particular application situation, where each aspect represents a different respect or criterion under which the items under question are being considered in some dimension, and suppose further that each relation R_i satisfies the Representation Condition 3.1 on page 46 for a corresponding utility function u_i. The aggregation of these functions can then be defined as an operation F that takes the outcomes of the utility functions for a given item as input, combines them in some way, and yields a new utility function:

$$u(x) = F[u_1(x), u_2(x), \ldots, u_n(x)] \tag{5.1}$$

It is also possible to define a domain D_i for each aspect i, such that the items differ for each utility function and the formula is expressed more generally as follows:

$$u(x_1, x_2, x_3, \ldots, x_n) = F[u_1(x_1), u_2(x_2), u_3(x_3), \ldots, u_n(x_n)] \tag{5.2}$$

The difference between the two is not essential and merely a matter of how to formulate the respective evaluations most conveniently, except that the more general formulation in theory allows for domains of different sizes, which would require additional normalization. To avoid such difficulties, I will assume Formula 5.1 in what follows but everything that is said also holds for the more general case.

Such aggregation problems are known in measurement theory under the label "conjoint measurement," since they naturally occur when a mix of features (i.e., aspects, in our terminology) is present in one form or another, and these features need to be measured in relation to some overall value or assessment, which might be another measured value or some stipulated aggregate of the individual values.[2] For example, the overall loudness of some sound derived from the loudness of the sound for the left and right ear is an instance of Formula 5.2 for $n = 2$.

A very general question one might ask about such value aggregation is what function F ensures that the overall utility $u(\cdot)$ adequately reflects a combination of the individual utilities without ignoring some of them or combining them in some unfair or arbitrary way. The question is vague because it is not clear what "fair" means in this context, but a very common answer, or at least a common stipulation, is to combine the utilities additively, using weighted sum for F:

$$u(x) = w_1 u_1(x) + w_2 u_2(x) + \cdots + w_n u_n(x) = \sum_{i=1}^{n} w_i u_i(x) \quad (5.3)$$

Weighted sum aggregation is well-understood and ubiquitous in decision-making. Notice that what is really going on here in the finite case is that n preorder relations R_i are combined into a new aggregate preorder relation, because we know that every utility function represents a preorder relation over a finite or countable domain out of the box.[3] These relations may be enriched with cardinal information if the individual utilities contain it, but even then, the individual utilities and their result represent an aggregate, complete ordering of the domain of items (viz., domains of attributes in the more general case). The additive model ensures that the outcome of the aggregation represents another complete preorder and not, for instance, a partial preorder, a semiorder, or some preferences with cycles like in an eligibility value structure.

Additive models have several properties derivable from the properties of addition. First of all, many combinations of individual utilities are equal, hence by Representation Condition 3.1 the respective combinations of rankings between items by the underlying ordinal value relations are equally good. On the one hand, this means that an additive model cannot represent every collection of preorder relations. On the other hand, this

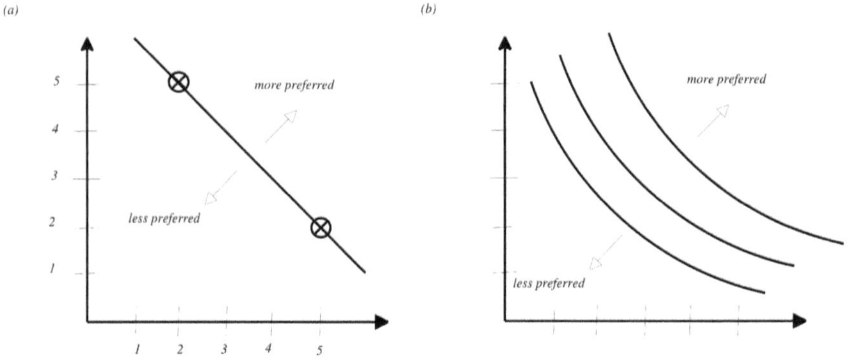

Figure 5.1: Examples of (a) linear indifference and (b) indifference curves for two components.

also implies that a vast number of comparisons between related items can be eliminated once two items have been assessed. For example, addition is commutative, i.e., $x + y = y + x$. Suppose that weights are equal, the use of a value predicate suggests two aspects for a given comparison, and that, for instance, $u_1(a) = 2$ and $u_2(a) = 5$. Then it follows by commutativity that $u(a) = u(b)$ whenever $u_1(a) = u_2(b)$ and $u_2(a) = u_1(b)$. In the example, $\langle 2, 5\rangle$ and $\langle 5, 2\rangle$ are equipreferred. It is also easy to see that if u_1 and u_2 are linear functions, then any point on the line defined by $\langle 2, 5\rangle$ and $\langle 5, 2\rangle$ is also equipreferred and that any line shifted into the direction of the upper right corner represents a set of items that are more preferred than a and equipreferred among each other. Correspondingly, any line shifted into the direction of the lower left corner represents items that are less preferred than a and are equipreferred among each other. This case is depicted in Figure 5.1a. In the general case when the utility are cardinal functions and may be nonlinear, indifference curves like in Figure 5.1b obtain.

The most controversial property of additive aggregation is that it requires preferential independence. Authors have used slightly different conditions and terminology, which are not always equivalent. I will lay out one of the strongest conditions called "conjoint independence."[4] To formulate it, suppose R is the weak preference relation obtained by aggregating weak preferences $R_1, \ldots, R_n$ for n aspects of betterness, and take four alternatives a, a', b, b'. The condition states that

$$aRb \leftrightarrow a'Rb' \tag{5.4}$$

must hold whenever the relations $R_1, \ldots, R_n$ can be partitioned into two sets $\mathcal{R}$ and $\mathcal{I}$ such that for every $R_x \in \mathcal{I}$ we have aI_xb and $a'I_xb'$ and for every $R_y \in \mathcal{R}$ we have aI_ya' and bI_yb'.

It is perhaps easier to see what this condition does by looking at vectors of outputs of utility functions $u_i(.)$ representing relations R_i and calling their elements $a_1, \ldots, a_n$, $b_1, \ldots, b_n$, and so on. The condition then states that if you substitute those elements in a and b on which they agree by other values on which a' and b' agree, this does not affect the overall judgment. For example, suppose the following vectors of real numbers represent the outcomes of the utilities of various aspects of a, b, a', b':[5]

$$a = \langle a_1, \ldots, c_i, \ldots, c_k, \ldots, a_n \rangle \tag{5.5}$$
$$b = \langle b_1, \ldots, c_i, \ldots, c_k, \ldots, b_n \rangle \tag{5.6}$$
$$a' = \langle a_1, \ldots, d_i, \ldots, d_k, \ldots, a_n \rangle \tag{5.7}$$
$$b' = \langle b_1, \ldots, d_i, \ldots, d_k, \ldots, b_n \rangle \tag{5.8}$$

Hereby, $i \ldots k$ can be any subset of aspects. Conjoint independence states that the outcome of the overall betterness relation between a and b does not depend on $c_i, \ldots, c_k$. Equivalently, if you replace $c_i, \ldots, c_k$ with other elements $d_i, \ldots, d_k$ that are equally good in both alternatives, and this is the only respect in which a and a' and respectively b and b' differ, then it must hold for the aggregate value relation that aRb if and only if $a'Rb'$. So in this example the difference between c_i and d_i may not influence the aggregate relation. If conjoint independence holds, then a is preferred over b if and only if a' is preferred over b'.

This independence criterion is very strong and sometimes violated in practical comparisons. However, when we aggregate additively by weighted sum, then conjoint independence is always satisfied. This follows from the properties of utility functions and addition. Because we use utility functions, all elements of the vectors are real numbers. If we set $K_a = a_1 + a_2 + \cdots + a_n$ without c and $K_b = b_1 + b_2 + \cdots + b_n$ without c, with unweighted sum as aggregation we obtain

$$K_a + c \geq K_b + c \Leftrightarrow K_a + d \geq K_b + d \tag{5.9}$$

as instantiation of condition 5.4. The constants c and d can be subtracted from the left- and right-hand side inequalities, which simply cancel out to one and the same condition $K_a \geq K_b$. It is easy to see that the same holds for weighted sum aggregation, provided that weights remain the same for c in a, b and d in a', b', and the same for $a_1, \ldots, a_n$ and $b_1, \ldots, b_n$.

5.3 Other Forms of Utility Aggregation

Multiplicative Aggregation. Multiplicative aggregation of utility functions is similar to weighted sum aggregation except that you multiply instead of adding. It is investigated by Pollak (1967) and Keeney (1974) who gives the following, slightly complicated definition:

$$1 + ku(x) = \prod_{i=1}^{n}(1 + kw_i u_i(x)), \tag{5.10}$$

where $0 \leq u_i(x) \leq 1$ and each utility function represents an underlying preorder R_i, $k > 0$, $0 < w_i < 1$ are weights for each aspect i, and $k > -1$ is a special non-zero scaling constant.

Although the original accounts were based on utilities of lotteries with quantified risks, the results concerning multiplicative utility aggregation can be used for the case when values under certainty is concerned. In Keeney and Raiffa's setting, a preference independence condition very similar to conjoint independence ensures that either an additive or a multiplicative model can be used to aggregate.[6] To determine the scaling constant k in the above formula, an item x must be chosen such that $u_i(x) = 1$, i.e., one that yields maximum utility for the respective attribute i, and then k can be computed from $1 + k = \prod_{i=1}^{n}(1 + kw_i)$ with known weights w_i by some iterative procedure. Keeney and Raiffa (1976) show that if $\sum_{i=1}^{n} k_i = 1$, then there is an additive utility representation like in 5.3; the more complicated multiplicative model is only needed when the weights do not sum up to 1. They also discuss preference elicitation methods and how to distinguish multiplicative from additive models.

The Choquet Integral. Another nonstandard way of aggregating preferences was pioneered by Schmeidler (1986, 1989) in decision-making under uncertainty. In this setting, Schmeidler uses the Choquet integral of Choquet (1954) to formalize a form of "probability" that does not satisfy the usual axioms of probability calculus, but instead allows for violations of the additivity axiom, i.e., it allows for the case that the probability of two disjoint events $E_i \cap E_j = \emptyset$ to be such that $P(E_i \cup E_j) \neq P(E_i) + P(E_j)$. Grabisch (1996) surveys other uses of the Choquet integral.

The Choquet integral can be considered an abstract way of generalizing addition. It allows for subadditive and superadditive aggregation. When the aggregation is subadditive, the result of aggregating may be less than the sum of the parts, whereas in the superadditive aggregation the result may be more than the sum of the parts. Although in the context of (supposedly) acceptable violations of probability calculus mostly subadditive operations were considered, superadditive aggregation is of particular philosophical interest because it formally represents the idea that the value of a whole might be more than the sum of the values of its parts. Based on suggestions by Moore (1903) this property is discussed under the label "organic unity" in the metaethical literature. Moore states: "The value of a whole must not be assumed to be the same as the sum of the values of its parts." Moore (1903, p. 28) This includes subadditive organic unity, but most of the subsequent discussion focused on superadditivity of value. A superadditive value aggregation method is one way of making the ideas behind the organic unity of value precise, although it might not cover all cases of organic unity.[7]

I will not lay out the classical Choquet integral for uncountably infinite domains, but instead follow Grabisch (1996) and Grabisch and Roubens (2000) who defines a finite sum for discrete application. First, some additional apparatus is needed. Let $\mathcal{S}$ be a set of subsets of a set Ω closed under union, i.e., for any $A, B \in \mathcal{S}$, it also holds that $(A \cup B) \in \mathcal{S}$. Let μ be a function from $\mathcal{S}$ into real numbers such that whenever $A \subseteq B$, then $\mu(A) \leq \mu(B)$. If in addition $\mu(\emptyset) = 0$ and $\mu(\Omega) = 1$, then μ is a "normalized fuzzy measure" on $\mathcal{S}$.[8] Assume that μ is such a fuzzy measure and that A and B are distinct subsets of $\mathcal{S}$, i.e., $A \cap B = \emptyset$. If $\mu(A \cup B) \leq \mu(A) + \mu(B)$, then μ is subadditive. In contrast to this, if $\mu(A \cup B) \geq \mu(A) + \mu(B)$, then μ is superadditive. If $\mu(A \cup B) = \mu(A) + \mu(B)$, then μ is additive. Notice that if μ is additive in this sense, then it is possible to define it solely in terms of singletons $\mu(\{a_1\}), \mu(\{a_2\}), \ldots$, for all $a_i \in \Omega$, because the function applied to any larger subset is a sum of the function applied to the singleton sets composed out of its individual elements, i.e., $\mu(\{a_1, a_2, \ldots, a_n\}) = \sum_{i=1}^{n} \mu(\{a_i\})$. This "lifting" from singletons to larger sets is generally not possible with subadditive and superadditive functions.

Suppose $u_1, u_2, \ldots, u_n$ are canonical utility functions normalized to the unit interval $[0, 1]$ such that each of the utility functions represents an aspect of betterness R_i (a preorder relation) over domain D_i and $u_i(x) = 0$ whenever there is no y such that xP_iy. Let $\Omega = D_1 \cup D_2 \cup \cdots \cup D_n$. Notice that this time the utilities are defined over different aspects of items, so we now assume that each aspect of an item is represented explicitly. This could be numerical value or a qualitative "item aspect." For example, suppose we are in a classical decision situation and try to find the best car for a particular purpose. In that scenario a_3 could be the engineering quality of car a, b_2 might represent the design of car b, c_1 might be the price of car c, and so forth. We denote variables as belonging to these aspect domains with subscripts, too, such that $x_i \in D_i$.

Now suppose a fuzzy measure μ is defined over the total domain Ω in the way laid out above. Furthermore, suppose that the indices of utilities and variables are ordered such that for given $x_1, x_2, \ldots, x_n$ it is the case that $u_1(x_1) \leq u_2(x_2) \leq \cdots \leq u_n(x_n)$. Based on this ordering, we can then define $A_i = \{x_i, \ldots, x_n\}$ from the given utilities. Given all that, finite Choquet aggregation may be defined as follows:

$$C_\mu(x_1, \ldots, x_n) = \sum_{i=1}^{n} [u_i(x_i) - u_{i-1}(x_{i-1})]\mu(A_i), \tag{5.11}$$

where for simplicity it is assumed that the (strictly speaking undefined) utility $u_0(x_0)$ is 0. This aggregation method sums up the differences between each next higher utility of an aspect $u_i(x_i)$ minus the utility of the aspect immediately below $u_{i-1}(x_{i-1})$ multiplied by the fuzzy measure over $\{x_i, \ldots, x_n\}$. This very flexible way of aggregating item aspects allows for dependencies between aspects that cannot be expressed by any of the methods discussed earlier. The fuzzy measure introduces a weight for each x_i that depends on the remaining items $x_i, \ldots, x_n$ ordered by their utilities. Since differences between utilities are multiplied by a fuzzy measure between 0 and 1, the utilities need to be on a ratio scale.

The Sugeno Integral. Based on Sugeno (1974, 1977), the Sugeno integral can be formulated as follows in the current finite framework based on (Dubois et al., 2001, p. 3):

$$S_\mu(x_1, \ldots, x_n) = \max_{i=1}^{n}[\min(u_i(x_i), \mu(A_i))] \tag{5.12}$$

Hereby, utilities need to be ordered like in a use of the Choquet integral. Minimum and maximum operations are also customarily used as so-called t-norms, related to logical conjunction and set intersection, and s-norms, related to disjunction and set union, in fuzzy logic, fuzzy set theory and possibility theory.[9] Generally speaking, minimum and maximum operations can yield radically cautious or optimistic aggregates and are in a sense information lossy because they do not compute a mean value. On the one hand, this is a deficiency if the utilities involved contain cardinal information. On the other hand, the Sugeno integral can be used in a purely ordinal setting because it does not presume that utilities are meaningful on a ratio scale. Other qualitative aggregation methods based on Social Choice are discussed in Section 5.4.

Generalized Additive Independence. This aggregation method was first proposed by Fishburn (1967). As the name suggests, it generalizes additive models by allowing some subsets of aspects to depend on others. Let $\mathcal{S}$ be a set of non-empty subsets of Ω, this time without additional restrictions like closure under union. The sets in $\mathcal{S}$ represent aspects of "better than" that depend on each other. For each of these, $S \in \mathcal{S}$ a utility function $u_S(.)$ is defined that represents preferences between items with respect to those interdependent aspects S. GAI aggregation is then defined as follows (Grabisch and Labreuche, 2018, p. 10):

$$U(x) = \sum_{S \in \mathcal{S}} u_s(x_s), \tag{5.13}$$

where x_S is a suitable restriction of item x to the aspects in S. For example, in the present case this restriction could be a tuple of "item aspects" $\langle x_j, \ldots, x_k \rangle$ consisting of those item aspects that belong to S. In the special case when each $S \in \mathcal{S}$ is a singleton containing one aspect, Formula 5.13 becomes equivalent to Formula 5.3 on page 75. Generally, however, the utility functions and corresponding preferences are now defined based on subsets of aspects, and this construction allows for having dependencies between aspects when items are compared with respect to them. GAI models are very general, so general that they have been considered unwieldy and have rarely been used for practical decision-making and value aggregation in the past.

5.4 Value Aggregation and Social Choice

In the previous sections we have aggregated utility functions. Representation theorems like 3.1 on page 46 and those of Section 3.3 couple these with underlying order relations, and so it is natural to think about how to aggregate these relations directly, without making use of utility representations. We will take a brief glimpse at this purely qualitative value aggregation and its connections to Social Choice Theory in this section.

In contrast to the previous sections, the aggregation methods in this section are purely ordinal, meaning that only the relations themselves and no additional cardinal information is decisive for the outcome. The task is to map n relations to one new relation that faithfully represents their aggregation into a final value assessment. We may ask the following questions about this process:

- What kind of input relations are allowed?
- What is the nature of the outcome relation?
- What could "faithfully represent" mean in this context?

Depending on how we answer these questions, we obtain different modes of qualitative value aggregation. In the simplest and best understood setting, the input relations are complete preorders, the outcome is a complete preorder, and a faithful representation is one that satisfies certain intuitively compelling criteria from Social Choice Theory.

Before going into these details, I would like to mention, however, an issue that I have deliberately suppressed so far. From the point of view of a theory of value structure, an overall aggregation seems to be a feature of applying value rather than a feature of value itself, and may be underdetermined outside of an application situation. However, an overall value *judgment* by an agent on the basis of values in a given situation can mean different things:

1. a comparison of a limited number of items, two items in the minimal case,
2. an assessment of all items under consideration, or
3. the election of one or more winning candidates among the items.

Moreover, these evaluations might have different purposes and covering considerations. They could be made for decision-making, but they could also be made part of a general comparison or evaluation of items or the whole set of items, and different goals and purposes may lead to different requirements.

The last two of the above situations have direct counterparts in Social Choice Theory. Preferences of voters among candidates are aggregated by a social choice function into one or more winning candidates, and, more generally, a social preference function aggregates preferences into a new preference relation that is supposed to represent the voters' collective preferences as best as possible.[10] The minimal variant of the first case above, on the other hand, is simpler than the other ones; when only two items are compared, for instance, other items can be pruned and the result needs to only represent strict preference or ties between two items.

There are good reasons not to stretch the analogy to voting too far. If all voters already agree unanimously on a winner, then there is no need for further voting. Hence, many voting methods have been invented for the explicit purpose of being able to obtain a result, such as electing one winner, under the premise that disagreements between voters cannot reasonably be expected to go away by further discussion. The voting method is a last resort in light of persistent political disagreement. Practical considerations also dictate voting when the number of voters is large, of course; thousands of people cannot resolve conflicts of opinion by discussion. In contrast to this, an individual agent can principally revise his assessments and thereby reduce conflict between value aspects. Moreover, voting requires particularly stringent criteria that may be relaxed for individual decision-making. Here is an incomplete list of properties that are held desirable in voting theory:

Unanimity. If a is the most preferred choice among all voters, then a is the winner.[11]

No Dictatorship. No single voter can determine the outcome of an election.

Anonymity. The outcome of the voting method does not depend on any labeling or ordering of the voters.[12]

Independence of Irrelevant Alternatives (IIA). The effect of a comparison of two candidates a and b by a voter on the result is not changed by a change in that or another voter's preferences about a third candidate c.

Equal Weight. Every vote has the same weight.

Unrestricted Domain. Every possible preference among candidates is allowed.

Restrictions of Manipulability. It should be hard to manipulate the result by strategic voting or collusion among voters. For example, it ought not be possible to make it more likely that the desired candidate turns out to be the winner by deliberately voting for a candidate *other* than the desired candidate.

Some of these such as Equal Weight and Restrictions of Manipulability are not required for aggregating value aspects. However, Arrow's famous theorem (Arrow, 1951) made only minimal assumptions and is also a problem for qualitative value aggregation. Arrow showed that every social preference function over three or more complete preorders that satisfies Unrestricted Domain and Unanimity has a dictator, i.e., there is no social preference function that jointly satisfies No Dictatorship, Unrestricted Domain, and Unanimity. Barbera (1980), Dardanoni (2001), Geanakoplos (2005), and Fey (2014) lay out proofs that are easier to access than Arrow's original proof.

The connection between Social Choice and qualitative value aggregation is straightforward. The voting situation described by Arrow corresponds to the standard model of betterness with multiple aspects, each of which is represented by a complete preorder. A particular ballot that a voter casts corresponds to a particular preorder representing an aspect of betterness in a particular situation of choice, the ballots of all voters in a particular voting situation (their "profile") correspond to a particular evaluation of items within a value domain, and the social preference function corresponds to a function that aggregates multiple value aspects into an overall notion of betterness of the same standard model type, i.e., a function from preorders to a preorder. Finally, a voter corresponds to a value aspect.

What does Arrow's Theorem mean in this setting? It states that every function that aggregates a value with three or more aspects into overall betterness within the standard model, and additionally satisfies Unanimity and Unrestricted Domain, will be such that in each particular decision situation the outcome is solely determined by one particular value aspect. Since Unanimity and Unrestricted Domain are no less desirable in the individual ordinal aggregation case than in voting, this theorem's consequence is fairly damning. There will always be one value aspect that is decisive in determining the entire aggregated value—that is bad, because it means that the other value aspects have no effect on the outcome.

Historically the first way to circumvent the theorem in Social Choice was to give up Unrestricted Domain. If the relations are all single-peaked, a specific criterion on their structure, then the aggregation will not necessarily be based on a dictator in the above sense.[13] However, imposing a restriction of the domain to single-peaked relations from the outside is neither desirable for Social Choice nor for value aggregation. Apart from the goal of evading the consequences of Arrow's Theorem, such a prescription does not seem to have any independent justification and appears to be arbitrary. Giving up IIA is more promising, although it is intuitively no less plausible than Unrestricted Domain at first glance. Notice that additive aggregation violates Unrestricted Domain since not all sets of input relations are compatible with it. As a remedy, I will describe two methods for qualitative value aggregation in the following paragraphs that circumvent Arrow's Theorem by violating IIA rather than Unrestricted Domain.

Minimization of the Kemeny Distance. The first method is to find a relation that is at a minimum (abstract) distance from all the input relations. For this purpose, a distance measure can be used that has been studied in statistics by Kendall (1938) and was later used by Kemeny (1959) and Kemeny and Snell (1972) for voting. It is often called Kemeny's Measure in the literature. In order to aggregate value relations $R_1, \ldots, R_n$ of a given sort T over the same domain D, you calculate the relation R^* in the space of all binary relations of sort T over D that minimizes the sum of the distances between R^* and $R_1, \ldots, R_n$ respectively.

How do we measure a distance between relations? Kemeny's Measure is derivable from the so-called inversion measure in combinatorics.[14] Suppose first, for simplicity, that all relations are complete strict preference relations, so no ties are allowed. For two strict preference relations P_1 and P_2, the inversion measure counts the minimum number of times needed to switch adjacent items in one preference ordering in order to get to the other preference ordering. For example, suppose $aP_1bP_1cP_1dP_1e$ and $bP_2cP_2dP_2aP_2e$ over the domain of items $D = \{a, b, c, d, e\}$. To get from P_1 to P_2 we first need to shift a down or shift the other elements up, which amounts to the same. You switch a and b, then a and c and then a and d. Since there is no shorter way of obtaining P_2, this is the inversion measure. So $I(P_1, P_2) = 3$.

For historical reasons, Kemeny's Measure is usually defined as twice the inversion measure, i.e., $K(P_1, P_2) = 6$. By an inductive proof on the size of the preference relations it can be shown that $I(x, y) = I(y, x)$ and $K(x, y) = K(y, x)$. The functions are symmetric. They also fulfill further criteria that are needed for a function to serve as a distance measure.[15] First, $K(x, x) = 0$ (reflexivity). Second, $K(x, y) \geq 0$ (positivity). Third, $K(x, z) \leq K(x, y) + K(y, z)$, which is called triangle inequality. Taken together, these properties ensure that distances are well-defined by the function and fulfill our intuitive requirements for what can count as a distance. For example, symmetry means that going from A to B is the same distance as going from B to A, and it is obvious why this should hold for whatever we call a "distance."

Bogart (1973) and Critchlow (1985) develop generalizations of Kemeny distance from strict orders to preorders with ties and partial strict orders. A simple way of achieving basically the same as what Bogart does is to give ties a score that is in-between a full preference reversal.[16] For example, if the distance from aPb to bPa is 2, then the distance from aPb to aIb is 1. Hence, the path from aPb to aIb and then to bPa has the distance 2 again. To further illustrate this measure, take a look at Figure 5.2 that depicts all

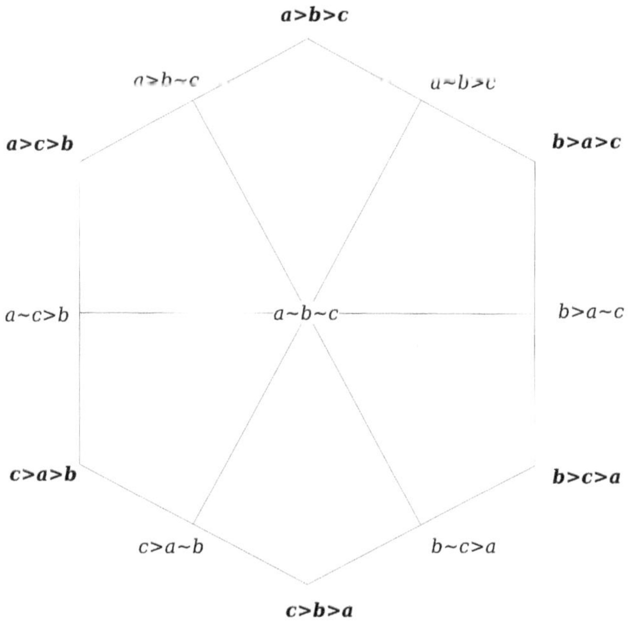

Figure 5.2: All 13 complete preorders between 3 items arranged by their Kemeny distances.

13 possible preorders of 3 items.[17] Each line segment between two adjacent nodes has score 1. Suppose we have the following three relations: aP_1cP_1b, bP_2aI_2c, and bP_3aP_3c. Table 5.1 lists the minimal generalized Kemeny distances of these preferences to all 13 nodes in the graph.[18] As is easy to see from the table, the solution to the distance minimization problem is in this case $bPaIc$ with score 4. However, solutions are not always unique. Consider the minimal paths for $cPaIb$ and $bIcPa$ in Figure 5.2, for instance. Clearly, $cPbPa$ and $aIbIc$ both minimize the distances to 1 and are therefore admissible value aggregations in this case. Minimizing the measure does not necessarily give a unique solution, but it is well-defined and based on basic combinatorial properties of orderings. While Kemeny and Snell suggested it for voting to circumvent Arrow's Theorem, it may also be used for the qualitative aggregation of value aspects.

	aPcPb	*bPaIc*	*bPaPc*	Sum
aPbPc	2	3	2	7
aIbPc	3	2	1	6
bPaPc	4	1	0	5
bPac	3	0	1	4
bPcPa	4	1	2	7
bIcPa	3	2	3	8
cPbPa	4	3	4	11
cPaIb	3	2	3	8
cPaPb	2	3	4	9
aIcPb	1	2	3	6
aPcPb	0	3	4	7
aPbIc	1	2	3	6
aIbIc	2	1	2	5

Table 5.1: Minimal distances of all preorders between 3 items to aP_1cP_1b, bP_2aI_2c, and bP_3aP_3c.

Borda Count with Averaging Ties. The second method I would like to suggest is Borda Count with Averaging Ties. The Borda count of an item is often minimized in the literature, giving the lowest score to the highest ranking item. To be able to compare it better to the other methods, we instead reverse it and maximize the score. In the end, the two methods are equivalent. What is important is that the Borda count is rank-based: It only takes into account the ordinal rank of each item in the relative ordering of an aspect.

To see how this method works, let us construct canonical utility functions based only on rank without any cardinal information. The highest ranking item among n items gets score n, the second highest score $n-1$, and so on, until the least preferred gets score 1. Additionally, ties are averaged in such a way that the sum of the scores is the same as if each item was in a strict ordering. For example, if $aPbIc$, then $u(a) = 3$, and $u(b) = u(c) = 1.5$, because then $u(b) + u(c) = 3$, which is the same as $2 + 1$ if bPc or cPb was the case. Why average this way? This method has the advantage that the sum of the scores for n items is always $\frac{1}{2}(n^2 + n)$, and this fact is useful for normalizing scores between relations defined on sets of different sizes without introducing unfair weights due to the number of items in a set.

Using this method to construct utilities for the example in Table 5.1, we get $u_1(a) = 3$, $u_1(b) = 1$, $u_1(c) = 2$, $u_2(a) = 1.5$, $u_2(b) = 3$, $u_2(c) = 1.5$, $u_3(a) = 2$, $u_3(b) = 3$, and $u_3(c) = 1$. Summing up, the result is $u(a) = 3 + 1.5 + 2 = 6.5$, $u(b) = 1 + 3 + 3 = 7$, and $u(c) = 2 + 1.5 + 1 = 4.5$. Hence, the unweighted sum of the Borda Rankings yields the ordering $bPaPc$, which has distance measure score 5 instead of 4 in Table 5.1.

As the example shows, the Borda method and Kemeny distance minimization may yield different results, although the difference is not huge. Both methods violate IIA and therefore do not fall prey to the undesirable consequence of presupposing a dictatorial aspect of betterness, which would follow from Arrow's Theorem if IIA was fulfilled. Since Kemeny's Measure is based on the inversion count and thus has a clear-cut and easy to understand combinatorial interpretation, it seems to be the better choice for qualitative value aggregation. In contrast to this, the Borda method seems ad hoc. However, Kemeny distance minimization comes with a huge practical disadvantage; it has bad computational complexity. Calculating it for more than four items is an NP-hard problem, which means that we do not know (and there likely isn't) any efficient way to minimize the distance of a large number of items. Diaconis and Graham (1977) has shown that Spearman's Footrule Measure is a reasonable approximation of the Kemeny distance, and minimizing this measure is computationally more efficient. To compute the footrule between two complete preorders over the same set of items, we simply sum up the absolute differences between the Borda Ranks of the items, i.e., $F(a) = \sum_{i=2}^{n} |u_i(a) - u_{i-1}(a)|$ for $n > 1$ aspects with canonical ordinal utilities (Borda Ranks) u_i that each represent a preorder. Minimizing this "city block" or "Manhattan" distance measure is fairly efficient. However, it remains only an approximation of Kemeny's distance minimization. In contrast, Borda's method has good computational complexity and has been studied extensively in voting theory.

It is worth taking a brief look at how those methods may be used to address the Condorcet Paradox of voting, which was the original motivation for the Borda method in voting theory. Here is a Condorcet case. There are three candidates a, b, c and at least three voters. The first voter prefers a over b and b over c, the second voter prefers b over c and c over a, and the third voter prefers c over a and a over b. So we have three strict preference relations aP_1bP_1c, bP_2cP_2a, and cP_3aP_3b. Clearly, there is no winning candidate. Schumm (1987) describes an example in decision-making with three attributes analogous to a Condorcet case.

So how do the methods described so far deal with such cases? When aggregating with weighted sum, different weights will usually ensure that one item is the most preferred because the corresponding attribute has the highest weight. Although ties between all items are possible, these are rare in practice once weights have been introduced, especially if some of the more sophisticated preference elicitation methods like those described by Keeney and Raiffa (1976) are used. If no weights are used, however, additive aggregation yields $aIbIc$ in such a case. The Borda method yields the very same result with the devilish scores of 6 for a, 6 for b, and 6 for c. Finally, a quick glance at Figure 5.2 tells us that $aIbIc$ is the closest to all three preferences in this case, too. The methods yield the same results for Condorcet cases.

If Borda and distance minimization are so great, why are they not used more often as voting procedures in the real world? For distance minimization the case is clear: It is hard to understand for voters and not computationally tractable for a large number of voters. In contrast to this, the Borda method is sometimes used. However, it also has some drawbacks for voting not mentioned so far. Modern Social Choice Theory is concerned with way more adequacy criteria than the ones mentioned above. For example, let the majority candidate be that candidate that gets the most first place votes. If 51 voters have preferences $aPbPc$ and 49 voters preferences $bPcPa$, then a wins by majority rule. However, b wins by the Borda method. This is sometimes conceived as a drawback, although it can be argued that the Borda result is fairer. However, consider the simple preferences $bPaPcPd$ and $dPaPcPb$. In this constellation a wins with score 6 according to Borda, even though it is not the top choice of anyone. Is that reasonable? Maybe. Suppose now that 51 voters have the first preference, and only 49 have the second preference. Still, a will win with Borda score 300, followed by b with score 253. This time, maybe there is a stronger "intuitive pull" towards candidate b who would have won by majority rule.

Yet another problem of rank-based methods is that they are particularly prone to being manipulated by strategic voting. If you suspect another judge might rank a very high but you want b to win, then you can simply rank a far below b. In one way or another, all voting methods are prone to this kind of manipulation due to the Gibbard-Satterthwaite theorem of Gibbard (1973) and Satterthwaite (1975), but rank-based methods like Borda give a manipulator some particularly large leeway for exploitation. That being said, the Borda method remains an excellent method for ranking candidates in a competition with several judges when those judges are not working against each other. In a cooperative setting in which individual committee members do not have ulterior motives, it makes a lot of sense to qualitatively aggregate grades of different disciplines or assessments of job candidates by different judges using the Borda method.[19]

The same caveat emptor as mentioned in the beginning of this section applies. At least in a single agent setting, manipulability should play no role for the evaluation of the appropriateness of a method for value aggregation. If someone is considering how to aggregate different aspects of betterness comparisons about given items in order to come to an overall betterness comparison and starts to think about how to wiggle here and there at individual comparisons in order to get another outcome, then there is nothing wrong with that in an individual choice situation. No value judgment is carved in stone and you should also test the robustness of the aggregation outcome. Similar procedure might also be advisable if one tries to lay out a more general structure of a value. If a seemingly insignificant change radically alters the outcome of the overall assessment, then this warrants some extra care and maybe taking into account additional, previously overlooked aspects. Violation of the majority rule seems equally acceptable in the value aggregation domain. If an item is the very best in one aspect of betterness but rather lousy in other respects, then this may be taken as a reason for not considering it best, all things considered. For example, if Aspect 1 stands for the quality of the blade of a knife and Aspect 2 for the durability and quality of the handle, and the betterness comparisons are $bP_1aP_2cP_3d$ and $dP_2aP_2cP_2b$, then it makes perfect sense to take a to be the overall best knife, and neither b nor d, which have the worst handle and the worst blade respectively.

All in all, the Borda count is a fairly good method for qualitative value aggregation. I will therefore use it as the basis of a more complex qualitative aggregation procedure in Chapter 9.

5.5 The Most General Aggregation Method?

Finally, a third way of looking at value aggregation needs to be mentioned that falls out of the scope of most of the decision-making literature and due to its potentially technical nature has also been ignored in the metaethical literature.

Consider Formula 5.2 again, the unrestricted aggregation scheme on page 74. We could simply choose to leave this template unrestricted in general and opt for specifying a particular function F instead. This function could have any form, as long as it is well-defined, and may be used to aggregate utility functions and the underlying preferences. Unlike the case of individual betterness relations, where general arguments such as money pumps may establish the rationality of a representational feature such as acyclicity, there does not seem to be any general argument of this sort for a particular method of aggregating different aspects of a value. We would only have to ensure that the function respects ordinality in case the utility functions are considered merely ordinal, and that we otherwise provide a convincing story why and in which way cardinal information is represented and measured. We may then develop a particular function F that expresses possibly complicated dependencies between different aspects of a value, which boils down to providing an analytic model of the value under consideration. Such a model could be supported by considerations that have nothing to do with questions of decomposability.

It should be clear why such unrestricted analytic models are rarely discussed in the literature on decision-making. The methodology in decision-making focuses on measurement, on practically useful, yet mathematically sound preference elicitation techniques. There will be one or more consultants who work together with one or more decision makers and domain experts to come up with practical solutions to a decision problem. These consultants need to elicit evaluative judgments from the decision makers and this involves cataloging the aspects of betterness that play a role in a value hierarchy, eliciting the decision makers' preferences and constructing utility functions, determining subjective and objective probabilities of outcomes of actions and of external events, and identifying the dependencies between attributes, if there are any. If a consultant (or a corresponding computer program) can prove that some preferences can be represented by an additive utility model, then this guarantees that a consistent decision can be made by maximizing overall expected utility and that the number of comparisons needed to construct corresponding utility functions and weights remains tractable.

Developing an analytic model is (almost) the opposite of this measurement process. After constructing utilities for individual value aspects, functional relations between them are spelled out and justified. An empirical model would then need to be tested, validated for its requirements, and possibly improved. In contrast, a normative model cannot be tested empirically, but it could partly be confirmed by practices or "intuitions," partly be justified philosophically. Economists develop such models all the time, for example in Public Choice Theory.

That being said, it is hard to imagine a moral philosopher defending such a model for a particular aspect of "better than." Until someone does it for a particular value, the analytic model option of value aggregation does not seem to bring many benefits, and it seems particularly hard to justify such a model from a normative perspective. To be fair, however, the aggregation methods discussed in the previous sections by themselves also do not have any normative justification. Just because a method is well-understood, mathematically elegant, or axiomatizable does *not* mean that it is normatively justified. As far as I can see, the normative justification of value aggregation methods is a blind spot in current metaethical research. I do not have a suggestion for solving this problem at the time of this writing either. However, choosing a method that has "technically" desirable properties like the ones discussed above and satisfies the mathematical requirements from measurement theory is a step in the right direction.

Finally, the aggregation of reasons instead of values needs to be mentioned. Is it an alternative? I believe that value aggregation is clearly better and more nuanced than an aggregation of reasons without a weighing conception of reasons according to which one set of reasons either completely defeats other reasons or not, or they remain in conflict and no decision can be made at all. Maybe reasons sometimes defeat or undercut others and can therefore be aggregated in this way, as it is suggested in research on Abstract Argumentation Frameworks based on Dung (1995) and work like Horty (2012). However, it is obvious that aggregating reasons is not the same as evaluating comparatively. There can be reasons for or against some decision, for instance, but in the end only some of them will win and the other reasons are defeated.

As a remedy, it is tempting to presume a weighing conception of reasons. However, weighing reasons also comes with many pitfalls that value aggregation avoids. One of these problems is that the perceived "strength" of a reason-giving argument, and, correspondingly, the perceived "strength" or quality of a reason does not represent the evaluative aspect of a reason for or against evaluating something in a certain way.[20] Consequently, whatever balance of considerations a weighing of reasons may achieve, it cannot be the same as evaluating items. A reason-giving argument for evaluating something in a certain way can be more or less convincing, more or less justified in a practical setting, independently of the suggested evaluation. For example, suppose a smuggler argues that democracy is better than tyranny because democracies are more open and have weaker security standards at the border, thus allowing the smuggling business to thrive. For various reasons we need not go into, this might be considered a relatively weak argument for democracy. Nevertheless, its evaluative component is clearly that democracy is better than tyranny. Although it seems in principle possible to come up with a theory of reason or argument aggregation that distinguishes between these issues and takes into account the above mentioned technical aspects of value aggregation, it is methodologically advisable to keep values and their structure apart from aspects of their justification. These justifications have a much broader scope and their soundness hinges on a vast number of areas such as ethics, economics, aesthetics, epistemology, and various specific domains from which they may draw in a particular context. Simply put, evaluation and justification are different intellectual faculties with different rationality requirements and standards.

Part II

Philosophy of Value Structure

Chapter 6

Problems of Value Analysis

Two philosophical problems are addressed in this chapter. First, we take a look at Moore's position that the good is primitive and cannot be further analyzed. This thesis is at odds with the central assumption that the structure of values can be disseminated and given some further normative justification. Second, the aims of a theory of value structure are contrasted with an inquiry of the meaning of evaluative adjectives on the one hand and with broadly conceived metaphysical theses about values on the other hand.

6.1 The Good as a Primitive

Readers familiar with the metaethical literature might have wondered why I have taken the complexity of values for granted so far, since the influential Moorean tradition of value analysis, "good" in particular, seems to be based on the very opposite idea. Moore (1903) famously argued that "good" is a primitive notion that cannot be further analyzed. If that was true, then the above cases for the complexity of values could not be based on an analysis of goodness and could not concern the meaning of value predicates.[1] So something has to be said about this.

The Open Question Argument is a positive argument against any suggested analysis of what it means to be good. Later, Langford and Schilpp (1943) coined the term Paradox of Analysis (PA) for a problem related to the Open Question Argument that is even more problematic and has stirred up many replies. There is some consensus in the literature that it has to be taken seriously as an argument, even by those who think it ultimately fails to be conclusive and can be solved in one way or another. I present both of these arguments separately in the following paragraphs and start with the Open Question Argument.

Moore's main point is that philosophers have erroneously conflated the property of being good with other properties, because good things often happen to have these other properties, too. For example, classical hedonic utilitarians like Bentham (1789) or Mill (1906) identify goodness and pleasure, because bringing about pleasure is good under normal circumstances.[2] In Moore's view, this conflation is based on a principal fallacy. He draws an analogy of "good" with color predicates like "yellow." Yellow objects have various properties, and some of them always coincide with an object having that color. For example, every yellow macrophysical object has a certain shape, is physical, has some weight, and so forth. It would be obviously false to conclude from this that "yellow" means the same as "having a certain shape," "having weight," "being a physical object," and the like. Instead, yellow is a primitive concept that cannot be further decomposed.[3] Moore argues that "good" behaves the same way as "yellow" in that respect:

> My point is that "good" is a simple notion, just as "yellow" is a simple notion; just as you cannot, by any manner of means, explain to anyone who does not already know it, what yellow is, so you cannot explain what good is. [...] [Y]ellow and good [...] are not complex; they are notions of that simple kind, out of which definitions are composed and with which the power of further defining ceases. (Moore, 1922, §7, p. 7)

In Moore's opinion, there are only two serious contenders to this primitivism: First, "good" has no meaning or only a derived one. While this possibility has been taken more seriously later by error-theorists such as Mackie (1977), Moore does not seem to consider it a serious option.[4] Second, uses of "good" can be analyzed and goodness is defined in some way. Against this view he raises a number of arguments. As Feldman (2005) lays out, none of them really state that a question is left open. Instead, Moore argues for three theses in Sections 13–14 of the Principia Ethica.

He argues against a definitional account of goodness according to which any use of "good" is supposed to be synonymous with a *complex* substitute such as "to desire to desire." He also argues against naturalist accounts according to which goodness is the same as being pleasant without a complex analysis of what "pleasant" means in turn. His conclusion is that goodness is primitive in thinking and cannot be further analyzed.

As Feldman (2005) notes, his first argument rests on the complexity of a potential substitute of a use of "good." For instance, suppose that goodness is defined as the desire to desire. We can then ask "...of the complex so defined, whether it is itself good." In a particular instance about item a, under the example reading of "good" this would be the question "Is it good to desire to desire a?" However, this question in Moore's opinion does not mean the same as "Is the desire to desire a one of the things we desire to desire?" Why not? According to how Feldman (2005) interprets this passage, this is because "to desire to desire" is more complex than "good" and cannot substitute it in any sentence. The two higher-order questions do not mean the same, even though we might be fooled to think so about the corresponding first-order pair "Is a good?" and "Is a something we desire to desire?" at first sight.

The second argument concerns naturalist reductions in which instead of a complex analysis naturalist synonyms such as "pleasant" are proposed. In such an account, one primitive notion is replaced by another primitive notion, but the substitute has some naturalist basis such as pleasure. The argument is simpler than the previous one. According to Moore, the meaning of "good" in concrete examples is distinct from the meaning of "pleasant" in the same context, and the same can be said about other primitive substitutes for "good." They are both primitive but different "in our minds." As Moore (1922, Sec. 14) lays out, this does not mean that pleasure cannot be conducive to goodness or that many pleasurable things cannot also be good. This may all be true, but at the same time we know upon reflection that pleasure cannot *define* goodness in the sense that "good" and "pleasant" would always be synonyms.

There is a way to interpret some of Moore's remarks about the first argument as concerning open questions, although the argument does not seem to be attributable to Moore at a closer look.[5] In this common rendition of the Open Question Argument, whenever you have a possibly complex property or set of criteria P that are supposed to serve as a definition of "good," you might ask "Is every item that is P also P?" to which the answer is trivially Yes. No question is left open. In contrast to this, the question "Is every item that is P also good?" seems to remain open. For instance, if goodness was defined by pleasure, then being pleasant should be able to serve as a substitute for being good. But "Is every pleasant item good?" appears to be an open, substantive question, whereas the corresponding question "Is every pleasant item pleasant?" is trivially true. This is the reading that forms the basis of Langford's criticism which will be addressed in the next section.

Finally, as Black (1944, p. 263) points out, it must be noted that Moore does not want his thesis about "good" to be understood as a thesis about natural language expressions. In Moore's view, it concerns the analysis of goodness in thinking. However, this does not help in the present case, since the multidimensional analysis of "better than" and other value predicates does not (need to) concern their meaning. It concerns aspects of uses of the value predicates, regardless of whether these pertain to their meaning, pragmatic content, or are part of the justification of the use of the value predicate.

6.2 The Paradox of Analysis

Let us now turn to the Paradox of Analysis that Langford raised against Moore in 1942. It expresses a more general skepticism about conceptual analysis. Moore acknowledged that he does not have a solution to it.[6] Langford (1968) characterizes it as follows:

> Let us call what is to be analyzed the analysandum, and let us call that which does the analyzing the analysans. The analysis then states an appropriate relation of equivalence between the analysandum and the analysans. And the paradox of analysis is to the effect that, if the verbal expression representing the analysandum has the same meaning as the verbal expression representing the analysans, the analysis states a bare identity and is trivial; but if the two verbal expressions do not have the same meaning, the analysis is incorrect. (Langford, 1968, p. 323)

The purpose of this alleged paradox is to show that there is a problem with Moore's position that goodness is not definable. If the Open Question Argument is merely an instance of the more general Paradox of Analysis, then this would state that any conceptual analysis of what is good—for example, analyzing what is good as what one desires to desire or as pleasure—would be trivially true if the analysis was correct, and this is clearly not the case: "When they say 'Pleasure is good,' we cannot believe that they merely mean 'Pleasure is pleasure' and nothing more than that" (Moore, 1922, §11, p. 14).

Langford's point is that this would a very general problem, and the criticism is justified because Moore asserts at several places in the Principia Ethica and later work that his arguments are meant in a general way and are meant to apply to any kind of analysis of goodness. Although Moore's original points about goodness are much narrower in scope, it is thus worth taking a look at how a multidimensional account of betterness might counter the Paradox of Analysis, too.

6.3 A Fregean Solution

Both arguments seem to be devastating for the current goal of elaborating the structure that underlies values, which is supposed to be filled with particular orderings by rational agents, including normative ethicists, based on well-wrought justifications. So they have to be addressed before this project can continue.

Starting with the Paradox of Analysis, various attempts of solving this puzzle have been made, and in my opinion the best way of dealing with it is along familiar Fregean footsteps. In reply to an exchange between Morton G. White and Max Black on Black's attempt of solving the alleged paradox, Church (1946) pointed out that it seems to be solvable by resorting to Frege's distinction between sense and referent (Frege, 1892) in the same way as in his Evening Star vs. Morning Star example. Discussing an analysis of "brother" (b) as "male sibling" (ms), he argues:

> In the reviewer's [Church's] opinion this is not merely an analogy, but the paradox of analysis is a special case of Frege's puzzle and is to be solved in the same way, on Frege's theory of meaning, by the distinction of sense and denotation ("Sinn und

> Bedeutung”). [...] But, if the analysis expressed by ‘$b = ms$’ is non-trivial, the names ‘b’ and ‘ms’ have different senses, hence the replacement of one by the other in a sentence may well change the sense (proposition) expressed. (Church, 1946, p. 133)

In my opinion, there is not much to add to this assessment. Refinements and related solutions have been proposed, but Church already addresses the core of the problem of the alleged paradox.[7] Although it is true that the analysandum of a conceptual analysis usually has a preestablished conceptual content and that whatever falls under the analysandum concept must generally also fall under the analysans concept, analysandum and analysans will usually have different senses and therefore the analysis can be informative without becoming incorrect. Of course, there are still many differences between Frege’s puzzle and providing an analysis of a value adjective like “good.” Frege’s puzzle was at least originally not intended as an explanation of conceptual analysis, but as an elucidation of the epistemic role of senses. However, the idea of a Fregean solution to the alleged paradox is that different expressions involved in an analysis have different senses, and so a “paradox” only occurs if extensions are confused with Fregean senses.

Does this reply also work for the more elaborate interpretations of the Open Question Argument? It does not seem to be needed for Moore’s first argument. This argument is based on the complexity of the explanans and seems closest to the Paradox of Analysis. However, Moore does not present a conclusive argument why a sentence with a more complex explanans cannot mean the same as the original, simple explanandum. Likewise, it is not entirely clear why he thinks that the complex analysis cannot be the same in our mind. From my point of view, a particular use of “good” and “better than” is only intelligible if it is understood as a proxy for multiple value aspects under a given covering consideration. These aspects are always more specific than the aggregative value judgment. Whether these aspects pertain to the justification of a primitive attribution of goodness or a primitive betterness comparison or whether they are part of the semantopragmatic content of a particular use of a particular variety of betterness under some covering consideration does not matter in this view. In other words, a Moorean need not take the complexity-based part of the Open Question Argument as an argument against a multidimensional account of value structure. If the aspects of a value in a given evaluative situation are taken as part of the reasons for or the potential justification of an evaluation, a multidimensional analysis remains compatible with the view that the attribution of goodness itself is primitive "in our minds" and takes part of the semantopragmatics of a use of "good."

What about the second argument then? This argument was targeted against primitive naturalist definitions for uses of "good." On the one hand, the same reply as above can be given. An aspect like how much an item pleases someone could be part of a multidimensional analysis of value structure in a given evaluative situation or be part of an abstract, general justification of certain evaluations ("generally, humans seek pleasure and avoid pain"). This does not need to enter our conception of what "good" means at that occasion. On the other hand, the claim that goodness really just is X, where X is some naturalist reduction like giving pleasure, would be a value monist conception of goodness that I do not endorse because it does not do justice to the trade-offs between aspects of betterness comparisons we are forced to make. I therefore reject these kinds of simplistic, value monist naturalist reductions, though for different reasons than Moore. They do not reflect the richness and reality of our evaluative practices and the variety of notions of betterness. However, multidimensional value structure remains compatible with more sophisticated naturalist conceptions of value.

Let us finally turn to the third variant of the Open Question Argument which is sometimes attributed to Moore. As mentioned before, this understanding of the argument is the basis of the Paradox of Analysis and should be treated like it. Either the analysis is trivial or it seems to be wrong. A Neo-Fregean solution is in my opinion the right approach to tackle this problem. If meaning is concerned, there is a deeper problem with such approaches related to the critique of analyticity by Quine (1951). While the details would go beyond the scope of this volume, it is worth noting that even if an analysis is taken to directly concern the meaning of a term, as Moore seems to suggest in some passages and denies in others, the analysis stays and falls with the merits of the theory that supports it.[8] Therefore, the seemingly analytic truth of statements like "Everything good is pleasant" would not have any epistemic priority, and, by the same token, the question that is seemingly not left open in the above example is only closed relative to the theory proposed, i.e., in this case relative to the naturalist reduction of "good" and its merits. Every theory can be contested, and so this version of the Open Question Argument is also not conclusive. However, as I will lay out in the next section and have mentioned before, there is no need to assume that a multidimensional analysis of a use of "better than" and the corresponding more general considerations about value structure concern the meaning of uses of "good" or "better than." Questions related to the semantic atomism versus semantic holism debate and the problems of analyticity need not concern a theory of value structure.

6.4 The Connection to Meaning and Value Metaphysics

In the remainder of this chapter, I want to address two fairly complicated questions concerning the theory of value structure and other areas of philosophy. This section is admittedly more cursory and sketchy than other sections of the book because there is simply not enough space to adequately address these issues in depth. They need to be mentioned briefly, however, in order to clarify the scope of the philosophical work on value structure. The first question is whether the theory of value structure ought not rather be based on the meaning of evaluative adjectives. The second question is how the (meta-)ethical literature on value metaphysics is related to the theory of value structure.

Regarding the first question, one might argue that a theory of value structure is ill-conceived, at least for some evaluative adjectives such as "good," because these denote thin value concepts. What if these only have minimal semantic content like "generally commendable" and otherwise serve a pragmatic function, for example expressing a general prescription like Hare (1952) proposed? Even for adjectives that denote thick value concepts such as "brave" and "lewd" one might argue that their semantic content is descriptive, whereas the evaluative function is pragmatic.[9] Shouldn't a theory of value structure depend on such semantic and metasemantic considerations?

One reply to this question is that specific (meta-)semantic approaches to evaluative language do not have much to do with value structure. Much of the literature in the philosophy of language skips over the requirements of value structure or makes implicit normative assumptions that would require further justification. For example, merely assuming that evaluative adjectives have semantic values on a ratio scale is inadequate, since the cardinal information needed for these scales cannot be derived from the comparative forms alone. As we have seen in previous chapters, neither comparisons by comparative forms nor intensifiers like "much" and similar expressions suffice to establish the existence of an underlying ratio scale. Moreover, the utility difference comparisons needed to clearly establish an interval scale on the basis of language use alone would require contorted uses of "better than" that are almost unintelligible. However, even when a particular candidate for the semantics or pragmatics of an evaluative adjective is well-justified, maybe based on empirical data about language use, it still does not follow from this that constraints about its meaning carry over to the value structure. Claiming that semantics illuminates value structure is akin to claiming that a semanticist can tell a physicist what "atom" means. On the one hand, if the lexical semantics of a word is purely descriptive, for example based on semantic fields and a componential analysis obtained by surveying native speakers, then it does not concern the normative business of value theory, except for the desideratum that a normative theory of X ought not deviate too much from the preestablished everyday meaning of "X."[10] On the other hand, if the semantic theory is supposed to be normative, reflecting what a word *really* means (however one understands this phrase), then the semanticist does the work of the respective domain expert.[11] However, physicists know better than semanticists what "atom" really means and ethicists know better than semanticists what "good" really means, because from this normative perspective "what a word really means" is merely a convoluted way of talking about the best current theory about what the word is supposed to denote or describe. For these reasons, one may argue that normative considerations about value structure may inform semanticists, insofar as their descriptive goals remain compatible with the normative constraints imposed, and data about language use may inform ethicists, insofar as it may reveal features of common value judgments, yet the two disciplines are independent of each other. Value structure may, but does not have to, describe the meaning of a particular use of a value adjective at a high level of abstraction. Aspects of betterness and their aggregation may also be taken as part of the pragmatics of a use of a value adjective, or they may be taken as part of a normative justification of the attribution of overall value.

Regarding the second question, we may start by clarifying the label "value metaphysics." Moore's position is that goodness is primitive, that it cannot be further analyzed. By the same token, there are various other positions about values that are not primarily supposed to be claims about the meaning of evaluative adjectives and their comparative forms. To name just a few of them, there is value realism,[12] expressivism,[13] error theory,[14] and there are various forms of moral relativism.[15] The buck-passing account of value based on Scanlon (1998) is also very prominent. According to this position, the fact that an item a is of value is explained by the normative statement that an ideal moral agent should have a pro-attitude towards a. Broadly speaking, all of these accounts are attempts of explaining what values are and what justifies their normative force. All of them make certain claims about the ontological status of values, and this dependence on the ontological status is the reason why they should be subsumed under the label "value metaphysics." What is the relation of these stances to value structure?

The metaphysical positions are normative. Even error theory is normative in the sense of stating that people err and make systematic mistakes when they assume or claim that values exist in reality. Nevertheless, most of the issues these approaches are concerned with are orthogonal and complementary to what is addressed by the theory of value structure. As far as many of these metaphysical positions are concerned, normative theses about the structure of comparatives can be regarded as constraints or desiderata with which these other theses about values must remain compatible. Conversely, a particular stance about the origin and normativity of values may be taken as a constraint for a thesis about value structure. For example, we will see in the next chapter that Wlodek Rabinowicz's position about parity is based on a fitting attitude analysis of value; to combine it with an approach that does not endorse the fitting value analysis therefore requires modifications. Other theories mentioned above concern how context enters value judgments. To these belong moral expressivism, contextualism and its opposite noncontextualism, as well as relativism.[16] These positions are compatible with different views about value relations and how they are aggregated and therefore complement the theory of value structure.

To summarize, descriptive lexical meaning theories may be informed by normative accounts of value structure, for example, when dictionary meaning as a blend of semantic and encyclopedic knowledge is concerned, but they are not themselves constraining potential accounts of value structure. In contrast to this, lexical meaning theories that are supposed to be taken to have a normative component are confused. As we will see in Chapter 8, even the seemingly innocuous claim that "better than" is transitive is controversial from a metaethical point of view, and so are many other presumptions about value structure such as completeness, the existence of an underlying cardinal scale, and the common practice of (sometimes silently) presuming additive value aggregation. These are normative questions of metaethics, albeit ones for which there may be no ultimate answers or only answers that resort to different "moral intuitions." As for metaphysical positions about values in ethics, a case-by-case analysis is needed. If Moore's position is taken as a view about everyday meaning, it remains compatible with making fine-grained normative assumptions about value structure. As a thesis about the nature of attributions of goodness to items it also remains compatible with multidimensional value analysis, as long as the underlying value structure is considered part of the justification of this attribution rather than the attribution itself.[17] Other metaphysical positions also address issues the theory of value structure is not concerned with. Even fairly radical error-theories about value can remain compatible with normative constraints of the structure of value comparisons such as the transitivity of "better than" or lack thereof. Thus, value structure is mostly independent of value metaphysics, although there can be interference and constraints in both directions.

Chapter 7

Parity

Parity is an important topic in the philosophy of value structure that needs to be addressed by any serious value theory. The discussion started with an article by Chang (2002). In this article and several follow-ups, Chang argued that there is a fourth value relation besides "better than," "equally good," and "worse than" that she calls "parity."

7.1 Motivation and Key Properties

As we have already seen in Chapter 5, many different value relations are aggregated into an overall assessment from a value pluralist perspective, so Chang's thesis needs to be qualified. According to her, parity is an additional kind of basic value relation among positive value relations that we use to evaluate items. Recall that in a unipolar approach "worse than" is the converse of "better than," so we can ignore this relation in what follows. Chang's thesis then states that if we compare two items a and b, a may be better than b, b may be better than a, a and b may be equally good, but a and b may also be on a par.

Items that are on a par are in some way not directly comparable, they are not equally good, but they are also not completely incommensurable with each other. Chang (2012) calls a complete lack of comparability "noncomparability" and argues that cases of noncomparability are merely formal, based on category mistakes. In contrast to this, parity is a form of lack of comparability by the traditional triad of value relations that still allows for some evaluation. Two items may be on a par without being equally good, noncomparable tout court, or one may be better or worse than the other.

As an example, she discusses Michelangelo and Mozart. One may judge them as being on a par, while refraining from considering them equally good or one better than the other in terms of creativity. Another typical example would be evaluating two substantially different careers such as becoming a lawyer versus becoming a professional clarinet player. Both careers have their merits and disadvantages, but both of them have them in different ways. Just like Michelangelo's creative achievements are not directly comparable with Mozart's, being a lawyer may not be directly comparable to being a professional clarinetist in an overall assessment. But if one of these choices is not better than the other, then why are they not equally good?

According to Chang, parity has (at least) two properties that distinguish it from equal goodness. First, if a and b are equally good, then if a is improved a little bit to an item a^+, then a^+ should be judged better than b. In her view, however, parity is not generally affected by such small improvements. If you judge the career as a lawyer and the career as a clarinetist on a par, then they may remain to be on a par if you learn that you would earn fifty dollar more per month as a lawyer than you have previously thought. We may call this the Small Improvements Arguments (SIA).

Second, parity is not transitive. Let Michelangelo$^+$ be better than Michelangelo in terms of creativity. According to Chang, it can make sense to claim that Michelangelo is on a par with Mozart while at the same time claiming that Mozart is also on a par with Michelangelo$^+$. However, Michelangelo$^+$ is not considered on a par with Michelangelo in this example (by construction). Hence, transitivity is violated.

As a more realistic example, suppose you consider work as a lawyer being on a par with work as a concert clarinetist. Considering your future work as a lawyer, you might conclude that working as an actuary is pretty much on a par with working as a lawyer. Actuarial science may be less challenging in the daily work, after you have passed all exams, but you judge that unless you become a top lawyer, work as an actuary would give you an initially higher salary while having more spare time for your family. Suppose, for the sake of argument, that these careers are still not equally good because of the Small Improvements Argument. You may still not be willing to conclude from all of this that working as an actuary is on a par with the life as a concert musician. For example, the reason for this evaluation could be that work as a lawyer comes with some kind of glamour and social prestige that is (again) on a par with that of a clarinetist, while working as an actuary does not have this feature. After all, many people do not even know what actuaries do.

Two more basic relational properties of parity should be uncontroversial. Parity is symmetric for different items. If a is on a par with b and $a \neq b$, then b is also on a par with a. According to Carlson (2010, p. 123), parity is irreflexive, though; if this is true, then it cannot be symmetric in general.[1] Since any item is comparable to itself, it is also equally good as itself, and if it is equally good as itself, then it cannot be on a par with itself because the two relations are supposed to exclude one another. This reflects the stance that being on a par is not an equivalence relation but rather a relation that obtains from comparing two different items under varying aspects. However, I will not follow this analysis in Chapter 9 and instead define parity in a way that makes it symmetric for different items and allows "equally good" and "on a par" to overlap. For the time being, we should note that there can be different versions of parity, some of which we will explore in more detail below.

Chang (2002) anticipates various counter-arguments against her conception of parity and Chang (2005, 2012) defends her position further. Two of these arguments shall be addressed here.

According to the first counter-argument, parity is merely a form of strong comparison failure. In this view, you cannot really compare Michelangelo and Mozart or two massively different future lives like being a concert clarinetist and working as a lawyer. Chang devises the Chaining Argument against this position. It is based on the intuitively compelling proposition that (i) "...between two evaluatively very different items, a small unidimensional difference cannot trigger incomparability where before there was comparability" (Chang, 2002, p. 674). Given that, she asks us to imagine a hypothetical scenario in which we start with "Talentlessi," Michelangelo's untalented counterpart, and consider a series of small improvements that gradually turn him into a good sculptor, an excellent sculptor, Michelangelo, Michelangelo^{+}, Michelangelo^{++}, and so forth. Since each small improvement is governed by principle (i), we can compare each of these hypothetical persons with Mozart. Some of them, like Michelangelo and Michelangelo^{+} are judged on a par with Mozart. Hence, parity is not a lack of comparability tout court, as the counter-argument assumed.

According to the second counter-argument, parity is just a rough version of "equally good," where "rough" can be understood in different ways: The comparison relation could be vague, it might be applied loosely, or may not be vague at all but is instead designed to make approximate comparisons. An account based on rough equality will be discussed in the next section in more detail, so vagueness shall be discussed first.

The idea behind a vagueness-based approach is that "equally good" may apply in some cases definitely and without controversy, yet in some borderline cases it becomes hard to judge whether or not two items are equally good. Recall Luce's coffee cup example from Chapter 2. In this example, it seems reasonable to claim that the predicate "sweet" can not be attributed to the coffee in a borderline case, yet at the same time it is also not fully justified to state that the coffee is clearly not sweet.[2] In a vagueness-based account of parity, in borderline cases of equal goodness we may call two items on a par but remain reluctant to consider them equally good.

A conceptual challenge of this view is that when vagueness is understood epistemically, as Williamson (1994) discusses in-depth, the reason why we would consider two items on a par is that we lack knowledge about them. This is not what Chang has in mind, though. In her view, parity is a genuine value relation that may or may not hold between two items. We are not unable to judge between two items whether they are equally good because we lack information, we judge them as being on a par based on all information we have, even if we are fully informed. One way to argue for this view is to say that it lies in the nature of the items that we cannot compare them with the traditional value relations and is not just a result of our lack of knowledge about these items. For instance, in the example when a career as a lawyer is compared with the career of a concert clarinetist, it is conceivable that no amount of additional knowledge about how those careers would turn out might make one better than the other or both equally good. As a way to salvage this vagueness-based account, one might thus try to understand "equally good" as an ontologically vague relation. I personally do not believe that there can be ontological vagueness, however, and in any case would be reluctant to assert that it holds when there are other possible ways of explaining parity. As a third option, "equally good" may be considered semantically vague. In this view, the vagueness is built into the meaning of the predicate just like in classical examples like "bald" and "orange." This would mean that there was a borderline where it is unclear whether two items are equally good or not, and whenever that was the case in an actual comparison, we would say that the two items are on a par.

Semantic vagueness is the most promising approach among these. However, it is still misleading. If we claim that two items are on a par whenever the attribution of their equal goodness is in a borderline zone and only call them equally good in clear-cut cases, then it is strictly speaking incorrect to state that "equally good" is semantically vague. After all, in such an account "equally good" is reserved for the clear-cut cases. Instead, there is a notion of rough equality behind equal goodness and parity that is used to model attributions of equal goodness and parity. Such accounts of rough equality have been proposed.[3] Notably, a suggestion by Gert (2004) is based on interval orders. Since he later retracted his proposal in light of a reply by Chang (2005), I will not go into the details of his account and instead lay out a generic way of using semiorders to deal with parity in the next section. As we will see in the next section, such a rough equality approach has descriptive shortcomings, and it is instructive to take a closer look at it to see why.

7.2 Using Interval Orders

Recall from Section 2.1 that semiorders are special interval orders and interval orders can additionally express subinterval relations.[4] Subinterval relations are needed for representing time intervals, as Allen (1983) and van Benthem (1991) elaborate, but they are not needed for representations of parity, because in such a representation any overlapping intervals will be instances of parity.[5] For that purpose, a semiorder suffices. Take S to be a semiorder relation defined over the domain of items under discussion, and let the strict part be L and the weak part be Q. As we know from Section 2.1, L is transitive and irreflexive like standard strict betterness, but Q is not transitive. Parity is represented by Q, it expresses a weaker

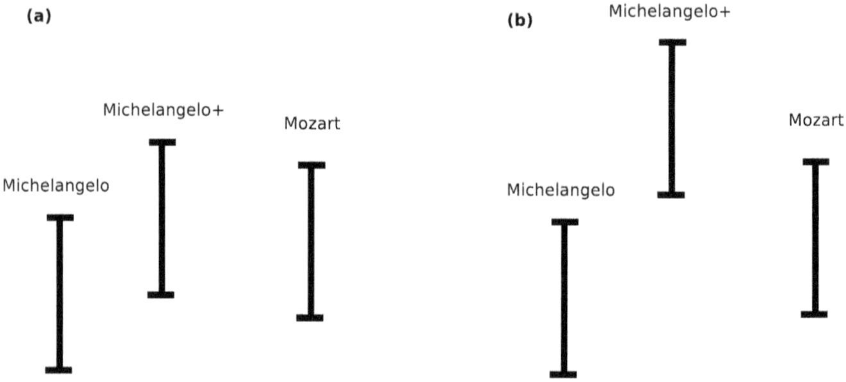

Figure 7.1: Two interval representations of the Michelangelo-Mozart example, where (a) Michelangelo is not L-better than Michelangelo$^+$ but all items are on a par, and (b) Michelangelo is L-better than Michelangelo$^+$ and both Michelangelo and Michelangelo$^+$ are on a par with Mozart.

form of equality that arises when two numerical intervals instead of two items are compared. Does this yield the desired result?

Since lack of transitivity has already been confirmed, let us check how this relation fares with the Small Improvements Argument. Figure 7.1 depicts two possible scenarios of the Michelangelo case. In scenario (a) Michelangelo and Michelangelo$^+$ are on a par with Mozart. That raises the question, however, how Michelangelo$^+$ can be an improved version of Michelangelo, if he is not better than Michelangelo. In scenario (b), Michelangelo$^+$ is better than Michelangelo, but both of them are on a par with Mozart. So scenario (b) seems to be on the right track with respect to explaining parity in relation to the Small Improvements Argument.

Is this an acceptable general solution? To investigate this question systematically, Figure 7.2 on page 115 depicts the relations between three intervals a, b, c, where the first branching shows the possible relations between a and b, the second one the relations between a and c, and the third branching lists the relations between b and c. In the notation chosen, $x > y$ means that the lower bound of x is above the upper bound of y interval, whereas $x \sim y$ means that intervals x and y overlap without specifying in which way they overlap. From that choice of representation it follows directly that aLb iff. $a > b$ and aQb iff. $a \sim b$.[6]

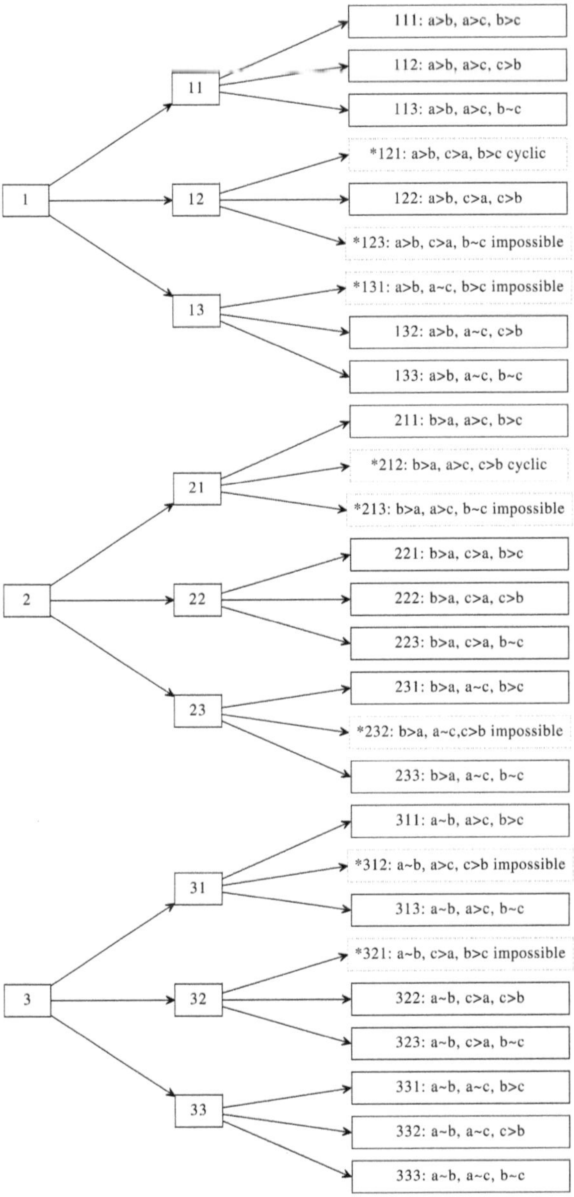

Figure 7.2: Relations between intervals a, b, and c, where the tree first branches for the relation between a and b, then for the relation between a and c, and then for the relation between b and c. In each case, either $x > y$, or $y > x$, or $x \sim y$.

Some of the branches lead to impossible constellations, as the figure indicates. Branches 121 and 212 create cycles in the strict part of the base relation cyclic, which is not allowed for a semiorder. Branches 123, 131, 213, 232, 312, 321 are also not allowed, because they lead to impossible relations between intervals. For example, in case 312 we would have aQb, aLc, and cLb. If aQb, then a and b overlap; but from aLc it follows that the lower bound of a is above the upper bound of c, and from cLb it follows that the lower bound of c is above the upper bound of b. Hence, a and b cannot overlap.

To see more clearly what is going on, let us take a look at the actual intervals and write $[\min_x, \max_x]$ for the interval associated with item x, where $\min_x$ is the lower bound and $\max_x$ the upper bound of the interval. Additionally, we assume that all intervals are of the same size.[7] Then the four relations are defined as follows:

Model 6 (Interval Model with Parity). *Let* $[\min_a, \max_a]$ *be an interval of real numbers associated with each item* $a \in D$*, where* $\max_x - \min_x$ *is the same constant size* k *for all* $a \in D$*, and derive the four value relations as follows:*

1. *a is strictly better than b iff.* $\min_a > \max_b$.
2. *a and b are equally good iff.* $\max_a = \max_b$ *and* $\min_a = \min_b$.
3. *a is strictly worse than b iff. b is strictly better than a.*
4. *a and b are on a par iff. either* $\max_a > \max_b$ *and* $\max_b > \min_a$*, or* $\max_b > \max_a$ *and* $\max_a > \min_b$.

Case 4 can be represented by relation Q, Case 1 by relation L, Case 3 as the converse of L as usual, and Case 2 as the absence of any of these relations, provided that no form of incomparability other than Q is allowed. In that setting, 133, 233, 313, 323, 331, and 332 in Figure 7.2 are the interesting cases in which transitivity of Q fails. For example, in scenario 331 we have aQb, bQc, but aLc. Is anything else needed to adequately represent parity? The representation seems fairly adequate, as long as parity is considered only as a relation for overall betterness and not in a multidimensional setting. The crucial case depicted in Figure 7.1 can be represented. It is the case when $\text{Mozart}_T > \text{Michelangelo}^{+}_{L}$ and $\text{Michelangelo}_T > \text{Mozart}_L$.

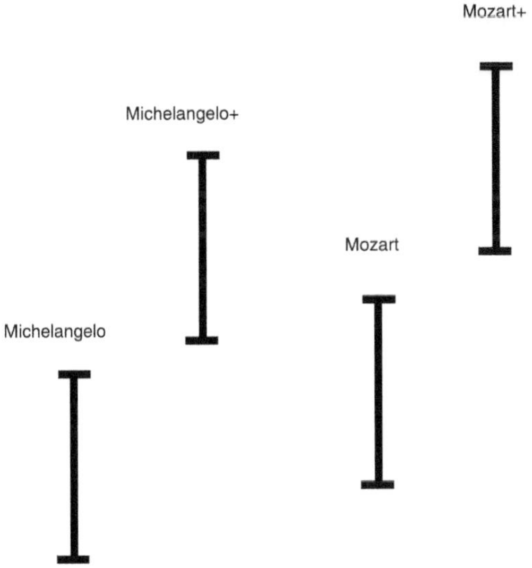

Figure 7.3: A problem for the semiorder representation of parity: Adding a better Mozart to the case of Figure 7.1b does not allow parity between Michelangelo and Mozart$^+$.

However, there is a problem with the representation that Rabinowicz (2010) lays out clearly.[8] The only possible interval configuration that allows improving Mozart to Mozart$^+$ in the above scenario is the one depicted in Figure 7.3. So Michelangelo cannot be on a par with Mozart$^+$ if there is also a Michelangelo$^+$ on a par with Mozart and Mozart$^+$. The Small Improvements Argument stipulates that it should always be possible to think of small improvements hypothetically, but the desirable parity case only works if three items are compared like in Figure 7.1b. This suggests that a semiorder representation is not fully adequate. It excludes (i) cases of the form aQb, a^+Qb, aQb^+, and a^+Qb^+, but allows (ii) cases of the form aQb, a^+Qb, a^+Qb^+, and b^+La. For further reference, let us call a parity relation that allows case (i) "quadruplic." The question is whether parity really needs to be quadruplic. It could be argued, based on a specific suggestion for determining or interpreting the intervals associated with given items, that b^+Qa cannot hold *because of* the underlying intervals.

Since in this particular semiorder model we interpret two items as equally good if they stand for the same interval, and we may simply stipulate that items cannot be on a par and equally good at the same time, the model adequately represents the requirement of irreflexivity. An item is not on a par with itself, but equally good to itself. Nevertheless, if a is on a par with b, and a stands for a different interval than b, then b is also on a par with a, and this follows from the above definitions.

7.3 Modeling Parity by Sets of Relations

Rabinowicz (2010) mentions another, more general argument against interval and semiorder accounts of parity. Many examples of being on a par suggest that parity only occurs when two items are compared across multiple aspects that may be related to each other, but are not directly comparable. For instance, one might argue that a musician's and a painter's creativity do not constitute the same value aspect. Both are ways of being creative, but you cannot directly compare them because composing differs vastly from painting. Likewise, choosing a career in law is substantially different from a concert clarinetist's life. It seems desirable to have an account of parity that somehow reflects this multidimensionality, whereas the semiorder-based account rather seems to represent rough equality within one and the same dimension or with respect to overall, all things considered betterness.

To lay out Rabinowicz's suggestion, it is best to start with his original proposal and address his own criticism and refinements afterward. Rabinowicz (2008) proposes an intersection model based on permissible preference orderings to define value relations under a fitting attitude analysis of value. Generally speaking, in a fitting attitude analysis the fact that something has value is explained in terms of fitting attitudes: Agents should have a pro-attitude towards items with value, and a contra-attitude towards items with disvalue. Rabinowicz uses the adjective "permissible" to express the deontic component of the analysis and the attitude of preferring one item over another as the attitude in question.

Based on these underpinnings, he considers a set K containing different permissible weak preference orderings. The idea behind this is that there is not just one such ordering, but several orderings may be permissible. Let R_i be the weak orderings in K. Although Rabinowicz does not state this explicitly, these may be considered the same relations as in the incomplete version of the preorder model we have seen in Section 1.3 of the first chapter. P and I are also defined as usual. The following value relations may then be defined on top of such structures:

Model 7 (Relational Set Model). *Let K be a set of incomplete preorder relations $R_i \in K$. The four value relations plus value incommensurability are defined as follows:*

1. *a is strictly better than b iff. a is preferable to b in every permissible preference ordering, i.e., aP_ib for every $R_i \in K$.*

2. *a and b are equally good iff. a and b are equipreferable in every permissible preference ordering, i.e., aI_ib for every $R_i \in K$.*

3. *a is strictly worse than b iff. b is strictly better than a.*

4. *a and b are incomparable iff. a and b are not comparable in any permissible preference ordering, i.e., $a \not{R}_i b$ for any $R_i \in K$.*

5. *a and b are on a par iff. a is preferable to b in some permissible preference ordering and b is preferable to a in another permissible preference ordering, i.e., there are $R_i, R_j \in K$ such that aP_ib and bP_ja.*

This approach's problem is that it is too general, as one would expect from an account that replaces one relation by a set of relations. Consider, for instance, strict betterness as defined above. Without further constraints, it is possible that a is preferable to b and b is preferable to c in every permissible preference ordering, yet there is a $R_i \in K$ such that cP_ia. So the transitivity of strict betterness is no longer guaranteed, and similar examples can be devised for the other definitions. K needs to be further constrained to ensure the desired properties.

As a remedy to this and other problems, Rabinowicz (2010, 2012) suggests to use degrees of favorings of individual items instead of preferences as a basis for the same overall construction. In this approach, there are functions $f_i \in \mathcal{F}$ from the total domain of items to "degrees of favoring" them. These are ordered by a transitive and asymmetric relation "$\succ$" he dubs "higher than," giving rise to a weak preference relation as follows: a is weakly preferred to b in favoring f iff. $f(a) \succ f(b)$ or $f(a) = f(b)$.[9] Permissible preference orderings K can then be defined from the class $\mathcal{F}$ of permissible assignments $f_i \in \mathcal{F}$ of degrees of favoring.

Model 8 (Rabinowicz Model). *Let D be the domain of items, $S \subseteq D$, and $f_i \in \mathcal{F}$ be a set of functions $f_i : S \to F$ from items in S to a set F of favorings, and let the favorings F be ordered by a complete transitive and irreflexive ordering relation "$\succ$" plus identity "$=$." For every $f_i \in \mathcal{F}$ there is a corresponding partial preorder $R_i \in K$ defined as aR_ib if $a, b \in S$, and $f_i(a) \succ f_i(b)$ or $f_i(a) = f_i(b)$; otherwise, if $a \notin S$ or $b \notin S$, a and b are incommensurable and R_i is not defined at a, b. The value relations are defined like for the Relational Set Model for the partial preorders in K.*

The main difference to Rabinowicz's earlier suggestion is that "strictly better than" and "equally good" are now guaranteed to be transitive, since "$\succ$" is transitive and so the weak preference relations in K are also transitive. Technically speaking, this is just a way of imposing the desired constraints on K. However, Rabinowicz finds favorings of this kind conceptually compelling for various additional reasons and provides further arguments for them.[10]

7.4 Trichotomic Parity

Carlson (2010, 2018) suggests to define parity in terms of the traditional value relations with incomparability modeled by incompleteness. Since it is based on the traditional triad of value relations "better than," "worse than," and "equally good," I will call his approach "trichotomic parity." We can assume that the base relation R is an incomplete preorder, with P and I defined as usual. Carlson's definition of parity is based on a notion "almost better than," which is, in turn, defined in terms of P. To get an intuitive understanding of this version of parity first, take a look at the graph in Figure 7.4. It depicts the four possible constellations in which two items a and b can be on a par. Item c in these graphs is "almost better" than the respective item on the other branch in cases (a) and (b) and "almost worse" than the respective item in the other branch in cases (c) and (d). For instance, in case (a) item c is almost better than b. In addition a and b are not directly comparable, but there is a superior item d that is much better than a and better than b. In this case a and b are on a par. Cases (b)–(d) work analogously.

The formal definition of "almost better than" is unfortunately a bit involved. Carlson (2018) has improved the original definition from Carlson

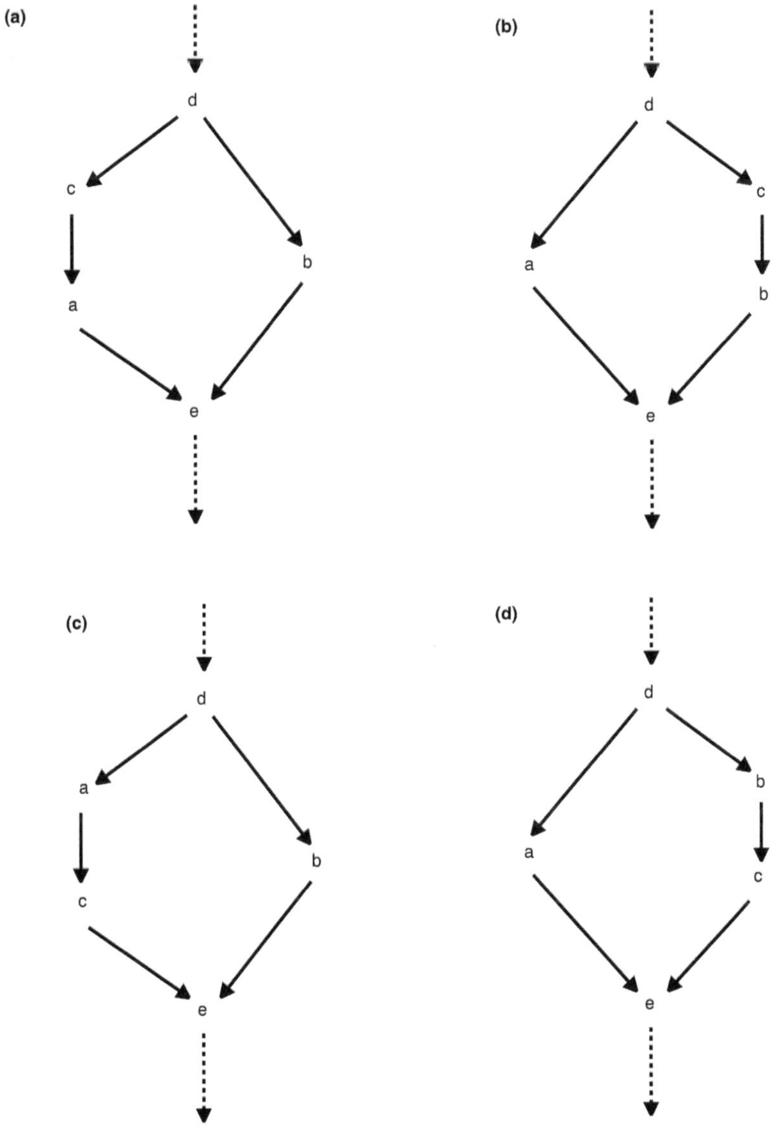

Figure 7.4: Trichotomic Parity (Carlson, 2010, p. 123): Items a and b are not comparable by the base relation R but are on a par, because an item c is either (a) almost better than b, (b) almost better than a, (c) almost worse than b, or (d) almost worse than a.

(2010) after John Nolt discovered a (minor) problem with it.[11] Following Carlson (2018, p. 532), let an item $a \in D$ be an upper semibound of a set $S \subseteq D$ iff. there is no $b \in S$ s.t. bPa. An item $a \in D$ is a minimal upper semibound of $S \subseteq D$ iff. a is an upper semibound of S and there is no upper semibound c of S such that aPc. Correspondingly, an item $a \in D$ is a lower semibound of $S \subseteq D$ iff. there is no $b \in S$ such that aPb, and an item $a \in D$ is a maximal lower semibound of $S \subseteq D$ iff. a is a lower semibound of S and there is no lower semibound c of S such that cPa.

We can now define a relation "almost better than," abbreviated by P^*, as follows: aP^*b iff. a is either (i) a minimal upper semibound of the set $\{x \in D \mid x\not{P}b\}$ or (ii) a maximal lower semibound of the set $\{x \in D \mid b\not{P}x\}$. Now that this relation has been defined, parity can be defined as holding between two items that are not directly comparable by the base relation R, but where one of them is almost better or almost worse than the other item.

Model 9 (Trichotomic Parity Model). *Let R be an incomplete base relation from which I "equally good" and P "strictly better than" can be defined as usual. Let P^* be the "almost better than" relation derived from R. Then two items a and b are on a par iff. $a\not{R}b$, $b\not{R}a$, and there is an item c such that (i) cPa and cP^*b, or (ii) cPb and cP^*a, or (iii) aPc and bP^*c, or (iv) bPc and aP^*c.*

The definition corresponds to the four cases depicted in Figure 7.4. Unlike the other accounts of parity discussed so far, trichotomic parity does not change the inventory of base value relations in any substantive way. An incomplete preorder relation may constitute the base of our overall value comparisons. Among the approaches discussed so far, it requires the smallest deviation from the standard model.

7.5 Comparison

How do different conceptions of parity compare to each other? As it turns out at a closer look, they mostly have the same basic formal properties. If intervals are used to represent parity in the way laid out in Section 7.2, then the relation derived from an interval order or semiorder relation representing those intervals is reflexive out of the box. However, as mentioned before, when using intervals directly for representing the relation between two items we can still give special significance to the case when the intervals are identical. According to the definitions in Model 6, parity is irreflexive, because two identical intervals define "equally good." Parity is also irreflexive in Rabinowicz's account, because it follows from the definitions in Model 7 that an item is always equally good to itself. Likewise, parity is irreflexive in Carlson's approach because neither of the clauses (i)–(iv) in the definition of Model 9 can be satisfied if b is replaced by another instance of a in them. For example, suppose aNa and consider clause (i). If there is a cPa, then it follows from the definition of "almost better than" that $c\not{P}^*a$, and so clause (i) cannot be fulfilled. Analogous arguments can be made for the other cases.

In all of the accounts parity is symmetric for comparisons between different items. If an interval associated with item a overlaps with that of b, then that of b also overlaps with that of a. If a is preferable to b in some permissible preference orderings and b is preferable to a in others, then this holds in both directions: If a is on a par with b but both are based on different preference orderings, then b is on a par with a. The property may be less obvious in Carlson's account. Suppose that a is on a par with b according to Model 9. Then one of clauses (i)–(iv) must obtain. Assume for a start that (i) holds. Then there is an item c such that cPa and cP^*b. But then either b itself is a minimal upper semibound of the set $\{x \mid x\not{P}a\}$, since by definition of parity $a\not{P}b$, or there is an item g such that gPb and g is a minimal upper semibound of the set $\{x \mid x\not{P}a\}$. In both cases, it follows from clause (i) in Model 9 that b is on a par with a, provided that $a \neq b$. The proofs for clauses (ii)–(iv) are similar.

Failure of transitivity of parity can also be shown for all of the accounts. We have already seen how this is the central feature of interval order and semiorder representations. As for Rabinowicz's account, let $K = \{R_1, R_2, R_3\}$ and the domain of items be $D = S = \{a, b, c\}$. Let cP_1aP_1b, bP_2cP_2a, and cP_3bP_3a. Then a is on a par with b, b is on a par with c, but at the same time c is better than a. Carlson (2010, p. 124) gives an example of failure of transitivity for his notion of parity. It is based on $D = \{a, b, c, d\}$ and an ordering $dPaPc$. Since b is not comparable to a, but dP^*b and bP^*c by definition of "almost better than," it follows that a is on a par with b and b is on a par with c. However, aPc holds as well.

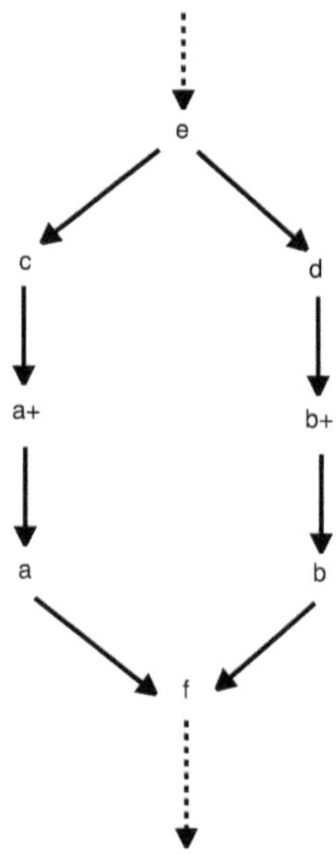

Figure 7.5: Trichotomic parity is quadruplic.

The accounts differ in other respects, though. We have already seen in Section 7.2 that interval-based parity according to Model 6 is not quadruplic. In contrast to this, both Rabinowicz's and Carlson's accounts are quadruplic.

To prove this for Rabinowicz's account, let $K = \{R_1, R_2\}$ and assume that $a^+ P_1 a$, $b^+ P_1 b$, $a^+ P_2 a$, $b^+ P_2 b$. We then swap the assessments for comparisons between a, a^+ and b, b^+ with respect to R_1 and R_2. For example, if $aP_1 b$, $a^+ P_1 b$, $aP_1 b^+$ and $a^+ P_1 b^+$, then $bP_2 a$, $b^+ P_2 a$, $b^+ P_2 a$, $b^+ P_2 a^+$. Since swapping the comparisons is possible for any two relations and we have chosen a, a^+, b, b^+ arbitrarily, this notion of parity is quadruplic.

For Carlson's approach we provide a construction of four items that stand in the required relations. Assume the scenario depicted in Figure 7.5. We have to show that in this scenario a^+ is on a par with b^+ and vice versa, a^+ is on a par with b and vice versa, a is on a par with b^+ and vice versa, and a is on a par with b and vice versa. We go through these cases and ignore the "vice versa" clauses in the proof, since these directions follow from the symmetry of parity for different items. Case 1: According to Model 9, a^+ is on a par with b^+ iff. there is a c such that (i) cPa^+ and (ii) cP^*b^+. Condition (i) is fulfilled for c in the figure. Condition (ii) is also fulfilled, since c is an upper semibound of the set $S := \{x \in D \mid x \not{P} b^+\} = \{b, c, a^+, a, f\}$. Case 2: We have to show that a^+ is on a par with b. In this case cPa^+ and a^+P^*b, because $b \in S$ and c is an upper semibound of S. Case 3: We have to show that b^+ is on a par with a. This case is analogous to the previous one, except that dPb^+ and dP^*a. Case 4: Show that a is on a par with b. Then a^+Pa and a^+P^*b, because a^+ is a minimal upper semibound for the set $S' := \{x \in D \mid x \not{P} b\} = \{c, a^+, a, f\}$. This concludes the proof that trichotomic parity is quadruplic.

Apart from these technical properties of parity, the three approaches differ quite substantially in their conceptual underpinnings, of course. The intervals on which a semiorder approach is based may be conceived in various ways. They may be epistemic upper and lower bounds of assessments of our comparisons or may represent other forms of uncertainty or measurement errors of value judgments. However, they might also be conceived as ontological and more principal in nature, for example reflecting a principal vagueness of evaluative comparative predicates. Or, they may be taken to represent the unwillingness or inability of a particular agent to distinguish closely related items. All of these possibilities lead to different conceptualizations of cases when the transitivity of equal goodness fails. However, semi- and interval order models are best considered qualitative formalizations of rough equality rather than parity in Chang's sense, because they lack quadruplicity.

Rabinowicz's revised approach is intriguing at first sight, since it on the one hand reflects our intuition that parity is multidimensional and based on comparisons according to different aspects of items, and on the other hand provides a possible link from qualitative comparisons to cardinal utilities. Although favorings are formulated without presuming that cardinal information is present, a favoring can also be understood as a sort of preference intensity. In that case a set of admissible favorings constitutes a ratio scale.

On the flip side of the coin, it is dubious that favorings are attached to individual items. As decision theorists like Keeney and Raiffa (1976) have argued, direct scoring in each aspect is not a good preference elicitation method and raises the question of how we use this information to make comparisons across multiple aspects. Reasonable aggregation methods require some kind of comparison between aspects, either by weighing or by ranking, but in order to arrive at such an assessment we need to know the highest and lowest possible utility value within each aspect. Eisenführ et al. (2010) illustrate this problem as follows:

> [I]n a test of vacuum cleaners, the attribute "safety" receives the weight factor 0.15, the attribute "handling" the weight factor 0.25, and so on. Does this really mean that handling is more important than safety? Without knowing the intervals of the attributes, the weights are meaningless. If the worst possible level of the attribute safety is attached to a device that delivers a deadly power surge every time it is turned on, any sensible consumer would obviously attach a weight of 1 to the attribute safety and 0 to any other attribute. However, if the attribute level interval ranges from "low risk of injury if opened improperly" to "no danger whatsoever," the attribute safety does not need to be weighted so heavily. (Eisenführ et al., 2010, p. 152)

Favorings seem to suggest that when a value is used in a decision situation, the decision maker can determine the choice-guiding intensity and relevance of each aspect of every item in isolation from other items and aspects, whereas in practice those assessments *need* to be based on comparisons.[12] Favorings therefore seem to be a step in the wrong direction when compared to Rabinowicz's original proposal. It is particularly doubtful, on a conceptual level, that favorings could be the basis of meaningful cross-aspectual comparisons, as their application for modeling parity suggests.

Carlson's account has none of these disadvantages but comes at the cost of lacking some explanatory power. It really just states conditions for one aggregate overall "better than" relation that must obtain when we say that two items are on a par, and in doing so lays out the minimal conditions for what seems to correspond to what Chang has in mind for parity. However, in contrast to Rabinowicz's approach it does not attempt to *explain* parity in terms of cross-aspectual comparisons. Ideally, such an explanation would be desirable, since there is such a strong intuition that two items can only be on a par if they differ substantially in some respects, but still belong to the same overall value category to be comparable. For example, it seems infelicitous to say that ten thousand chocolate bars are on a par with a painting, even if these are comparable in certain aspects like monetary value. The items belong to different value categories, so to say. In contrast to this, there is no such problem with Chang's example of Mozart versus Michelangelo or with choosing different professions like working as a lawyer and working as a musician. Items from these domains can be on a par, it seems, because we can compare them across relevant aspects that are related to each other, even though they are not the same aspects. A painter's creativity differs considerably from a composer's creativity, making Mozart and Michelangelo hard to compare with the conventional value relations. Both are types of creativity, though, and therefore we can judge the two artists on a par. Ideally, a notion of parity would model the cross-aspectual comparisons involved, whereas Carlson's approach only characterizes the end result.

I will lay out in Chapter 9 how to explicitly take into account cross-aspectual comparisons in a multidimensional setting, but the resulting notion of parity will differ from the one defended by Chang (2002, 2005). Carlson's approach matches Chang's requirements more closely.

Chapter 8

Spectrum Cases

Spectrum Cases are scenarios in which items are arranged so that the transitivity of intuitively plausible "better than" comparisons seems to fail. Since Temkin (1987) introduced them, they have fueled a controversy about the transitivity or failure of transitivity of "better than" comparisons. Temkin (2012) discusses them in most detail. As it turns out, the problem is hard to tackle and every solution proposed so far has some downsides. Although I argue in this chapter that lexicographic approaches are the most promising way to handle Spectrum Cases, the lack of a decisive criterion for resolving the disputes about them remains troubling.

8.1 Typical Scenarios

Temkin (1987) originally discussed the Mere Addition Paradox of Parfit (1984) as an example of a scenario that illustrates a transitivity failure. However, Parfit's example also concerns population ethics, which comes with a host of additional problems. Cleaner examples can be found in subsequent discussions by Temkin (2012) and Rachels (1998, 2001). We will look at two Spectrum Cases in what follows, a hedonic example with "better than" comparisons and a scenario based on "worse than" comparisons. Other examples in the literature have the same structure and differ only with time intervals and dimensions under consideration.

For the hedonic example, consider the amount of pleasure for an individual agent over time. In this case, items are possible states of affairs.

Figure 8.1: Hedonic Spectrum Case: Even though in every pairwise comparison of adjacent items $a_j P a_i$ when $j > i$, at some point k the pleasure during the time interval is so low that the judgment becomes $a_1 P a_k$.

Suppose that a_1 is a state of affairs in which a particular agent has a life with an extremely high amount of pleasure for a month, after which the amount of pleasure returns to some neutral low but positive base value. Now assume that a_2 has only a very slightly lower amount of pleasure than a_1 but lasts two months, that a_3 brings a little bit less amount of pleasure than a_2 but lasts six months, and so on. For each adjacent pair a_i, a_j ($j > i$), the difference in pleasure is barely noticeable, but a_j lasts much longer than a_i. Given that, the argument against the transitivity of "better than" is as follows: When we compare a_1 and a_2, we clearly judge that $a_2 P a_1$, and when we compare a_2 with a_3 we clearly judge $a_3 P a_2$. Generally, we seem to judge $a_j P a_i$ for any two adjacent items with $i < j$. However, at some point k any reasonable agent will judge that $a_1 P a_k$. Hence, the strict betterness relation P is not transitive. Figure 8.1 illustrates this example.

Let us turn to comparisons by "worse than." The two aspects under consideration are pain and duration. The structure is similar to the previous example. Suppose item a_1 is that you suffer an extreme amount of agony for one month. In scenario a_2 you receive slightly less pain but still have to endure excruciating torture, and a_2 lasts two months, a_3 means a little bit less pain than a_2 and lasts for four months, and so forth. The claim is that many people would consider a_2 worse than a_1, a_3 worse than a_2, and so forth, until at some point k they would judge that a_1 is worse than a_k. Hence, "worse than" is not transitive.

Before going on, we need to discuss some common but in my opinion not very fruitful responses. A natural reaction is to dismiss Spectrum Cases as intuition-pumping and point out that they are based on unrealistic scenarios. However, according to Temkin the realism of the scenarios is fairly irrelevant; his point is that we are able to evaluate fictitious scenarios intuitively and that our initial intuitions about Spectrum Cases are clear and robust.[1] It is always difficult to discuss purported or real intuitions, but in the end I agree with Temkin. People do make value judgments that support the conclusion that transitivity fails in Spectrum Cases, and if they deny them, then usually because they sense a "trap" and have already reflected philosophically about the transitivity of comparative forms of evaluative adjectives. It takes a certain willingness to seriously engage with the thought experiments posed by Spectrum Cases in order to acknowledge the problem. Merely claiming that the problem does not occur in practice is not a satisfying reply.

Another standard reply is to attack the hedonic underpinnings of the examples. Despite being a legitimate critique, it leads astray. It is possible to reformulate the examples in non-hedonic ways. Consider welfare levels of an individual agent instead of pleasure in the first case, for instance. This does not change the structure of the example or our judgments. Some value domains like monetary value lead to additional problems that might complicate their evaluation, and aggregating value across different individuals like in Parfit's Repugnant Conclusion is also more problematic than comparisons for one agent, yet in general Spectrum Cases can be formulated in many different value domains.

I will not consider these replies any further in what follows. Attacking intuitions is fine but does not solve the problem. If one person has an extremely strong intuition that "better than" is transitive and therefore the judgments in Spectrum Cases must be "wrong," and another person has an equally strong intuition that the value judgments in the Spectrum Cases are plausible and "right," then the problem remains. Attacking specific features of the examples themselves is also fruitless because they can be reformulated in other value domains and with other values and durations. It only takes one working example to support Temkin's point that the transitivity of "better than" is not compatible with other assumptions that underlie Spectrum Cases.

8.2 Ways to Preserve Transitivity

What sets Spectrum Cases apart from many other examples of cyclic value comparisons is that they exemplify failure of strict betterness. Thus, semi-order and interval order representations cannot solve the problem. As we have seen in Chapter 2, Hansson (2001) lays out minimal criteria for monist value relations that allow for the nontransitivity of strict betterness. However, most authors who replied to Temkin have focused on the idea of explaining what goes on in Spectrum Cases without giving up the transitivity of strict betterness.

One reply may be called the Analyticity Objection. We have already seen Broome's position that all comparative forms are transitive by virtue of their meaning.[2] This view is supported by the literature on the semantics of scalar adjectives like Kennedy and McNally (2005). However, as I have argued in Section 6.4, such approaches need to be taken with a grain of salt. Whatever point of view one has about the problematic notion of "linguistic evidence," it is hard to dismiss value judgments in Spectrum Cases solely by pointing out that some other, perhaps more customary judgments seem to indicate that value relations are transitive. Spectrum Cases provide evidence to the contrary, supporting the thesis that not all comparative forms of scalar adjectives are transitive.

It is wrong to talk about linguistic evidence in this context, though, because the judgments in question rest on moral intuitions about the examples. They are normative, moral judgments. If they can be further justified, they have to be justified with arguments in ethics, not by resorting to word meaning only. Insofar as ethics is a rational endeavor, the situation should be the same as in any other discipline. Bloomfield discusses an example from zoology to make a similar point:

> There is nothing in the structure of morphemes like *wolf*, *fox*, and *dog* to tell us the relation between their meanings; this is a problem for the zoölogist. The zoölogist's definition of these meanings is welcome to us as a practical help, but it

> cannot be confirmed or rejected on the basis of our science [linguistics]. (Bloomfield, 1933, p. 162)

Lexical semantics cannot decide which theory is well-confirmed or true; that is the task of domain experts in each subject area. Hence, we have to understand the Analyticity Objection as a normative position concerning value comparisons. The "right" view about the meaning of "better than" makes it transitive. Although this position may still appear to beg the question, it has a certain overall appeal. The idea behind it is that someone who concludes from a Spectrum Case that "better than" is not transitive makes a mistake. As I mentioned in Section 2.5, I consider this a legitimate point of view. To put it in terms of rationality principles, the objection ultimately says that the transitivity of value comparisons normatively outranks other considerations that play a role in Spectrum Cases. It is in that respect similar to claiming that the law of the excluded middle is a foundational logical principle that outweighs considerations against it in specific examples. Although this Analyticity Objection is rather weak as an argument by itself because it attempts to justify a normative position by resorting to existing meaning, it can be made stronger with additional arguments for transitivity, for example by pointing out that reasonable utility representations require strict betterness to be transitive.

As a seemingly easy way to maintain transitivity, it is tempting to give up completeness.[3] Suppose in the chain of pairwise comparisons between a_1 and a_k there are two incomparable items. Then transitivity between comparable items is not violated, and the cycle is avoided. This solution denies that our judgments between adjacent items are as clear as they seem to be. In contrast, Temkin claims that comparing adjacent items is unproblematic: We unambiguously judge that a tiny little bit less pleasure over a much larger duration is better than a tiny little bit more pleasure over a much shorter duration, and if a particular skeptic does not agree with a particular case, the example can be modified to make the difference in duration sufficiently large and the difference in the other aspect sufficiently minuscule. If there is some uncertainty, reluctance, or other failure to compare two items, then it should primarily occur between a_k and a_1 once we take a step back and look at the situation as a whole. Although giving up completeness suffices as a remedy to the problem from a technical point of view, it does not match our assessments in pairwise comparisons of adjacent items, which seem to be the least problematic.

Another reply is that Spectrum Cases are merely Sorites Puzzles illustrating the vagueness of "better than" and "worse than." For instance, one might argue that it is not clear whether a_{k+1} is better than a_k at some point because the level of pleasure has gotten so low. One might even argue that this is so, because there is epistemic vagueness about what counts as pleasure in such a case. Clearly, the "life of potatoes and muzak" (Parfit) is not a life of pleasure, but what about a life of excellent potatoes with molten butter and a bit better music? This argument seems to be on the right track, but, as Temkin and others have pointed out, Spectrum Cases do not have the typical structure you would expect from a vague comparison predicate. There is a transition from clear-cut cases to a vague zone and back to clear-cut cases in a classical case of vagueness. For example, certain colors are clearly red, then there is a zone of reddish-orange colors, and then there are clear-cut cases of orange color. This would suggest a zone of uncertainty between adjacent items, but this is exactly what Temkin denies. The pairwise comparison of adjacent items is not the problem, according to Temkin. The problem is, instead, that if we step back and take a look at a_1 in relation to some later item like a_k, we might at some point k revise our assessment. What he calls "essential comparability" is a feature of certain situations that requires us to take a look at the scenario as a whole, rather than only at pairwise comparisons, and in such situations we may get a failure of the transitivity of "better than." In contrast to this, Sorites Puzzles are based on vague predicates like "bald," where clear-cut baldness because of no hair at all is on one side of the spectrum, not being bald at all is on the other side of the spectrum, and the unclear cases occur somewhere within.

Nebel (2017) develops a counter-argument similar to the Analyticity Objection. He observes that if "good" is defined in terms of "better than" in one of the ways laid out in Section 4.2, then it follows from the non-transitivity of "better than" that either all items until the k-th item are good, or that none of the items in the whole spectrum is good, or that the positivity of "good" does not hold. To see this, suppose first that some item a_i in the ordered spectrum at position i $(i < k)$ counts as good. By positivity, any better item a_j with $a_j P a_i$ is also good. However, once there is a cycle, $a_1 P a_k$, it follows that all items before k are good. Suppose, as a second case, that no item before k is good. Then there can be no good item at all, since $a_1 P a_n$ for $n \geq k$ and a_1 is not good. So if positivity holds and "better than" is not transitive, then either all items in the spectrum until the tipping point are good or no item in the whole spectrum is good. However, it seems at first glance that if such claims make sense at all under the already counter-intuitive assumption of cyclic betterness judgments, then it seems more reasonable to assume that there are Spectrum Cases where a_1 is good, for instance, or those where a_{k-2}, a_{k-1} and a_1 but no other items are good. These possibilities are incompatible with the positivity of goodness. To Nebel this is enough to justify a reductio ad absurdum of the original argument that the transitivity of "better than" fails in Spectrum Cases.

Nebel's argument is a valid objection but also feels a bit contrived. It is far from being clear why the positivity of "good" should have more weight than the transitivity of "better than." On the contrary, the cycle in the betterness assessment allowed by nontransitivity appears to be the source of the problem. Notice that in a typical Spectrum Case there is no strongly eligible item either, so the "better than" judgments cannot be used for decision-making. Unless one decides, as a remedy, to consider a_1 the best item and discard the judgments $a_2 P a_1$ upon closer inspection, the only solution for choice guidance is to collapse the cycle into one class of equally good items: Choose any of the items $a_1, \dots, a_{k-1}$. In that case, it is plausible to assume that all of $a_1, \dots, a_{k-1}$ are good, maintaining positivity. The failure of positivity is the result of rejecting that solution, yet the solution is rejected not because of the failure of positivity, but rather because the lack of the transitivity of "better than" without further constraints allows for implausible cycles without eligibility. So the initial assessment that it should be possible to only have some items before k to be good should be rejected and then positivity can be maintained. Even in this case the cyclic "better than" assessments have implausible and impractical consequences such as lack of choice guidance and lack of a reasonable utility representation. Hence, the transitivity of "better than" is a more fundamental normative rationality principle than the positivity of "good." Nevertheless, even though it does not provide an entirely conclusive reductio ad absurdum, Nebel's observation provides an important additional argument in favor of the transitivity of "better than."

Klocksiem (2016) lays out a promising way to preserve the transitivity of "better than" while doing justice to at least some of the intuitions behind Spectrum Cases that make them plausible in the first place. It is based on work by Rachels (2001). Rachels's "quasi-maximizing theory" is based on four principles, one of which is of particular interest. According to the Lexicality Principle, "[p]leasures sufficiently different in intensity differ lexically" (Rachels, 2001, p. 215). This is meant to be understood in the following way. When we compare the pleasure of a_1 with the pleasure of a_k, these differ in quality, thereby giving rise to lexicographic comparisons between them. Generally speaking, lexicographic comparisons are based on the idea that you first apply one set of criteria, and only if you cannot evaluate which item is better apply a second set of criteria, and so forth, until an evaluation can be made. In this particular application, the intensity of pleasure in a_1 is so high that it outranks any duration of the lower pleasure of a_k, which is why transitivity fails in combination with his other principles called Conflation and Duration.

Rachels himself accepts the nontransitivity of "better than" and adopts it as one of his principles.[4] However, as Klocksiem (2016) notices, the Lexicality Principle describes different qualities of pleasures based on the *relative* intensity between them. If instead absolute thresholds are used for making lexical comparisons, then "better than" can remain transitive. How so? Take any three items a_i, a_j, and a_k, where a_k is below an absolute threshold and the other items are above it, and suppose that a_i has more pleasure than a_j but is shorter in duration.[5] If it is granted that all items are comparable, then either $a_iPa_jPa_k$ or $a_jPa_iPa_k$, or maybe even a_iIa_j and a_iPa_k, a_jPa_k. In any case, since a_k is below the threshold at which the amount of pleasure starts to count, it will always be outranked by alternatives above the threshold. Overall betterness remains transitive in this setting, no matter what other value judgments are made, since a_1Pa_k holds in any case.

8.3 Why a Lexicographic Approach?

This section is concerned with some more general arguments for a lexicographic approach. One way of interpreting the examples is to take (sub-)values and value aspects to change in quality within a dimension, and these kinds of qualitative changes of values occur naturally in our intuitive value judgments. These kinds of qualitative changes support non-compensatory value aggregation methods, and the lexicographic approach is a special instance of these.

Before continuing, we need to clarify what "compensatory" and "non-compensatory" means in this context. Let us assume for simplicity that all aspects have cardinal utility representations, that $u(.)$ is the aggregate utility function and that $u_1(.), \ldots, u_n(.)$ are the utility functions for each aspect.[6] We may call an aggregation method compensatory in aspect i iff.: if $u(a) > u(b)$, there is an item b' such that $u_j(b') = u_j(b)$ for all $j \neq i$, and $u_i(b')$ is such that after aggregation $u(b') > u(a)$.[7] An aggregation method is compensatory for a subset $S \subseteq \{1, \ldots, n\}$ of two or more aspects iff.: if $u(a) > u(b)$, then there is an item b' such that $u_j(b') = u_j(b)$ for all $j \notin S$ and all $u_i(b')$ with $i \in S$ are such that after aggregation $u(b') > u(a)$. As a special case, we may stipulate that aggregating items is always compensatory when it is based on a set that contains only one aspect. An aggregation method is fully compensatory iff. it is compensatory for every non-empty subset of aspects. Let us further call an aggregation method noncompensatory in aspect i if it is not compensatory in aspect i, noncompensatory for a subset of two or more aspects S if it is not compensatory for S, and fully noncompensatory iff. there is no subset S of two or more aspects for which it is compensatory.

The commonly-used additive aggregation discussed in Section 5.2 is fully compensatory. For any aspect and any non-empty subset of aspects, there is always a number that can compensate for other aspects. However, it is easy to find hypothetical evaluative situations for which this is highly implausible. Many value aspects seem to belong to qualitatively different values, especially with respect to their moral relevance. For example, suppose that one aspect is that n people receive a free chocolate bar and ignore, for the sake of argument, the costs behind the "free" chocolate bars—imagine, for instance, that they materialize out of thin air. Since receiving one chocolate bar gives pleasure to most of us and is not substantially unhealthy, we can assume that n chocolate bars distributed to n people yields nk positive value for some constant k. We can set k to 1. Now suppose getting those chocolate bars to n people requires murdering someone. When a fully compensatory value aggregation method is used, then there is a number m such that the disvalue of murdering someone is outweighed by the value of m people obtaining a chocolate bar each. This is always the case for a fully compensatory aggregation method, no matter how bad a disvalue might be. However, this is clearly unacceptable in this example. The value of n people getting one chocolate bar each is of a completely different quality than the disvalue of murdering someone. So we ought not accept that the two aspects can be freely weighed against each other.

As a particular instance of noncompensatory aggregation in subsets of aspects, a general lexicographic approach gets the example right. Murdering five is worse than murdering one person and providing the gift of a chocolate bar to a thousand people is better than to only a hundred people insofar as the overall value is concerned. In each value category the aggregation might very well be additive. However, there is no way to justify a murder so that n persons can each get their free chocolate bar, no matter how large n is. They belong to different kinds of values, and, as one may add, getting one free chocolate bar is likely not morally relevant at all, not just not in this example but not in general either.

To some readers the above example might seem contrived. A response to it could be that we rarely, if ever, need to make such comparisons in practice. Indeed, although noncompensatory decision-making methods have been investigated and used in practice,[8] they are often not needed. In practice, the outranked aspects are often not considered in the first place and it is rarely useful to keep a second set of aspects ready in case the first one yields a tie.[9] Moreover, even when such aspects are taken into account they will be dominated by more important aspects. In an additive model with weights it is always possible to adjust the weights for aspects to make a counter-intuitive conclusion go away. This is not cheating, but part of the rational decision process.

However, from the fact that a lexicographic layering of aspects is not always needed in practical decision-making and may be undesirable from a technical point of view, it ought not be concluded that it is not needed for an adequate representation of value structure. First, the above example is just one of many highly implausible scenarios that compensatory models of value aggregation do not exclude. The problem with compensatory aggregation is more general; the very idea is dubious that any aspect of a value and any other (sub-)value can be traded off *in principle* with any other aspect of a value and any other (sub-)value that enters an overall "better than" comparison. Why should we think so? Second, scenarios like the above one do occur in practice, and perhaps even more often than one might think at first glance. Substitute "affordable access to oil" for "chocolate bars" and you get a more controversial case. Many people would in that case consider the two aspects compensatory, but others might not. Now suppose that instead of affordable access to oil we are talking about access to tuna. It is much harder to justify the view that the value aggregation should be fully compensatory in this example. This shows that commonsense valuations can meander between compensatory and noncompensatory aggregation in dependence on what is at stake and the value domains under consideration. Hence, a purely compensatory aggregation method like weighted additive sum is not adequate for representing value structure in general in a multidimensional setting.

It is important to emphasize that a lexicographic outranking of value aspects is always up for debate and that compensatory value trade-offs must always be considered as a possibility. Adopting a noncompensatory approach to value aggregation is a double-edged sword. A disadvantage of absolute thresholds is that borderline cases around the threshold can have seemingly paradoxical consequences. Why should the threshold be at exactly this place and not a little lower or higher? This question will rarely have a clear-cut answer. Like in approaches to vagueness in legal reasoning, where the same problem occurs, the solution is almost always a matter of what one might call "normative sociology" and politics, based on criteria like fairness, division of power, and practical coherence among agents and within the same agent over time. The right solution is usually to stipulate a threshold, if there is a need for a determinate value assessment, and defend its reasonableness with a mixture of normative and practical considerations. For aspects of "better than" comparisons such arguments can draw from a rich tradition in aesthetics and moral philosophy. That in the end there is often a certain arbitrariness to thresholds does not by itself speak against their use. Criticisms of particular thresholds and disagreements about where to place them are not inherently more problematic than any other discussions of values comparisons; different people endorse different values.

The sword is double-edged because it is easy to erroneously presume that one aspect outranks another when there are good arguments why they should be compensatory. There are often strong social and institutional pressures involved in such judgments. For example, statistical deaths occur in many areas of policymaking. Realistically speaking, the lives of people have to be traded off against the costs of safety measures in domains such as health care and product safety. If the cost of a preventable statistical death was infinitely higher than the cost of some safety measure, this would generally lead to unacceptable results. For example, people can be easily saved from aviation accidents by grounding all airplanes indefinitely, but this is not a reasonable position. It is reasonable, however, to ground airplanes that have a known technical defect. The problem with any such measures is that decision makers face strong social pressures not to make trade-offs involving statistical deaths explicit and to claim that lives have to be saved at all costs. These pressures can cloud judgments and move people towards lexicographic comparisons in areas in which, upon closer examination, a compensatory aggregation of value aspects is more justified. Hence, even though there are examples that strongly suggest lexicographic outranking, there may be less of them than what popular public morality dictates.

On a similar note, if moral considerations in the deontic tradition always outweighed aspects concerning personal and prudential value, the result would be a tyranny of morality. Even if priority is given to morally relevant aspects of a value comparison (whatever is taken to constitute these), some permeability and trade-offs between these aspects and other types of value must be allowed at least in cases when the stakes are low.[10] On the other side of the spectrum is the position of sum utilitarianism according to which all aspects of value (prudential, moral, hedonic, etc.) can be weighed against each other and even summed up between agents. If the lexicographic approach to value structure is on the right track, this view is not plausible either. Instead, the right approach lies in the middle. It is based on a careful justification of different *qualities* of value aspects, which constitute a ranking between subsets of value aspects.

Chapter 9

A Theory of Betterness

In this chapter, I present a general formal approach to value structure based on the discussion in previous chapters. It serves as an example of how a reasonable theory of "better than" and other gradable value adjectives may look like and illustrates the main features of lexicographic "better than" comparisons.

9.1 Overview

In the previous chapter, arguments for a lexicographic model were laid out. Generally, when domains can be infinite, this is achieved in decision theory by rejecting the Archimedean Axiom for utility functions. Together with other axioms, the Archimedean Axiom ensures that within each value aspect preferences are structured in such a way that every range of utilities remains fully compensatory with any other range of utilities. In combination with a compensatory aggregation method like weighted sum, this ensures that the whole model is compensatory. Rejecting the axiom allows for preferences that cannot be represented by ordinary utility functions from items into real numbers, because the real numbers might not be rich enough in structure. Consider, for instance, a single utility function and the claim that the disvalue of one or more otherwise preventable deaths cannot be outweighed in any way. This means, in essence, that the disvalue of a preventable death is infinitely large in comparison to what is contributed in value otherwise, or, to put it in terms of value only, that the value of a scenario (=item) which involves preventing a death is infinitely higher than the value of any scenario in which such a death is not prevented. This fact can be expressed by defining utilities as functions from items to the hyperreal numbers. The hyperreal number system is an extension of the real numbers that contains numbers that are infinitely larger and numbers that are infinitely smaller than any real numbers.

However, if only the aggregation of different value aspects is supposed to be noncompensatory and domains remain finite, there is a more straightforward way of achieving the same effect. We only need to bundle aspects into different ranks and then ensure that the overall "better than" relation or a corresponding utility function is built in a way that takes into account these ranks. The construction used in the next section ensures this by ordering subsets of aspects with a preorder relation that determines the rank of a set of aspects. If two subsets A, B of all aspects have the same rank, they are aggregated with a compensatory method like weighted sum. For instance, $u(x) = \sum_{i \in A \cup B} u_i(x)$ for those u_i that are defined for x. If in contrast to this the rank of A is $k+1$ and the rank of B is k, then we have to ensure that the utility functions are constructed to satisfy the inequality $\sum_{i \in A} u_i(x) > \sum_{j \in B} u_j(y)$ for any items x, y comparable with respect to the aspects in A and B respectively. This can be achieved by a recursive definition that sets $u_i(x) = 1 + \max_y \sum_{j \in B} u_j(y)$, for any $i \in A$ whenever A ranks directly above B. Not every item should be comparable to any other item within any aspect in this setting, though, and so the definitions have to be carefully adjusted to deal with noncomparability and corresponding partial relations and utility functions. The details are based on the theory by Rast (2020a) and laid out in the next section. After this tour de force through the formal aspects of the approach, its benefits and limitations are addressed in Sections 9.4 and 9.5.

9.2 Formalization for Ordinal Value

Basic definitions. Let $E = \langle A_n, \mathcal{D}, \mathcal{S}, \mathcal{R} \rangle$. In this tuple, A_n is a finite set of n aspects $\{1, 2, 3, \ldots, n\}$, $\mathcal{D}$ a set of aspect domains indexed by A, where $D_i \subseteq \mathcal{D}$ for any $i \in A$, $\mathcal{S}$ a set of sets of comparable items indexed by A, where $S_i \in \mathcal{S}$ and $S_i \subseteq D_i$ for any $i \in A$, and $\mathcal{R}$ is a set of binary relations R_i over S_i respectively. For each R_i, the weak and strict parts I_i and P_i are defined as usual. Each binary relation $R_i \subseteq S_i \times S_i$ is used to order items in S_i. These relations are reflexive and cycle-free in their strict part, so weak eligibility models are excluded in this approach. The total domain of items may contain real or hypothetical entities. We will not assume that items are negatable like propositions. They are objects that may be evaluated under varying value aspects.

If all ordering relations are preorders, we may speak of a preorder model, and if they are all semiorders, we may speak of a semiorder model. I will assume preorder relations in what follows unless otherwise noted, so we have the standard view with respect to S_i and possibly incomplete preorders with respect to D_i. An item a is incomparable with other items in aspect i, short $N_i(a)$, iff. $a \in D_i \;\; \& \;\; a \notin S_i$. An item a is noncomparable with items in aspect i, if $a \notin D_i$. This reflects a distinction made by Chang (2012). However, in contrast to her view we will assume that noncomparability is not always formal like a category mistake. It may also result from the lexicographic ordering of aspects and the multidimensional setting in general. Two items that are noncomparable in one aspect may be comparable under another, perhaps even similar value aspect. While noncomparability denies that an item falls under a value aspect in the first place, incomparability means that we have prima facie reasons to evaluate a under a given aspect. This may be the case because a naturally fits the underlying dimension, for instance. At a closer look, upon reflection, it may then turn out that a cannot be compared to other items with respect to a given aspect.

Two aspects may be compared in terms of how their items can be compared. Aspects i, j are incommensurable with each other iff. for all $x \in S_i$, $N_j(x)$ and, vice versa, for all $x \in S_j$, $N_i(x)$. This means that the items in those aspects are either comparable by the first or by the second aspect, but not by both at the same time. Notice that the structure, as I have laid it out so far, allows domains of items to overlap freely, and that is how things should be. Items can be evaluated under many different aspects.

A tuple E is an evaluative structure if the following nontriviality conditions hold in addition to the conditions mentioned above:

1. For all $x \in \bigcup \mathcal{D}$, there is at least one $S_i \in \mathcal{S}$ and $i \in A$ such that $x \in S_i$.

2. For all $i \in A$, $|S_i| \geq 2$.

For the lexicographic aggregation we need to order the aspects themselves additionally. This ordering gives rise to values of different quality. Let a lexicographic evaluative structure (LES) $\langle E, \succeq \rangle$ consist of an evaluative structure E and a preorder relation $\succeq$ over the set of aspects in E. If $\succeq$ is complete, we speak of a complete LES, otherwise of a partial LES. Aspect equality is defined as $i \sim j$ iff. $i \succeq j$ and $j \succeq i$, and aspect outranking as $i \succ j$ iff. $i \succeq j$ and $j \not\succeq i$.

A value can be defined directly in terms of its aspects as a non-empty subset of the set of a value structure's aspects. Two values U, V are incommensurable iff. for all $i \in V$ and all $j \in U$, i and j are incommensurable. Two values U, V are mutually exclusive iff. for all $i \in V$ and all $j \in U$: if $x \in S_i$, then $x \notin D_j$, and vice versa, if $x \in S_j$, then $x \notin D_i$. Two values U, V are distinct iff. $V \cap U = \emptyset$. Moreover, in a partial LES two values V, U are partially noncomparable iff. "$\succeq$" is not defined between some $i \in V$ and some $j \in U$ and fully noncomparable iff. "$\succeq$" is not defined between any $i \in V, j \in U$.

Multidimensional Parity. I would like to propose a kind of parity in this setting that is not exactly the same as what Chang (2002) has in mind. In a multidimensional theory, parity has to be a cross-aspectual notion. This means in an ordinal setting that it needs to be based on the rank of items according to two or more different aspects. The rank may in turn be computed from the bottom up, or it may be calculated starting with the topmost (=best) items in an aspect. The first method is slightly more general because it does not need to stipulate that the items are bounded from above. It seems easier to presume that there are one or more worst items than to presume that there are one or more best items. Intuitively, however, parity seems to be a positive value relation that should be defined in terms of distance from the best items. At least the typical examples in the literature like the Michelangelo vs. Mozart example suggest that interpretation. If the models are finite, the difference does not matter since in that case there are always best and worst items as long as the ordering relation is acyclic and the above nontriviality condition is fulfilled. We can define a ranking function $L_i(x)$ for aspect i and items $x \in S_i$ as follows:

$$L_i(x) = \begin{cases} 1 \text{ if there is no } y \in S_i \text{ such that } xP_iy; \\ L(y) + 1 \text{ if } xP_iy \text{ and there is no distinct } z \\ \text{such that } xP_iz \text{ and } zP_iy. \end{cases} \tag{9.1}$$

A function from items and aspects to integers calculates the top distance of $x \in S_i$ within aspect i: $T(x, i) := [\max_y L_i(y)] - L_i(x)$; if $x \notin S_i$, $T(x, i)$ is undefined. The idea of a multidimensional notion of parity is now that two items are on a par with respect to two aspects, if one is comparable to items in the first aspect but not in the second, and vice versa for the other item, but they are roughly the same distance from the top in the respective aspect in which they can be compared to other items. Formally, items a, b are aspectually exclusive with respect to aspects $i, j \in A$ iff. $a \in S_i \;\&\; b \notin S_i \;\&\; b \in D_i \;\&\; b \in S_j \;\&\; a \notin S_j \;\&\; a \in D_j$. Two items a, b are on a par with respect to two aspects $i, j \in A$ iff. (i) a and b are aspectually exclusive with respect to i, j, (ii) $|T(a, i) - T(b, j)| \leq \delta$ for constant $\delta > 0$, and (iii) $i \sim j$. Let us call this parity between two items "aspect parity." The constant δ in the definition is a threshold for the rough equality of top distances. Using this notion, the definition of parity is straightforward. Within a value structure two items a, b are on a par iff. for every distinct pair $i, j \in A$ of aspects such that $a \in S_i$ and $b \in S_j$, a and b are aspectually on a par with respect to i, j.

While aspect parity might occur frequently, overall parity is a rather demanding notion. The more aspects are at play, the less likely will two items be completely on a par according to this definition. This is how things should be. Cases of full parity seem to be rare, maybe as rare as moral dilemmas. Once additional aspects for comparing two items a and b are taken into account, the impression that two items are on a par may go away.

In contrast to Chang's position, this view about parity under multiple aspects of betterness makes it doubtful that parity is really a genuine value relation as opposed to a feature of using existing value relations for evaluation. To argue that it can be a genuine value relation in this setting amounts to showing that particular items have a finite list of aspects of betterness and that these fulfill the above conditions. Although I do believe (and assume above) that the number of aspects is finite, any particular set of aspects is always chosen by an evaluator. The strongly value-realist thesis seems dubious to me that there could be an evaluator-independent fixed set of aspects such that two items can only ever be evaluated under these and no other aspects to correctly represent an underlying complex value. However, one would have to argue for this thesis in the course of arguing for the thesis that parity is a genuine value relation. Nevertheless, the above definition of parity remains compatible with this stronger thesis that Chang seems to have in mind. Approaches to the selection of aspects can be more or less realist and more or less evaluator-dependent, and I would like to remain agnostic about this issue, as it clearly depends on more general metaethical considerations that go far beyond the scope of this volume.

9.3 The Aggregation Problem

As we have seen in Chapter 5, the problem of how to aggregate values into an overall assessment has no unique solution unless a lot of additional conditions are added, some of which are of a technical nature. The problem is that in addition to finding the right measurement-theoretic conditions, modeling value must also involve a normative justification. Despite lacking such a justification in general, I have made a case for lexicographic aggregation. This regulates the aggregation of value in aspects when one outranks the other, but not the aggregation when two aspects i, j have the same lexicographic level, i.e., whenever $i \sim j$. In light of the previous discussion, it is fair to assume that there could be different justifications for aggregating value at the same level. However, in Section 5.4 of Chapter 5 we have also seen that in an ordinal setting not every aggregation method fares equally well with respect to Arrow's Theorem. A method that violates the Independence of Irrelevant Alternatives (IIA) condition while at the same time having other desirable features and not appearing completely ad hoc is preferable to a method that satisfies all the conditions of Arrow's Theorem. Two such methods were laid out as examples, minimization of the Kemeny distance measure (or, equivalently, a generalized inversion measure) and the Borda count from Social Choice. I choose the latter for simplicity and because it can be generalized more easily to a setting with cardinal utilities. However, I will deviate from the exposition in Chapter 5 with respect to summing up Borda scores. In Social Choice we would under normal conditions just sum up, since individual voters for typical applications of voting methods ought not have different weights. In contrast to this, I will assign weights between aspects, because it is highly implausible to assume that any aspect of a "better than" comparison weighs exactly the same as every other aspect. Still, the weights of all aspects at each level need to be normalized to prevent anomalies. As a requirement on weights, if A_k is the set of all aspects at level k and w_i is the weight of aspect i, then $\sum_{i \in A_k} w_i = 1$ must hold.

Introducing weights in this way deviates from a purely ordinal, rank-based approach and presumes that evaluators are able to consider the relative importance of aspects between each other once these have been identified as residing principally on the same aspect level. This relative importance can only be determined if all utilities are constructed in exactly the same way on the basis of Borda scores. From a technical point of view, the underlying scale of these functions is not ordinal, but a ratio scale, since we are using weights. Conceptually, we remain in the ordinal realm, though, as Borda scores only represent the ordinal rank of items among each other. While measurement-theorists might find this methodology impure, I believe it to be justified because we are not measuring anything. Instead, we construct the utilities from betterness comparisons and, independently of that, compare aspects among each other by assigning weights to them that add up to one. This conceptually ordinal nature of the approach also means, however, that in the next chapter we will not be able to use expected utility theory with the utility functions defined in this way, nor can concepts like the Principle of Diminishing Marginal Utility be expressed in the current setting. For the time being, our utilities remain ordinal except for the weighing of aspects among each other. I will discuss modifications to account for cardinal utilities later in Section 9.5.

A canonical ordinal utility function for an aspect can be constructed in a way similar to the one laid out in Section 3.2 of Chapter 3, except that we have to take care of aspect levels this time, which complicates the apparatus. A few auxiliary definitions are needed. The following function yields the set of items that reside at the same level with respect to an aspect i for any $x \in S_i$:

$$Eq_i(x) := \{y \in S_i \mid L_i(x) = L_i(y)\} \tag{9.2}$$

Based on this definition we can define a function that yields the set of items that are equally good with respect to aspect i and given level x in aspect i:

$$E_i(x) := \{y \in Eq_i(z) \mid \text{for any } z \text{ such that } L_i(z) = x\} \tag{9.3}$$

The starting score at each level is determined by the following recursive definition:

$$\mathcal{O}_i(1) = 1 \tag{9.4}$$
$$\mathcal{O}_i(x+1) = \mathcal{O}_i(x) + |E_i(x)| \tag{9.5}$$

This function returns the number of items at a level plus the previous starting index. Taking into account the number of items that are equally good at each level of an aspect i, this starting function can be used to define the Borda Rank with Averaging Ties for a given aspect k and level x as follows:

$$B_k(x) = \frac{1}{|E_k(x)|} \sum_{i=\mathcal{O}_k(x)}^{\mathcal{O}_k(x)+|E_k(x)|-1} i = \frac{1}{2}(|E_k(x)| + 2\mathcal{O}_k(x) - 1) \tag{9.6}$$

An example shall illustrate how this somewhat unwieldy formula works. If we have a strict ordering, the rank is easy to determine by counting from the worst to the best. For example, consider the ordering $aPbPc$ between $n = 3$ items. With a bit of abuse of notation, the Borda ranks can be assigned as $c = 1$, $b = 2$, and $a = 3$.[1] Their sum is 6. The whole purpose of the apparatus above is to ensure that the sum remains the same, can be computed by a neat analytic formula, even when a preorder relation with ties is used for comparisons. These ties need to be averaged in a way that ensures that the total sum remains the same. Suppose, for instance, we have $aIbIcPdPeIfPgPh$ with $n = 8$. Averaging the Borda ranks yields scores $h = 1$, $g = 2$, $e = f = \frac{1}{2}(3+4)$, $d = 5$, $a = b = c = \frac{1}{3}(6+7+8)$. Formula 9.6 defines the rank of items at a given level with averaging ties in a way such that the total sum for n items is given by the analytic formula $\frac{1}{2}n(n+1)$. For example, in the previous case the level of b is 5 and the corresponding averaged Borda rank is $(7+8+9)/3 = 7$; the total sum of the scores of all items remains 36 like in a strict ordering of 8 items.

This means that canonical ordinal utilities defined in terms of the Averaging Borda Rank can be normalized to the number of items without introducing unwanted distortions. To achieve this, a function for items $x \in S_k$ is defined as $v_k(x) = B_k(L_k(x))$. Using this function, we may in turn define canonical utilities which are independent of the size of the domain S_i of comparable items of an aspect. For each aspect i, ordinal utility is given by the averaging Borda rank for comparable items $x \in S_i$ as follows:

$$u_i(x) := \frac{2v_i(x)}{|S_i|(|S_i|+1)} \tag{9.7}$$

In this formula, $n = |S_i|$ is the number of items in the domain over which aspect R_i is defined and the value $v_i(x)$ in aspect i is normalized to this size by defining $u_i(x) := v_i(x)/\frac{1}{2}n(n+1)$. In combination with Definition 9.6, this construction of canonical utilities ensures that $u_i(x)$ is normalized to a real number between 0 and 1 and remains independent of the size of the corresponding aspect domains. Consequently, aspect utilities are comparable with each other to a limited extent, even though they are based on ordinal Borda scores in each aspect and the domains S_i and S_j of two aspects i, j may vary in size.

Finally, we define a lexicographic aggregation function based on these ordinal utilities that ensures that the aspect levels given by ordering "$\succeq$" are respected, but aggregates ordinal utilities within the same aspect level in a traditional way by computing a weighted sum. To start with, we need to define aspect level and the class of aspects at the same level in a similar way as defined above for items within an aspect. This is simpler this time, as we do not need to take care of averaging and aggregation issues.

Let $\ell(i)$ be the level of an aspect with respect to the preorder $\succeq$ between aspects. Like Formula 9.1, it can be defined recursively:

$$\ell(i) := \begin{cases} 1 \text{ if there is no } j \text{ such that } i \succ j; \\ \ell(j) + 1 \text{ if } i \succ j \text{ and there is no distinct} \\ k \text{ such that } i \succ k \succ j \end{cases} \tag{9.8}$$

Now it is straightforward to define the set of $\sim$-equivalent aspects at a given level k as $Eq(k) := \{i \in A \mid \ell(i) = k\}$. For the weight w_i at aspect level k such that $w_i > 0$ and the sum of all w_i at k is 1, the utility of an item x at aspect level k given by "$\succeq$" is

$$u^k(x) := \frac{1}{|Eq(k)|} \sum_{i \in Eq(k)} w_i u_i(x). \tag{9.9}$$

This is the ordinary weighted sum aggregation at a level. It requires the relations $R_i \in Eq(k)$ to be preferentially independent for additive models. We may use the notion of conjoint independence from 5.2 of Chapter 5 for this purpose. Consider those cases in which any aspect level k and for any items a, b, a', b' relations $R_1, \ldots, R_n \in Eq(k)$ can be partitioned into two sets $\mathcal{R}$ and $\mathcal{I}$ such that for every $R_x \in \mathcal{I}$, we have aI_xb and $a'I_xb'$ and for every $R_y \in \mathcal{R}$ we have aI_ya' and bI_yb'. Preferential independence then holds at k if in any such case $u^k(a) \geq u^k(b)$ if and only if $u^k(a') \geq u^k(b')$. When this condition is fulfilled, then Definition 9.9 guarantees that the relations are faithfully aggregated at level k.[2]

As long as the preferential independence condition is fulfilled at each aspect level, we can take into account the maxima at each level to obtain the desired lexicographic outranking of higher against lower levels. Again, this is normalized to a value between 0 and 1. The maximum utility at an aspect level k is defined as:

$$M(k) := \max_x u^k(x) \tag{9.10}$$

Value aggregation at the highest applicable level can take into account the maxima of all previous levels. For all $x \in D$ such that there is a highest aspect level k at which some $u_i(x)$ is defined, the aggregate utility $u : D \to \mathbb{R}$ is

$$u(x) := u^k(x) + M(k-1) + M(k-2) + \cdots + M(1). \tag{9.11}$$

If this is normalized, it must be normalized as $u(x)/\max_y u(y)$ for any $y \in D$, and not just to the highest aggregate utility of items defined up to aspect level k. This is so, because other items in the domain could have utilities defined at aspect levels higher than k (unless k is already the highest aspect level, of course).

Bear in mind that the utility at a level in Definition 9.9 and corresponding aggregation in Definition 9.11 is defined for a given item a only up to the highest level k for which a utility $u_i(a)$ is defined ($i \in Eq(k)$). Items may be comparable by aspects at lower levels, but whenever $m > k$, any aggregate utility of an item a that is comparable by aspects at an aspect level k will be lower than any aggregate utility of another item b that is only comparable at an aspect level m. So the construction in 9.11 is equivalent to a pruning step that eliminates items that cannot be compared within the highest level aspects. The above definitions are one way of defining such an outranking. Instead, we could also have specified them by some algorithm. The only tricky part in specifying this type of aggregation for finite domains is to ensure that ordinal utility functions are normalized and canonical. Once we have such utility functions, we have the means to construct overall utilities that respect aspect levels regardless of the size of the aspect domains.

9.4 Explaining the Puzzles

How does this theory fare with the puzzles presented so far? Let us start with multidimensional parity first. As mentioned above, this notion is fairly demanding in the sense that it is less likely to obtain, the more aspects are taken into consideration. This is to be expected from a notion of parity that is not just rough equality of the overall comparison. In contrast to this, if only two aspects are taken into consideration as being relevant, and these are aspectually exclusive to each other, then aspect parity may obtain easily. Aspect parity states that two aspects exclude each other, indicating a change in value quality between them, but that two items are roughly at the same top distance with respect to the corresponding aspect according to which they are comparable. For example, one aspect may be the creativity of a painter and another aspect may be the creativity of a composer. Michelangelo and Mozart are not directly comparable since these aspects do not represent the same type of creativity. Nevertheless, since both artists reside in the top range of those artists they are directly comparable with, they are on a par with each other insofar as creativity is concerned.

The account assumes a modeling perspective that requires us to disregard irrelevant features of the comparison. Maybe Mozart also painted in his spare time, and if we included that, then the aspectual exclusivity condition would not be fulfilled. It makes sense to exclude such factors when talking about parity, however, since otherwise the parity assessment becomes doubtful. For example, suppose Mozart was a lousy hobby painter, whereas Michelangelo was a quite gifted lute player who wrote a number of decent pieces for lute. Including this information may change our assessment and may allow us to conclude that Michelangelo was overall more creative than Mozart. I believe that this is true for all examples of parity discussed in the literature. The more aspects we include, the more should we be inclined to come to a "better than" assessment rather than claiming that two items are on a par. Notice further that mere reluctance to come to a verdict does not for itself indicate parity—this should be regarded as a case of weak incomparability, as discussed in Section 1.4 of Chapter 1.

A major difference between multidimensional parity and Chang's notion of parity is that in her view a judgment of two items being on a par excludes judging that one of them is better than the other. In contrast to this, multidimensional parity does not explicitly disallow mixed value comparisons. Although such a constraint could easily be added, it would be no more than a façon de parler. Gricean maxims alone should exclude double value ascriptions, as the conditions for parity are rather specific. A statement of the form "a and b are on a par and a is better than b" would violate the Gricean maxim of quality because asserting that two items are on a par implicates that any small differences that would make one better than the other do not count—or should be actively disregarded—in the given comparison context. Being equally good, on the other hand, is more specific than being on a par, even if both conditions are fulfilled. Thus, saying that a and b are on a par while knowing that they are exactly equally good would also violate the maxim of quality. So parity really is another mode of comparison, which like rough equality is based on the idea that certain small differences between items may in a specific comparison context not matter for the overall comparison. This matches the intuition that when someone claims two items a and b are on a par, it is perfectly fine for someone else to have the viewpoint that a is better than b. Even the same agent can have both views, as long the agent is aware that the respects in which a is better than b do not really matter when they are on a par.

Arguably, this pragmatic way of dealing with the exclusion of "better than" and "being on a par" might not satisfy authors like Chang and Parfit who seem to suggest that there may be something about the items under comparison which prevents one of them from being better than the other when they are on a par. The model is compatible with the view that evaluators ignore certain differences, do not make them explicit, or do not want to commit to them, but it seems incompatible with the thesis that it may in certain cases in principle not be possible for one of them to be better than the other independently of what evaluators think about them. To be honest, I do not find this thesis compelling and am not aware of any conclusive argument for it. On the contrary, I believe that it is principally possible to either look closer at the existing value structure or find additional aspects according to which one item might be slightly better than another item when two items are on a par, and that this move can only be blocked by restricting the set of admissible aspects based on general metaethical considerations or by claiming that the underlying betterness comparisons of one or more individual aspects involve rough equality, i.e., require a semiorder representation. However, I want to emphasize that I only deny this thesis for overall "better than" comparisons, all things considered, and not for individual, more specific notions of betterness such as medical goodness, instrumental goodness for a certain purpose, moral goodness, and so forth. If we compare items under a certain covering value, say, medical goodness, and we say that two items a and b are on a par, then it may very well be the case that we cannot say that one is healthier than the other or that one is equally healthy as the other. However, one can still be slightly better than the other.

How is this possible? The reason is in my opinion that aggregating aspects filtered by a particular notion of goodness as covering value may not necessarily yield a "better than" or "equally good" assessment *under that particular covering value* if the items are on a par, because the covering value may have a built-in imprecision. This kind of imprecision may even be required by the respective notion of betterness. We may still be able to judge one item better than the other, all things considered, as long as this overall betterness judgment does not pertain to the covering value. Two items can be on a par with respect to a covering value, even though one is overall better than the other upon close inspection.

For example, when two plans for airports are compared, these are not compared with respect to goodness, all things considered, but with respect to what plan counts as better than another in the urban planning scenario. Two plans can be on a par in this area, even if one is strictly speaking overall better than the other because it allows the decision makers to save 50 dollars. Of course, the reason for this is that a 50 dollar cost difference *should not* play any role in urban development and taking it into consideration would lead the planning process astray. Multidimensional parity allows one to disregard small differences between items on a par with aspects at the same lexicographic level while remaining comparable under a more encompassing notion of overall betterness. The lack of exclusivity of parity is a feature rather than a disadvantage.

To further illustrate this feature, consider a hard choice between a career as a lawyer and a career as a clarinet player again. Suppose these are on a par for someone. Despite that, the career as a lawyer may be overall better in general and at a closer look, when all kinds of comparison aspects are taken into account, if it pays one or two hundred bucks more per month. The additional money need not be considered entirely worthless, as would be the case when the difference fell prey to lexicographic outranking. However, *for the more specific purpose of evaluating the goodness of major life choices* the two careers may remain on a par. My explanation of this seeming paradox—which is, I agree, somewhat counter-intuitive and requires a pragmatic explanation like the one mentioned above—is that goodness for the purpose of comparing whole careers or ways of life requires some built-in imprecision that the notion of parity offers. The strict overall betterness judgment does not need to be absent, which would amount to ignoring the additional income of the lawyer, but no longer tracks the more specific and less precise form of goodness under consideration. Saying that the two careers are on a par is more felicitous than stating that one is better than the other in this case, since comparing whole careers ought not take into account small differences between salaries. The threshold for multidimensional parity (δ in Section 9.2) may thus be said to depend on the covering value and contextually vary with the purpose for evaluating.

Multidimensional parity also fulfills the formal criteria discussed in Chapter 7. Aspect parity is irreflexive, since the same aspect cannot be aspectually exclusive to itself. It is symmetric for different items (though not in general, as this would imply reflexivity), since $|T(a,i) - T(b,j)| = |T(b,j) - T(a,i)|$ for any distinct items a, b and aspects i, j, and aspectual exclusivity and "$\sim$" are symmetric. To show that it is nontransitive, we construct a model in which a is on a par with b, b is on a par with c with respect to aspects i, j, k, but a is not on a par with c. This is easy to construct; suppose, for instance, that $a, c \in S_i$, $b \in S_j$. Then a is on a par with b if $|T(a,i) - T(b,j)| \leq \delta$, and b is on a par with c if $|T(b,j) - T(c,k)| \leq \delta$, but since i and k are not aspectually exclusive, a cannot be on a par with c. An example could also be created without resorting to aspectual exclusivity by setting $|T(a,i) - T(c,k)| > \delta$. This reflects the fact that the absolute difference gives rise to a semiorder representation with nontransitive equality.[3] Quadruplicity is equally obvious. We construct a model in which $i \sim j$, $a, a^+ \in S_i$, $b, b^+ \in S_j$, $a, a^+ \notin S_j$, and $b, b^+ \notin S_i$. To achieve that, we may simply set $|T(a,i) - T(b,i)| \leq \delta$ and $|T(a^+,i) - T(b^+,j)| \leq \delta$ while $a^+ P_i a$ and $b^+ P_j b$ hold. Clearly, all four items are on a par. Since it is based on mutual aspect parity, the much stronger general multidimensional parity has these properties, too. However, as noted above, the more aspects are taken into consideration, the less likely this demanding notion of parity will obtain. Cases of multidimensional parity are indicators that the underlying conception of betterness is fairly specific.

Let us turn to Spectrum Cases now. A key idea of a lexicographic approach to "better than" is that value aspects are not constituted by a one-on-one mapping from underlying natural dimensions because values can change in quality within one and the same dimension. In the hedonic example of Section 8.1 from Chapter 8, there is a threshold at which the value of an amount of pleasure shifts from counting as a positive value to becoming insignificantly low for the overall comparison. The pleasure above that value is of a different quality than the pleasure below it. As I argued in Chapter 8, this is not at all an alien idea. For example, we may consider a certain temperature range as being pleasantly warm. At a certain point when the temperature declines, we may no longer consider it pleasantly warm, though still somewhat warm, and then it might cease to be warm at all, become chilly, cold, bitter cold, and so forth. By the same token, with respect to the overall comparison between all scenarios a certain amount of pleasure may be deemed worth having and will therefore outrank lower amounts of pleasure.

To express this in the above framework, we may assume that there are two mutually exclusive aspects. Aspect 1 concerns scenarios (=items) with a certain duration and a level of pleasure that is clearly worth having. Aspect 2 are scenarios which might be longer than those in Aspect 1, but the amount of pleasure is not high enough to really count as worth having in the fictive scenario as a whole. Hence, we have $1 \succ 2$ as lexicographic aspect ordering. Meanwhile, items in this case consist of a certain amount of pleasure and a duration, and, generally speaking, an item a with a much longer duration but only slightly lower pleasure than b is better than b. So when in a sequence $a_1, a_2, \ldots, a_{k-1}, a_k, a_{k+1}, \ldots, a_n$ the item a_k is the pivot element for the absolute threshold, the resulting ordering in the lexicographic model is as follows (from best to worst):

$$a_{k-1}, a_{k-2}, \ldots, a_1, a_n, a_{n-1}, \ldots, a_{k+1}, a_k \tag{9.12}$$

While this might seem counter-intuitive to some people, it should be kept in mind that the ordering of each half between a_k is given by the assumption that an item a with a much longer duration but only slightly lower pleasure than b is better than b. It comes from the idea that the overall "utility" of a scenario is *pleasure* $\times$ *duration*. Let us call this the "combination principle." Maybe this principle is wrong, but that is irrelevant to the lexicographic ordering of the aspects. If the amount of pleasure starting from a_k is too low to compare items directly with items before a_k in the sequence, other than pointing out that it is consistently outranked in comparison to those items, then any other ordering should also be centered around a_k.

Suppose someone judges, upon sincere reflection, that the combination principle does not hold and that a_1 (or, a_4) is the best item. This would change the example and might make the lexicographic ordering obsolete, but it does not have to make it obsolete. A different ordering of the left side of the spectrum due to different underlying criteria and justifications is consistent with maintaining the proposed division into two aspects and their ranking.

It may also be reasonable to reject the composition principle for the other half of the spectrum and, for instance, stipulate that $a_k I a_{k+1} I \ldots I a_{n-1} I a_n$. This is always possible if a threshold is interpreted as indicating that some dimension of an aspect is no longer relevant to the evaluation as a whole.[4] Like in the previous case, this interpretation does not (have to) change the aspects and their lexicographic ordering. Notice further that a lexicographic model like the above one is much more general than merely stipulating that certain dimensions or aspects become irrelevant in certain contexts. It allows for the ordering and aggregation of outranked aspects, and which aspect levels are decisive depends on the items under consideration. There could be hard constraints like costs, laws, and moral considerations, for instance, that would limit the items under consideration to a subset of items only. If so, in a general lexicographic approach like the above one, some aspects may become relevant, even decisive for the evaluation that were outranked in the larger set. On a final note, a standard additive weighted sum model occurs as a special case when $i \sim j$ for all aspects $i, j \in A$. The lexicographic approach is a generalization of some base model, in this case a generalization of a standard additive model of value aggregation.

9.5 Towards a General Axiology

In light of the discussion in previous chapters it is clear that despite its generality the model of this chapter has limitations. In this section, the drawbacks and advantages of some extensions and modifications are discussed.

First of all, we have assumed incomplete preorder relations for each aspect. What about semiorders or relations that allow for cycles? For the semiorder representation of aspects the same approach as above can be used. The result may be interpreted as a new semiorder relation by choosing a threshold δ such that aRb iff. $u(a) - u(b) > \delta$ and aIb iff. $|u(a) - u(b)| \leq \delta$ like in Representation 2 on page 49 of Chapter 2. This means that the result of aggregating value is interpreted with a rough "equally good" relation, which is possible for both semiorders and preorders as inputs of aggregation. The representation by partial ordinal utility functions has an advantage over using the underlying relations directly in this case.

As for cyclic base relations like the ones we have discussed in Sections 2.3 and 2.4, only a reduction of the cycles to a partial preorder model seems to make sense, like already mentioned in Section 3.3. The idea is that a preorder relation is generated by collapsing the largest cycles such that aI^*b for the new relation R^* whenever items a, b occur in the largest R-cycle of the cyclic relation R. After this step, aggregation of aspects $i \in A$ can proceed with the respective R_i^* relations as laid out above. However, as I mentioned previously, this kind of procedure in a sense defeats the purpose of having an eligibility model in the first place.

Maybe there is a better way of aggregating weakly or strongly eligible relations into a faithful weakly or strongly overall betterness relation. In any case, the above method based on Averaging Borda Ranks and ordinal utility representations is not well-suited for this purpose.

Another, perhaps more pressing question is how to deal with cardinal utilities. Let us first deal with the easier case when *all* aspects have ratio scale utilities u_i that represent underlying partial preorders R_i for those items for which they are defined. It is immediately clear from this change that the ordinal top distance $T(i, x)$ of an item x in aspect i ought no longer be used in such a setting. Instead, it is natural to use the utilities' actual distance, since these already contain enough information and distances are meaningful on ratio and interval scales. So the top distance needs to be defined as $T(i, x) := [\max_y u_i(y)] - u_i(x)$. Likewise, the canonical definition of utilities is omitted, of course; the utilities are now given or measured directly in one way or another and should be normalized to the interval $[0, 1]$. They can be aggregated at each aspect level k like in Definition 9.9. The lexicographic aggregation works as before, taking into account the sum of the maximum utilities at lower levels as in Definition 9.11. The result of such an aggregation may be drastically different from the aggregation of corresponding ordinal utilities defined in the way laid out above. This is to be expected, since we now have rich information in the form of utility differences of varying extent.

The hard question is whether it makes sense to allow mixed models in which some aspects have cardinal and others ordinal utility representations. This is exactly how different aspects of betterness often seem to pan out in real life. Some aspects are based on extensively measurable dimensions. For example, costs, maximum or average speed, energy efficiency, the quantity of certain environmental pollutants in air or water, durability, flexibility, and strength of materials belong to these categories. Other aspects are not based on such dimensions and harder to measure. To these belong, for instance, perceived happiness, pleasure, preferences, the desirability of items, comparisons by subjective worth, comparisons based on the violation or satisfactions of deontic rules, and comparisons based on aesthetic judgments. It is very hard, if not implausible, to justify the existence of cardinal utilities in such dimensions, even when there are good reasons for individual "better than" comparisons in a corresponding value aspect. So it seems as if models with a mixture of cardinal and ordinal utilities would be most adequate.

Unfortunately, such models are problematic. The ordinal aggregation laid out above is based on the idea of constructing canonical utilities that are independent of the size of domains of items. Using weighted sum rather than mere summing up of the normalized Borda Ranks is already problematic, based on the presumption that we can give meaning to the relative importance of aspects despite their being ordinal. The justification for this deviation from pure ordinality is that we use these weights for comparing the relative importance of aspects given the range of items under consideration and the best and worst items in each aspect, but without taking into account any further comparisons within these aspects. In a similar vein, we can use weighted sum aggregation for cardinal utilities, as long as they fulfill the requirements laid out in Section 5.2 of Chapter 5. Using weighted sum for both ordinal and cardinal utilities changes the game, though. Levels of canonical ordinal utilities are meaningful, because they merely represent items' relative ranks. Adding them up is justified for the same reasons as Borda counts can be used for voting—like in Social Choice, there are reasons for and against this method of aggregation, and some of them carry over to the value aggregation problem. However, it is doubtful that such ordinal utilities can be compared in a meaningful way with cardinal utility levels. The intensity of a cardinal utility, its actual value for a given item, is given by considerations that only marginally concern an item's rank. If a has a higher rank than b, i.e., aP_ib, then $u_i(a) > u_i(b)$ by being a representation of the underlying preference relation. However, these utility functions contain way more information and the utility distances between items may vary drastically. Recall that the highest non-normalized Averaging Borda score of an item is the averaged score of the best items. In our setting, it is n for a domain of n items if there are no ties. Why would that value be comparable at all to the maximum value of a cardinal utility, which is usually given by extensive measurement in the underlying dimension? There is no reason why. That is the problem.

In decision-making, it is common practice to "quantify" ordinal aspects of comparisons and then aggregate them together with cardinal utilities. This has the effect of postulating that they are on an interval or ratio scale without justifying this decision. The rationale for this practice is similar to the rationale I gave above for introducing weights between canonical ordinal utilities. Maybe we can, to a certain extent, judge the relative importance of aspects between each other even when some of them are ordinal and some of them are cardinal, as long as the maximum and minimum items of each aspect are fixed and well-known. We can then seek to find the exchange ratio between those two aspects using standard preference elicitation techniques like those laid out by Fishburn (1970b), Keeney and Raiffa (1976), Keeney and Raiffa (1993), and Eisenführ et al. (2010).

The other way of dealing with the problem is to ignore the cardinal information of cardinal utilities and only use their rank for aggregation. While being fully compatible with the method laid out above and less problematic from a measurement-theoretic perspective, this approach discards a lot of valuable information.

We thus face the conundrum of either introducing spurious information without proper justification or discarding existing information that should go into an overall evaluation. There is, as far as I can see, no entirely satisfactory solution to this problem. No matter which route is chosen, mixed models will always be problematic. Realistically speaking, it is probably best to go the first path, treat ordinal utilities with care when we come up with initial comparisons in that aspect, make them canonical and normalized to the size of the domains, and later treat them as if they were fully comparable to other, possibly cardinal utilities. Although this can lead to distortions when ordinal and cardinal utilities are compared and aggregated, this is still better than ignoring the ordinal aspects in the first place. In the worst case, if we feel unable to come up with an exchange ratio between two vastly different aspects of an overall betterness comparison, then we may still be able to decide whether one outranks the other.

Chapter 10

Risk

So far, we have only taken a look at value structure under certainty. This is in my opinion how any investigation of value structure should start, because evaluation by comparatives of value adjectives like "better than," "braver," "more pleasurable than," "preferable to," and "healthier than" does not necessarily concern any future events. Problems of uncertainty and risk become important, however, once potential courses of action are considered or when possible future states of affairs are evaluated whose existence hinges on the occurrence of uncertain events. This chapter deals with how to deal with quantifiable risk in the theory of the previous chapter.

10.1 Risk versus Uncertainty

It is customary in the literature to speak of risk whenever the probabilities of future events are known or at least well-confirmed and quantified. Throwing a die and playing lottery are paradigmatic examples of quantified risk. Although definitions differ in detail from author to author, most authors agree that the term "risk" is used more or less as a substitute for "probability of an event" whenever the occurrence of that event is associated with disvalue rather than value, whereas "probability" is neutral in that respect.[1] For example, we talk about the risk of losing money in a gamble but about the probability of winning money in a lottery, because losing money is bad. Other than that, quantified risk and probability describe the same thing, or at least I will make this assumption from now on and ignore other uses of the term.

In contrast to risk, uncertainty is generally used as an umbrella term for all kinds of situations in which the actual probabilities of future events are either not known or are uncertain themselves. Uncertainty comes at a degree. The term "Knightian uncertainty" is sometimes used to describe the most drastic form of uncertainty about future events, the case when their future probabilities are almost completely unknown. This is the case whenever we lack *any* analytic causal model to predict the future event under discussion and also lack correlations good enough for making predictions. Technological developments and scientific breakthroughs in the far future are uncertain in this sense, since we know from the history of humanity that these changes can be drastic and unexpected. Although we might speculate about them, the probabilities of specific events of this type cannot be estimated. The same applies to unforeseen failures of a machine after a thorough risk analysis has been conducted. If the failure is not foreseen at all, then no probability can be determined for it. This is the most severe form of uncertainty.

Less radical forms of uncertainty can be modeled with intervals of probabilities. For instance, one might estimate that the probability that a specific event occurs in the future lies between a lower probability of 0.3 and an upper probability of 0.7. In such a case, uncertainty is modeled by risk, though often this risk is interpreted in Bayesian terms as a subjective rather than an objective probability. Into this category fall the Dempster-Shafer theory of evidence by Dempster (1968) and Shafer (1972), plausibility theory of Halpern (2003), and subjective logic of Jøsang (2016), for example. In addition to these broadly-conceived probability-based approaches there are also very general representations of uncertainty with a more qualitative flavor, representations that are not directly based on probabilities such as possibility theory of Dubois and Prade (1988, 2009) and ranking theory by Spohn (1988).

Addressing these theories in detail would go beyond the scope of this book. In a nutshell, all of them generalize probability theory, albeit in different ways. For example, the rule of standard probability theory $P(\overline{A}) = 1 - P(A)$ does not hold in Dempster-Shafer theory, but when there is no uncertainty, then ordinary probabilities may be derived from a Dempster-Shafer representation. So it makes sense to start with probability theory and standard representations of risk. However, one problem that needs to be mentioned right from the start is the fact that ordinal value relations cannot be easily combined with probabilities. Standard expected utility theory requires a ratio scale, and even though we have assumed this for technical reasons in the previous chapter, the account remained ordinal from a conceptual perspective. Only weights between aspects were allowed, but not necessarily aspect intensities or meaningful differences within each aspect. The ordinality of the account precludes the use of standard expected utility theory, and we will return to this problem later.

10.2 Basic Notions

As is well-known, there are further distinctions in decision-making between expected utility theory going back to Ramsey (1931) and von Neumann and Morgenstern (1944), subjective expected utility theory of Savage (1954), Jeffrey-Bolker decision theory of Jeffrey (1965), and causal decision theory like the study by Joyce (2008). I will not go into these details in what follows and instead make a case for Choquet expected utility in Section 10.4. The reason for this is independent of the debate between the positions just mentioned, which concern the expressiveness of the event modeling and its interpretation. Despite being of great philosophical interest, the more fine-grained representational problems behind the above brands of decision theory go beyond the scope of this book.

Although some familiarity can be presumed, let us quickly repeat the foundations of probability theory. A set $\mathcal{S}$ of subsets of an event space Ω is a σ-algebra if (i) it follows from $A \in \mathcal{S}$ that the complement $\overline{A}$ of A in Ω is also in $\mathcal{S}$, and (ii) whenever $A_1, A_2, \ldots, A_n \in \mathcal{S}$, then $(\bigcup_{i=1}^{n} A_i) \in \mathcal{S}$. The second condition means that if a countable number of sets are in the σ-algebra, then the union of these sets is also in it. Since in set theory $A \cap B = \overline{\overline{A} \cup \overline{B}}$ (De Morgan's Law for intersection), it follows from the two conditions that any intersection of a countable number of sets in the σ-algebra is also in it.

A function $P : \mathcal{S} \to [0, 1]$ defined on a σ-algebra of an event space Ω is a probability function if the following conditions hold:

$$P(\Omega) = 1 \tag{P1}$$

$$P(\emptyset) = 0 \tag{P2}$$

$$P(A \cup B) = P(A) + P(B) \text{ if } A \cap B = \emptyset \tag{P3}$$

If an event space is finite, it is customary to speak of discrete probabilities and every element in the event space is an elementary event $e \in \Omega$. If so, then it follows from the above axioms that any probability of an event that consists of a set of elementary events can be expressed as the finite sum of the probabilities of those elementary events. In other words, every probability is uniquely defined by the probabilities of the elementary events and the above rules. As a typical example, the event space for a six-sided die is $\Omega = \{e_1, e_2, e_3, e_4, e_5, e_6\}$. If the die is fair, then any elementary event is equally likely and thus has the probability $1/6$. A more complex event like throwing an even number then has a probability composed out of the elementary events; in this case, supposing that $E = \{e_2, e_4, e_6\}$, we obtain $P(E) = P(\{e_2\}) + P(\{e_4\}) + P(\{e_6\}) = {}^1\!/_6 + {}^1\!/_6 + {}^1\!/_6 = {}^1\!/_2$ by repeated applications of P3.

As is well-known, this does not work for continuous event spaces. In the continuous setting, probabilities need to be defined by probability density functions because the underlying event space does no longer have elementary events: The probability of the occurrence of a particular value in a continuous event space is 0! This creates some technical complications that I wish to avoid. Since we have assumed finite domains of items throughout this book, we may continue to stick with discrete probabilities. However, much of what follows could be extended to uncountable domains without much ado.

So how can probabilities be combined with what has been said about value structure so far? There is no general answer to this question, as it depends on the modeling purpose. A simple way to include probabilities is to consider a finite set of states of affairs W, each of which contains or brings about a number of items, and to define a probability measure over it. This works fine if we are interested in the probabilities that certain events occur and want to evaluate these events. However, it is a limited model for decision-making, where each action generally can have several possible outcomes. In the decision-making tradition it is customary to define risky prospects as lotteries and consider hypothetical choices. Talking of a lottery can evoke misleading intuitions, though; instead, I will use the term "prospect" in what follows.

A prospect represents the probabilities of the outcomes of possible courses of actions and choices we make. Each of the possible outcomes must have a fixed probability, and these probabilities must add up to 1. Prospects may also represent the occurrence of independent events in nature with several possible outcomes, each of which has a determined probability of occurring. For example, a prospect might represent a volcano outbreak and the probability of different consequences this might have, or it could represent different possible consequences of a failure of a valve in a nuclear power plant. Finally, nested prospects may be taken as a mixed representation of actions and contingent events that may effect them.

Let $W = \{w_1, w_2, w_3, \dots\}$ be a finite set of state of affairs that may obtain. A prospect consists of (i) a number of states of affairs with associated probabilities, or (ii) another prospect with an associated probability. All probabilities of states of affairs and embedded prospects must add up to 1 in a given prospect. Prospects may only be nested finitely and events of an embedded prospect need to be probabilistically independent of events in the prospect that embed it. It is usual to depict prospects (lotteries) as trees, where an action or initial event is at the root, the edges are labeled with the probability, and at the end nodes there is either a state of affairs as an outcome or another prospect. To link states of affairs in prospects with evaluation, a function $D : W \to \mathcal{P}(D)$ from states of affairs to subsets of the total domain of items is used. This acts like a domain function in modal logic.

As an example of a non-nested prospect, throwing a fair coin may be represented by two states of affairs w_H, w_T and the prospect $(w_H, {}^1\!/_2; w_T, {}^1\!/_2)$. By the same token, throwing a fair die can be represented by the prospect

$$(w_1, {}^1\!/_6; w_2, {}^1\!/_6; w_3, {}^1\!/_6; w_4, {}^1\!/_6; w_5, {}^1\!/_6; w_6, {}^1\!/_6).$$

As an example of a nested prospect, consider the following game. You throw a fair coin, and if it falls tail you obtain \$4. Otherwise you throw it again, and if it falls head you obtain \$10, but you get \$0 if it falls on tail this time. This prospect–$((H, 0.5; T, 0.5); T, 0.5)$–is depicted in Figure 10.1a. Since each coin throw is probabilistically independent of the previous one, the probability of hitting Head twice is $0.5 \times 0.5 = 0.25$. Since the branches of each non-nested prospect must add up to 1, this nested prospect can be

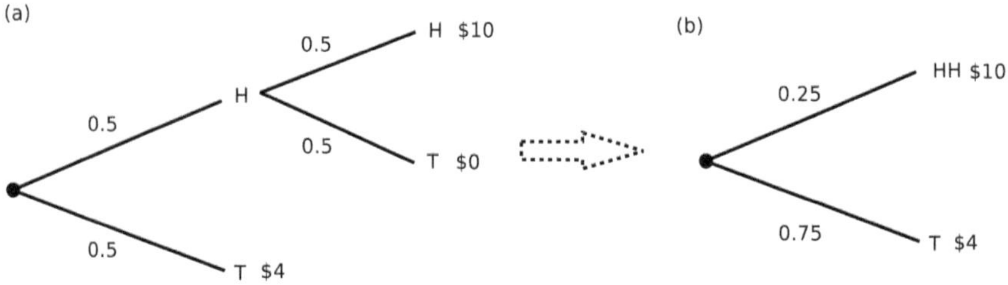

Figure 10.1: Example of flattening a nested prospect.

replaced by the non-nested prospect $(HH, 0.25; T, 0.75)$ in Figure 10.1b. Of course, this new prospect does not represent a coin throw but rather the game as a whole. If you were asked to bet between Head and Tail based on this prospect and if you use the Expected Value to decide, which will be laid out in the next section, then you should choose Tail, since 75% of \$4 is \$3 whereas 25% of \$10 is only \$2.50.

However, this kind of flattening is not compatible with all ways to evaluate prospects. With standard expected utility it works because in this approach the utility function transforms the final value at leaves of the tree. In contrast to this, flattened prospects may not give the same result as nested prospects when probabilities are weighted like in Prospect Theory of Kahneman and Tversky (1979). In such a theory it can make a difference whether 0.5 is weighted in the nested prospect or 0.25 is weighted in the flattened prospect. Because of such potential complications with non-traditional evaluation procedures, it is better not to generally assume that prospects can be flattened. Instead, to evaluate a nested prospect we start with the most deeply embedded prospect and evaluate it like a non-nested prospect. The resulting utility value then replaces the prospect in the embedding prospect, and we proceed in this way until all of the tree has been evaluated. In the above example, for instance, we first evaluate the second throw of the coin and obtain \$5 as expected value, and subsequently calculate the values \$2.50 and \$3 for the embedding prospect. This procedure avoids making assumptions about flattening that might yield incorrect results with less traditional evaluation methods. To keep things simple, I will furthermore assume that the evaluation of an embedded prospect results in a new state of affairs that represents the value of the evaluated prospect. This state of affairs is taken to bring about one item in the highest aspect level of the collapsed prospect that represents its value. That simplification is admissible because the intermediate states of affairs in a nested prospect are not evaluated in isolation. Given that, we may write x_i for the state of affairs i in a prospect x and $P(x_i)$ for the probability of x_i and for simplicity ignore nested prospects in what follows.

There are a few more things to note about this modeling. First, we should demand that states of affairs exclude each other, even if two distinct states of affairs can bring about the same item. Moreover, I will not assume that W forms a σ-algebra in what follows, because this is not what states of affairs are intended for. They are not representing everything that is possible. Instead, a prospect is taken to represent all possible outcomes of an action or consequences of an external event, hence the probabilities of all resulting states of affairs must sum up to 1. Consequently, we need to sometimes assume a state of affairs that serves as a catch-all-clause and ensures that probabilities add up to one.

10.3 Expected Value

We are now ready to introduce some basic distinctions. To simplify notation, the following abbreviation for the utility of the items at a state of affairs w is used:

$$U(w) = \frac{1}{|D(w)|} \sum_{a \in D(w)} u(a) \tag{10.1}$$

Given that, the compensatory Expected Value of a prospect of size n is

$$\mathrm{EV}(x) := \frac{1}{n} \sum_{i=1}^{n} P(x_i) U(x_i). \tag{10.2}$$

This version of expected value sums up the utilities of items in the states of affairs of a prospect. Suppose that we use the above formula to compare two certain prospects x and y, i.e., two prospects that yield states of affairs w_x and w_y with certainty respectively, to the effect that we compare the states of affairs directly. Using the above formula would remain compensatory in the sense that the expected values of x and y in this case take into account and sum up the utility of items that may reside at different aspect levels in w_x and w_y respectively. Although *within* each state of affairs items at a higher level will always outrank those at a lower level, as laid out in the previous chapter, items at different aspect levels still enter the comparison between the two prospects. In that sense, expected value according to EV remains compensatory.

This may rarely be desirable and justifiable. Whether this type of compensatory comparisons makes sense depends on how we look at the aggregation of the value of items at states of affairs, and consequently also between prospects. The question is whether this process is also lexicographic or whether it should be additive. EV brings back compensatory comparisons, this time between states of affairs and prospects instead of items alone. Generally speaking, however, reasons for allowing lexicographical comparisons between items should carry over to the case when states of affairs that bring about different items are compared with each other. For instance, if one possible outcome of an action results in a state of affairs w_1 that brings about an order of magnitude more statistical deaths than another possible outcome w_2 that brings about many items with very small positive value that belong to a lower-ranked value quality than the value of avoiding statistical deaths, then this lexicographic outranking of the value of the items in w_2 should enter the overall evaluation of the expected value of the corresponding prospect. The value of w_2 should not be able to outweigh the value of w_1 for the same reasons as this ought not be possible when we directly compare items.

To get a noncompensatory version, only items at highest aspect levels ought to be taken into account. Recall that $Eq(k)$ according to Definition 9.8 on page 149 yields the aspects at level k and that $\ell(.)$ denotes the lexicographic level of an aspect. Based on this, we may define the aspect levels of an item as follows:

$$\mathcal{L}(x) := \{\ell(i) \mid \text{ for any } i \text{ s.t. } x \in S_i\} \tag{10.3}$$

We can then define $A^*(x)$ as those aspects whose aspect level for item x is highest:

$$A^*(x) = Eq(\max \mathcal{L}(x)) \tag{10.4}$$

The set of items at a state of affairs comparable with respect to the aspects with highest level is then

$$D^*(w) := \{x \in D(w) \mid x \in S_i \text{ for some } i \in A^*(x)\}, \tag{10.5}$$

and we can use this for redefining the utility function. Let $U^*(w)$ be the utility defined like in Definition 10.1 except that $D(w)$ is replaced with $D^*(w)$ and recall that we write x_i for the i-th state of affairs in prospect x. The Noncompensatory Expected Value is then defined just like the compensatory version:

$$\text{EV}^*(x) := \frac{1}{n}\sum_{i=1}^{n} P(x_i)U^*(x_i). \tag{10.6}$$

Despite the minor difference in the formulation, the conceptual difference between these two versions of expected value is not trivial. Suppose we compare two states of affairs w_x, w_y by comparing two prospects x and y with certain states of affairs w_x and w_y like in the case discussed above. Suppose the highest aspect level of items at w_x is γ and the highest aspect level of items at w_y is δ. Then, if $\gamma > \delta$ we can conclude from Definition 9.11 and Definition 10.6 that $\text{EV}^*(x) > \text{EV}^*(y)$, since $u(a) > u(b)$ whenever a is an item at w_x and b is an item at w_y. This time we have a guarantee that lower ranking aspects cannot outweigh higher ranking aspects when comparing different states of affairs, hence also when comparing different prospects with the same probabilities but different outcomes. However, EV* still evaluates states of affairs in a somewhat compensatory way, because it allows outranked items to be decisive for making an uncertain prospect preferable to another uncertain prospect when the probabilities they assign to their outcomes differ.

Generally, this seems to be the right approach. We would like the lexicographic ranking of aspects to be decisive for comparisons between certain outcomes, but not for it to also govern the interplay between this evaluation and probabilities. A more radical approach would ensure that only states of affairs contribute to comparisons, both within prospects and when these are compared among each other, when these bring about items at the respective highest aspect level among all aspect levels of the items in the states of affairs involved.

Such a principle leads to very counter-intuitive scenarios. It categorically favors any future state of affairs w that brings about items with evaluative aspects that lexicographically outrank evaluative aspects of items in other states of affairs, no matter how small the probability of w's occurrence is in comparison to the probability of those other states of affairs. It can lead to a complete disregard of the probabilities involved. The problem with such a radical proposal is that almost anything may occur with very low probability. As a typical example, some activists claimed that after it had been upgraded there was a small chance that the Large Hadron Collider (LHC) at CERN might create a black hole that would destroy Earth. Although most physicists agreed that this was impossible, even just the slightest doubt would raise the subjective probability of the extinction event slightly above zero. Under the reasonable assumption that a certain extinction event outranks any certain gains, that an extinction event belongs to a different kind of value in comparison to normal benefits for humanity (though perhaps it could be weighed against the extinction of another intelligent species), radically noncompensatory expected value would thus have favored almost any course of action that led to the closing of the LHC.

Although people have sometimes brought up the Precautionary Principle in support of such radical decision principles, this way of looking at extremely small probabilities is counter-intuitive and in the end based on an irrational fear of the virtually impossible. There may be an incredibly small chance that Elvis lands in a UFO on Trafalgar Square tomorrow and announces that we should praise our new alien overlords, or else humanity will be destroyed. However, this possibility ought not at all influence our actions today. There needs to be a weighing of very small probabilities with the value or disvalue the respective event brings about. If not, actions are essentially dictated by a decision maker's creativity in painting doomsday scenarios whose (dis-)value outranks the merits of any other courses of action.

EV^* avoids this pitfall. It treats small probabilities right by fully taking them into account while at the same time doing justice to the lexicographic ranking of evaluative aspects of the underlying betterness comparisons. However, neither EV nor EV^* allow us to formalize risk attitude such as avoiding risk in favor of certainty or assessing risks in a pessimist or optimist manner. This is the subject of the next section.

10.4 Choquet Expected Utility

In expected utility theory the risk attitude of an agent is modeled by making the utility function nonlinear. The expected utility of an event x is then its probability times its utility, $EU(x) = P(x)U(x)$, or, in our setting, formulas EV and EV* with a non-linear utility function U for states of affairs. If an agent's utility function is convex, then the agent is risk averse, if it is concave, then the agent is risk prone, and if it is linear, then the agent is risk neutral and expected utility coincides with expected value. This way of defining risk attitude makes sense as long as utility functions are measured jointly with subjective probabilities and as long as there are reasons to presume that the utilities reside on a ratio scale.

Consider, for instance, a prospect in which an agent may win $10 with a probability of 0.5 and nothing otherwise. The expected value of this prospect is $5. One way to look at this is that that a risk neutral agent would be indifferent between this prospect and the prospect of getting $5 for certain. The "certainty equivalent" of this prospect is $5. Most people are risk averse, though, and would rather get the $5 for sure. This means that the expected utility of the uncertain prospect must be lower, for instance, $4. In other words, the agent is only willing to pay $4 for the lottery or bet, and this value is the uncertain prospect's certainty equivalent under the new utility function. Since $5 is more than $4, a utility-maximizing risk averse agent will choose the certain win of $5 if there is a choice. In contrast to this, a gambler might prefer the uncertain prospect, meaning that the expected utility of the uncertain prospect would be higher than the expected value, say $6. That means that the gambler is risk prone and may even be willing to pay money for taking a risk, as gamblers do when they play at the casino.

In the current setting, this standard view about expected utility is not very compelling for several reasons. First, we are not measuring probabilities and utilities jointly. We have instead assumed, throughout this book, that betterness judgments give rise to canonical utilities and these judgments are made under certainty. The canonical utilities introduced in the previous chapter could also be called ordinal value functions instead. In such a setting, risk attitude should be independent of the evaluation under certainty. Arguably, the same could be said about the classical view, as the cardinal utility functions in it also serve to encode nonlinearities in an agent's evaluation under certainty such as the Principle of Diminishing Marginal Utility, but it can be justified in this setting if both aspects are measured jointly. We cannot make this assumption in the theory of value structure because in this theory these different features of a decision situation are not measured jointly. In a sense, they are not measured at all. Value structure is supposed to reflect normative assessments, not just what individual agents prefer, and is based on a rejection of the Preference Satisfaction Principle.[2]

Another problem with expected utility in the current setting is that we are not generally using cardinal utilities and the above canonical utilities are derived from ordinal comparisons. Although we have deviated from this assumption already for weighing aspects and for the expected value principles, making the utility functions themselves nonlinear is more far-reaching. Nonlinear utilities cannot be justified from the "better than" judgments only. So if we introduce expected utility in the current setting, the underlying utility functions cannot be canonical ordinal utilities. They would need to be based on a ratio scale from the start, with the modifications I have described in Section 9.5 of the previous chapter.

Finally, we cannot easily speak of a concave or convex utility function in the current approach since the inputs may not be ordered on the x-axis. The basis of our utility functions are items, which are not necessarily themselves ordered by a natural dimension. To work around this limitation, decision theorists customarily use money as a general exchange medium for value, like in the above examples. However, this would be misleading in an approach that takes different aspects of betterness seriously and allows one to outrank another. In my point of view, an aspect or subvalue of an overall "better than" comparison can have a genuine, unique quality that detaches it from the natural dimension on which it resides. One dimension can support mutually exclusive value aspects. Converting any such aspect to monetary value—or, correspondingly, to abstract "utils" on a ratio scale—is not compatible with this type of value pluralism, since the conversion would only be admissible in a fully compensatory model.

How, then, can risk attitude be expressed in the current approach? A seemingly easy way to fix the above problems is to transform probabilities instead of utilities in a nonlinear way. This idea seems very natural: Why should risk attitude be modeled as the shape of the utility function which describes the values of items under risk and certainty? So let us explore the transformation of probabilities instead. According to the "simple weighing" approach a nonlinear function $\pi : [0,1] \to [0,1]$ is used to transform each probability of a state of affairs. This function should be continuous and also satisfy the conditions $\pi(0) = 0$ and $\pi(1) = 1$. The expected utility versions of EV and EV* are then like these formulas, except that $P(w)$ is replaced with $\pi(P(w))$. In this approach, an agent is risk averse if π is concave and risk prone if π is convex, whereas we obtain the expected value when π is the identity function.

This simple weighing approach was used in psychology from time to time since the 1950s and received more scrutiny by economists with the publication of Handa (1977).[3] It was also used in the first version of Kahneman and Tversky's prospect theory. In their psychologically-motivated theory, the probability weight was a function that overemphasized small probabilities and slightly undervalued high probabilities.[4] Simple weighing turned out to be problematic at a closer look, however, and was discarded at the beginning of the 1980s when several scholars realized independently of each other that it violates the property of first-order stochastic dominance.[5]

I will not attempt to explain why the simple weighing account is unsatisfactory and instead refer the reader to Wakker (2010).[6] The solution to the problems of the simple weighing account is to use Rank-dependent Utility Theory (RDU) instead, which is closely related to the Choquet method for value aggregation we have seen in Chapter 5 and is also sometimes called Choquet Expected Utility.[7] This type of "non-expected utility theory" goes back to Quiggin (1981, 1982), and Schmeidler (1986, 1989) and was later used in Cumulative Prospect Theory by Kahneman and Tversky (1992).

Rank-dependent utility is most comfortable to describe if prospects are pre-ordered. Instead of allowing any kind of ordering of the outcomes x_i of a prospect x like until now, we order the prospect from best outcomes to worst $x_1, x_2, \ldots, x_n$, where x_1 is the state of affairs for which $U(x_1)$ is highest, $U(x_2)$ is second highest, and so on until the worst state of affairs $U(x_n)$. Following Wakker (2010, p. 171), ranks are then taking into account the probability of an outcome x_i with its relative ordering i in the prospect and weighted with a weighing function π as follows:

$$\mathrm{RDU}(x) := \sum_{i=1}^{n} \left[\pi(P(x_i) + \cdots + P(x_1)) - \pi(P(x_{i-1}) + \cdots + P(x_1))\right] U(x_i), \quad (10.7)$$

where it is additionally assumed that the weight for $i = 1$ is $\pi(P(x_1))$. So in this approach the weight of a probability is not a function of that

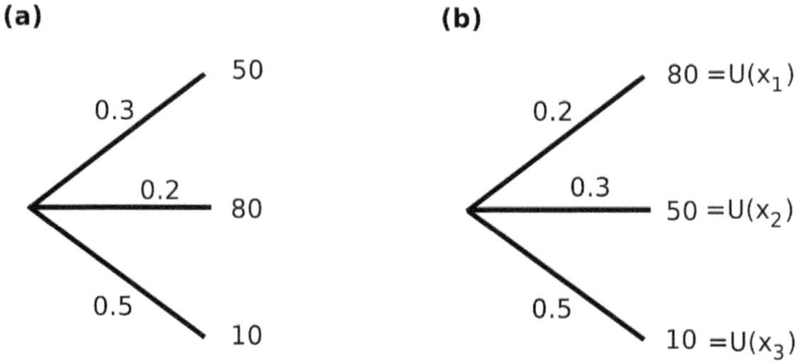

Figure 10.2: Example of a non-nested prospect, (a) unordered and (b) ordered for applying the RDU principle.

probability like in the simple weighing approach. Instead, it consists of the difference between the probability rank of the respective state of affairs and the probability rank of the next best state of affairs, both transformed by the weighing function π.[8] A corresponding function RDU* may be defined in the same way except for using $U^*(x)$ as aggregate utility function, i.e., the version in which lexicographically outranked aspects of items at a state of affairs are pruned away.

As an example taken from Wakker (2010, p. 166), suppose x is the prospect in Figure 10.2a. We first have to order it from best to worst outcome like in 10.2b. In the ordered prospect, $U(x_1) = 80$, $U(x_2) = 50$, and $U(x_3) = 10$. Let the weighing function be $\pi(x) = x^2$. We then get as RDU value of the whole prospect:

$$\begin{aligned} &\pi(0.2) \cdot 80 + [\pi(0.2 + 0.3) - \pi(0.2)] \cdot 50 + [\pi(1) - \pi(0.5)] \cdot 10 \\ &= 0.2^2 \cdot 80 + 50(0.5^2 - 0.2^2) + 10(1 - 0.5^2) \\ &= 21.2 \end{aligned} \tag{10.8}$$

In the rank-dependent utility model, risk attitude can be expressed just like in the simple weighted model, but this time in a technically more sound way. To keep the new types of risk attitude apart from the expected utility model that transforms utilities, it is customary to use the terms "optimism" and "pessimism." Suppose the probability weighing function is weakly increasing, i.e., $\pi(x) \geq \pi(y)$ whenever $x \geq y$. Under that assumption, an assessor is pessimistic if the probability weighing function is convex and optimistic if it is concave. If $\pi(x) = x$ and the utility function is also linear, then RDU returns the expected value. As an example, let x be a simple prospect $x = (\$100, 0.5; \$0, 0.5)$, for example representing the throw of a fair coin that gives you a hundred dollars or nothing with a 50 percent chance. In this case the difference between simple weighing and rank-dependent weighing collapses, which simplifies the example. Since the expected value is positive, the prospect is always a desirable option. How desirable is it in comparison to getting $50 for sure?

Suppose, first, that $\pi(x) = x^2$. The convexity of that function means that, except for the extreme points 0 and 1, probabilities are lower than the expected value. The RDU utility of x is $25 whereas the expected value of the prospect is $50. The outcome is considered "worse than what one might normally expect," and getting $50 for certain is preferable.

In contrast to this, suppose $\pi(x) = \sqrt{x}$. Then, the RDU utility of x is much higher than the expected value, about $70.71. This can be interpreted as being optimistic, as a way of overemphasizing probabilities.

We will address the rationality of these risk attitudes in the next section. What the examples show is that risk attitudes can be expressed with Choquet expected utility by weighing probabilities, while the utility functions involved remain linear and may be based on the canonical utility construction of the previous chapter. Of course, the construction still requires us to assume that there is an underlying ratio scale that makes the multiplication with the rank-based weighted probabilities meaningful. However, it does not require us to transform the utilities themselves. They can remain linear, based on the canonical way of constructing them from ordinal comparisons, as long as we do not consider risk attitudes, and may be thought to reflect value assessments under certainty. Furthermore, the account can also be combined with full-fledged cardinal utilities. If the utility functions are nonlinear and based on eliciting this nonlinearity in addition to the underlying value comparisons (in each aspect), then they can express principles like the Principle of Diminishing Marginal Utility that was motivated by Bernoulli's solution to the St. Petersburg Paradox.[9] In contrast to traditional expected utility theory, the two different sources of nonlinearity—risk attitude and attitude towards the amount of value or relative evaluative rank of an item—are kept apart in this representation, making the RDU approach with arbitrary utility functions principally more expressive than classical expected utility.[10]

10.5 On the Rationality of Risk Attitudes

In the previous section, we have deviated from a purely normative perspective by talking about risk attitudes. The corresponding normative question is whether we *should* be risk averse, risk prone, pessimistic, or optimistic in certain situations. This question is not easy to answer because there are arguments for and against using only the expected value.

Perhaps the strongest argument against risk attitudes is that they seem to be a purely psychological matter, as the term suggests. Even if we rename them somehow, it is unclear what other than an emotional reaction to risk they could represent. Even though risk avoidance is understandable from a psychological perspective, it is far from clear why it should have a normative impact. Consider any risk averse agent such as an agent who evaluates the prospect mentioned above with an RDU utility of $25 and an expected value of $50. The difference between the two values means that the agent should be willing to pay some positive amount of money to swap the risky prospect with one that yields $50 for certain. This means that anyone who can afford making 50-50 gambles in the long run can make money from this decision maker by offering such swaps for a fee. How is the loss of money in the long run rational? Recall that money is just used for convenience and only serves as a proxy for value in general.[11] The risk averse decision maker is willing to pay for getting less value (in the long run) than what they would gain in the long run when accepting risky prospects. That behavior seems irrational.

Notice that this concerns the risk attitude and not the evaluation under uncertainty. Although the St. Petersburg Paradox could be used to justify concave utility functions and one might argue that risk aversion cannot be separated from this because both aspects of decision-making are measured jointly, this reply is not viable in the current setting with weighted probabilities. Distorting probabilities seems unjustified from a normative point of view, whereas distorting utility functions reflects an aspect of potentially subjective evaluation. Even if the evaluation is not subjective and pertains to value structure, there may be good reasons for allowing nonlinearities of value. If this was all there is to say about risk attitudes, then the conclusion should be to only allow expected value from the perspective of normative evaluation.

However, there are various counter-arguments to this view. First of all, in practice we rarely encounter situations in which clear-cut quantified risk is available and no uncertainty is involved at all. If the risks themselves are uncertain, not fully known or come with a margin of error, and this uncertainty cannot be modeled explicitly for lack of data, then it seems rational to generally avoid this uncertainty. One (radical) way of avoiding it is to avoid risky prospects. Generally, in such situations prospects with more evenly spread risks or no risks at all will be preferable. Uncertainty about a risk may mean that a quantified probability of a desirable gain may be lower than indicated, or that the quantified risk of an undesirable loss is higher than indicated. Why, then, go for the risky prospect if there is a less risky alternative? Avoiding epistemic uncertainty is a general epistemic virtue. Knowing more is always better, one might argue, so it seems also desirable to avoid risks whenever there are doubts about them.

Even when risks are certain, for example in gambling situations, it may make sense to be slightly risk averse because in practice there are often irrecoverable losses that need to be prevented. Imagine you are offered to buy lotteries for $5 that allow you to win $20 with a 50% chance, nothing otherwise. That is a winning lottery, so you should go for it. Or so it seems. However, suppose you only have $10 and these are really important to you. For instance, imagine that you need these $10 to take the train home or otherwise you would have to walk for many hours. The rational thing to do in this scenario is not to play, since the $10 are that important to you. Obviously, if someone offered you a positive amount of money *for sure* in the same scenario, there would be no good reason to decline.

Losses may be too high. In a unipolar setting like ours, this can be expressed by considering states of affairs that allow us to avoid these losses to bring about items in a value aspect that outrank items at states of affairs that do not avoid the loss. If this lexicographic comparison mechanism is not available, risk aversion may also achieve the desired effect as long as the certain option does not incur the respective loss. One way to avoid bad luck is not to gamble, and that can be rational even if the gamble for itself would allow you to win in the long run. To prevent high losses is also the idea behind insurances, where the fact that the insurance company wins money implies that their clients would lose money in the long run. The trade is desirable and rational because it allows the clients to share risks with others and therefore prevent unlikely, though catastrophic losses.

There may also be rare cases when being risk prone is advisable. Suppose, for instance, you have a generous discretionary salary. This is just a fancy way of saying that you have a lot of money left each month after you've paid all the usual running costs for food, water, electricity, and so on. Maybe you have so much money left that you don't even have an idea what to do with it. Billionaires have this problem. Imagine you're one of them and someone offers you to pay $5 for a lottery ticket that will give you $100 with half a percent chance. The expected value of this prospect is $-4.5, so it seems irrational to play it. Nevertheless, it may not be irrational for you if you don't care about the likely loss of $5 in the given situation. The $5 may be considered a superfluous benefit of your discretionary income: Whether or not you have them does not matter to you in your current situation. If almost nothing is at stake and the price of a gamble is high enough, then it may make sense to be optimistic in a particular gambling situation. Being repeatedly or always optimistic will still lead to losses that are too high and should therefore be avoided; but you may afford to be optimistic from time to time and gain a lot from this with a bit of luck.

This last scenario is not modeled in the current approach. To model it with optimism we would have to allow the risk attitude to depend on the value aspect of the items brought about by the scenarios under consideration. As an alternative, we may use utility transformations and not probability weighing to model the example. For example, one might distinguish between states of affairs that bring about billions, millions, hundreds of thousands, thousands, and tens of dollars, and lexicographically rank the corresponding aspects. Being a billionaire is in this view of a different value quality than being a millionaire, and so forth, and the evaluation of scenarios differs with respect to the aspect they belong to. I do not see any *normative* reason why within a "billionaire aspect" of monetary changes the agent cannot remain indifferent between small changes in monetary value while at the same time obeying the principle "more is better" within the other aspects in which an agent has tens, thousands, and hundreds of thousands of dollars in the respective scenarios. This can be achieved by using a semiorder representation for monetary value of items within the billionaire aspect.

In summary, the examples suggest that it is rational to avoid disastrous losses by avoiding risks with positive expected value and that it is also rational to sometimes take risks whenever potential losses would lead to an outcome that is good enough. The question is: What normativity lies behind this rationality, which at the moment only seems to be supported by intuitions?

This question is not easy to answer. The strongest arguments for using only expected value are based on money pumps. Take the last scenario, for example. It seems that the indifference about small monetary gains and losses in the utility function $U_{\$B}$ for the money aspect of the billionaire's evaluations would allow for a money pump. Since the billionaire is indifferent between the two options, they might be willing to swap an item with x dollar value for one with $x - 5$ value. If this process is repeated—maybe there is an incentive to swap in another aspect of the items—then the billionaire would lose money again and again.

However, this money pump can be blocked either by assuming that value aspects change between options farther apart or by requiring the decision maker to take a look at the beginning and end points of a series of actions. A diachronic money pump only works as long as it is set up in a way that does not allow a decision maker to take a look at arbitrary states of affairs in the sequence of choices that incur the loss. However, being narrow-minded is not a requirement of rationality. As I have argued in Section 2.5 of Chapter 2, a rational decision maker should look at the scenario as a whole and determine that a sequence of trades will create a loss that is much larger then the indifference threshold of the underlying interval- or semiorder. As laid out in Section 3.7 of Chapter 3, once $U_{\$B}(a) - U_{\$B}(b) > \delta$ for some threshold δ, this represents the case $aP_{\$B}b$ and after aggregating all aspects may also result in the judgment that a is better than b. At some point in a series of switches, the threshold will be exceeded. The money pump against the billionaire rests on the idea that comparisons of an initial state with later outcomes in a series of trades or comparisons between multiple hypothetical choices are not possible, but they *are* possible, since otherwise the Dutch book example could not even be formulated. Money pumps of this type live off the idea that the outside evaluators know more than the decision maker and can be resolved once the decision maker gains the same knowledge as the outside evaluator. For that reason, I do not find them convincing as counter-arguments to the above examples.

The lesson to learn from the above examples is in my opinion that a rational agent *should* sometimes be risk averse and *may* sometimes be risk prone, but that the reasons for weighing probabilities in this way differ from case to case. One reason why being risk averse is rationally justifiable is that quantified risk almost always comes along with some amount of uncertainty about the risk, and that it is an epistemic virtue to avoid uncertainty, provided this does not itself bring about high disvalue. Obtaining more information costs money and other resources, yet this is often money well spent. Another justification for being risk averse is to avoid catastrophic losses and resource exhaustion when dealing with multiple risky prospects. In both cases, it is better to be risk averse in the particular decision situation. The case of "wasting" money from your discretionary salary by being risk prone is different. The potential loss of a small number of gambles is irrelevant, or at least at a lower aspect level than the potential gains, but a more cautious person could also justify the choice not to gamble on the basis of these potential losses, as insignificant as they may be. From a normative perspective disregarding the losses is allowed, since there is already enough of value anyway, but the choice seems to be personal and may indeed be based on the psychology of the decision maker.

Although these considerations are only based on a few examples, they suffice to show, in my opinion, that there is not one rationality principle governing decision-making under risk. Instead, there are different norms of rationality at play which at times may conflict with each other. For example, one such principle is "If x brings about value, then more of x is better." This is not generally true and only holds for certain value aspects, for example it tends to hold for monetary value. However, the principle is defeasible and can be overruled by other considerations. In the above example it may be overruled once the agent has attained a certain amount of wealth. In this case, a satisficing interpretation may rationally justify a semiorder representation: If you have enough money, then you can afford to be indifferent about losing or gaining a little bit of it. The reason why this is justified is, of course, that money has only value as an exchange medium and that small losses or gains play no role for *other* values that affect the quality of life. As another example, the justification of risk aversion because of uncertainty is based on the principle that it is generally good to learn more about the world and avoid uncertainty, which can at times conflict with bare utility maximization that does not take this epistemic virtue into account. A clever bookkeeper can trick a risk averse agent to swap risky prospects for less risky ones for a small fee, even when these have the same expected value, and thereby gain money in the long run. The deviation from expected value cannot be justified only by looking at overall utility gains and losses, it can be justified only with an additional epistemic principle.

That being said, using expected value without weighing probabilities is generally the safest choice if care is taken to adequately include the effects of potential catastrophic losses in the outcomes. It is the safest choice because it does not allow any Dutch book against the decision maker. The reason for this becomes clearer in the rank-dependent utility framework than in traditional expected utility theory, which mixes up nonlinearities in our assessments of value with risk attitudes. Transforming probabilities means nothing else than distorting them, and that is in itself a dubious practice. If the risk assessments reflect objective probabilities of stochastic processes, then the distortion by a weighing function is not rational, if taken in isolation, in the sense that it overtly misrepresents reality. It may only *become* rational in a particular decision situation in conjunction with other criteria and rationality postulates that override the call for representing known probabilities accurately. Risk attitudes other than risk neutrality are rationally justifiable in certain situations, but are not rational for themselves.

10.6 Limitations

Finally, I would like to address some limitations of the approach on value structure laid out in this book and discuss to what extent structural requirements of value representations are normatively justifiable. We need to make two distinctions before we can tackle these questions. First, as laid out in previous chapters, general value representations need to be distinguished from representations of choice situations in decision-making contexts. My take on general value representations is that they need to allow for a technically sound aggregation method. Since it is hard, if not impossible, to find a convincing non-trivial aggregation method when strict "better than" comparisons are allowed to be cyclic in one or more aspects, the lexicographic aspect ranking solution to Spectrum Cases is preferable to giving up the transitivity of overall betterness. As shown in Section 9.3, value aspects can be aggregated in such an approach, albeit in a way that considerably departs from the standard view in economics. As for choice-guiding value representations, the existence of a sound aggregation method is also a minimal requirement, since in practical choice situations there are almost always multiple value aspects to consider. This also rules out cyclic strict betterness comparisons, unless one is willing to bite into the sour apple and defend an aggregation method that trivially conflates preference cycles with equal goodness or indifference between the items in the cycle. So in both cases the aggregation requirement leads to some constraints on value structure.

However, the problem of how to aggregate value aspects (viz., subvalues) into overall betterness does not have a unique solution. I chose the Borda method from Social Choice in Chapter 9 to aggregate items within each aspect, and also assumed that we are capable of evaluating the relative importance of aspects between each other. There are other methods, though. For example, the minimization of the Kemeny distance measure mentioned in Section 5.4 is certainly also sound from a technical perspective. Other than weighing the pros and cons of each method by using additional criteria known from the Social Choice literature and evaluating how these apply to the value aggregation case, there does not seem to be an external criterion for deciding which aggregation method is normatively justifiable. Even when someone would come up with a convincing set of rationality postulates that one and only one of the possible qualitative aggregation methods passes, the uniqueness of the solution is always relative to these postulates. This is a problem of the decision-making literature in general. Many authors use "rational" almost synonymously with "axiomatized" and stipulate that their set of axioms is the right one. However, other sets of axioms are usually available.

A second distinction needs to be made between evaluation for policymaking and individual evaluation. Policymaking involves decisions and evaluations that concern many people at once. Often, the decision makers are not the people who are most affected by the possible outcomes of a decision. In contrast to this, although individual decision-making may also affect other persons, the number of persons affected is usually much smaller. Another crucial difference between the two cases is that in policymaking value aspects—or, features, criteria, and attributes—are often based on data measured by various parties involved. Most of the time, this data will not be presented in raw form but as reports by expert panels and research institutes. These reports may involve costs of construction, safety measures, failure and attack models, etc., and they may involve a decent amount of statistical inference and modeling. In contrast to this, in individual evaluation and decision-making such expert testimony rarely plays a role, and if probabilities are involved these are usually subjective estimates that may not reflect the objective probabilities of events. A third key difference is that policymaking is a group-based process with many procedural and legal constraints, whereas just one agent is involved in individual evaluation and decision-making.

The model laid out in Chapter 9 and the previous sections might be suitable for representing the values of individual agents and also for representing intersubjective values on an abstract level. However, it does not take into account the additional requirements of policymaking. Although the Borda method is sound for aggregating value aspects proposed by different agents from a Social Choice perspective, and could therefore be used in group decision-making once agreement about the ranking of value aspects has been reached, group decision-making might need to satisfy additional constraints. Procedural fairness needs to be warranted, legal requirements need to be fulfilled, and mechanisms to ensure a democratic power division may be needed. For instance, there may be moral arguments for having public hearings, for additionally protecting minorities affected, for dealing with the difference between decision makers and affected people, for due process of decision-making, and for vocation of the decision-making process at higher instances. These requirements play no role in individual evaluation and when value representations are considered in the abstract.

Because of these differences, a representation of value structure and accompanying method of making recommendations for decisions based on those values can only ever play a small role in the overall process of policymaking. Fairness of the process cannot be reflected directly in the value structure—it might be based on other values but it is not part of the above value structures that are aggregated into an overall betterness assessment.

Another limitation is that procedural, legal, and moral norms are not part of value structure, even though they will need to be taken into account in decision-making. This limitation may also affect individual decision-making. Sometimes it is possible to "encode" rule-like statements that represent norms and deontic rules in value comparisons. For example, if a norm says that you should do p under certain circumstances, then a state of affairs in which you do p is better with respect to that norm than one in which you do not do p. The lexicographic model still fares a bit better with respect to norms than the standard view, since its noncompensatory nature allows for using aspects as hard constraints. We can say that doing p is a must, for instance. However, some deontic rules and norms are probably better treated as hard constraints that act as a filter. Only those courses of action ought to be considered whose possible outcomes satisfy these hard constraints. The remaining deontic rules and norms are then integrated into the lexicographic value structure based on how good, bad, or neutral following and ignoring them would be.

Notes

Chapter 1 Basic Monist Value Structure

1. See Pareto (1900, 1906) and Samuelson (1938, 1947).
2. Not every value-related activity leads to an agent-relative value. A value is agent-relative only if it is a value *for* that agent but not necessarily for others. Moreover, the benefactor of an agent-relative value may be someone else. For instance, it may be good for John to occasionally bake a cake for his husband Matthew. The value is relative to John, as it might not be good for other people to bake cakes for Matthew (or, if it is, then it may be good for other reasons than those John has). At the same time, the benefactor is Matthew. The goodness of John's actions can be independent of whether John himself likes baking or the cakes he creates.
3. See Smith (2007), cf. Stojanovic (2015).
4. Alternatively, one might argue that "excellent" is a primitive superlative, meaning "among the best."
5. See Hansson (2018a, pp. 512–514).
6. Some authors also write 2^D for the Cartesian product of a set D with itself.
7. Unfortunately, in some of the discussion of Temkin's Spectrum Cases it has become customary to use "intransitive" for failures of the transitivity of "better than" when in fact the term "nontransitive" should be used. As long as everyone is aware of them, such unusual conventions do no grave harm, although they might cause some confusion.
8. I have chosen the last example to illustrate the independence of our judgments about transitivity from the individual value judgments. Nobody in his right mind thinks that oligarchic kleptocracy is better than democ-

racy, but *if* it is, and democracy is better than tyranny, *then* it is also better than tyranny.

9. Buridan's ass is sometimes mentioned in the context of rational choice among equally good alternatives. However, although it might pose a problem to the concept of free will, like many others I fail to see how it can be regarded as a genuine challenge to rational choice. If an arbitrary choice among alternatives conceived as equally good is taken as not being rational, then in my view this indicates an unnecessarily narrow view of rationality rather than a genuine problem with rational choice.

10. See Raz (1986, p. 342), cf. Orsi (2015, pp. 102–103).

11. See Chang (2015, pp. 212–214).

Chapter 2 Relaxing Requirements

1. See Vincke and Pirlot (1997, pp. 14–15).

2. Gilboa (2009, p. 67) uses a definition equivalent to the above one, based on a shortcut notation. Yet another way to specify a semiorder is by composing relations. We may write RP for the relation Q composed out of R and then P. This operation is defined as follows: RP is that relation Q such that aQb holds if and only if there is a c such that aRc and cPb is the case. (Be advised that composition is also sometimes written in the opposite order.) Writing aR^db for $b\not Ra$, which is called the dual relation of R, the properties can then be defined as follows: R is Ferrers if $RR^dR \subset R$, and R is semitransitive if $RRR^d \subset R$.

3. See Williamson (1994) for an in-depth defense of an epistemic conception of vagueness.

4. The term "instrumental goodness" is borrowed from von Wright (1963) who discusses and contrasts it at length with other forms of goodness.

5. See Hansson (2001, p. 25).

6. Note that this condition does not make sense if I is not transitive, like in semiorder models, because in that case we can have aIb, bIc, and aPc. Suppose a is weakly eligible; then, by repeated application of top-transitivity of weak eligibility we would get that b and c are weakly eligible, too, directly contradicting the assumption aPc.

7. See Hansson (2001, pp. 26–32).

8. See Hansson (2018b, p. 568).

9. See Hansson (2018b, pp. 569–570).

10. Money pump arguments under certainty are discussed by Davidson et al. (1955); cf. Schick (1986, pp. 116–118). Decision-making under risk is the subject of Chapter 10.

Chapter 3 Utility Functions

1. In this context, it must be noted that Mill distinguished between high and low pleasures and therefore cannot be counted as a value monist, even though the higher pleasures had priority.
2. The issue in this example is trivial but it is worth noting in this context that the verb "to exist" is used in its strong sense in mathematics, meaning that entities of the respective sort can be constructed. Mathematicians also sometimes use the verb "to exist" in a much weaker sense as meaning that the entities can be defined in a way that it can be proved that no contradictions arise—where these assumptions may, in turn, sometimes even hinge on assuming that supporting theories are consistent. Showing existence by construction is always more desirable.
3. As an alternative to this construction, one might set $u(a_i)$ to the number of those $b \in D$ such that a_iPb and $u(a_i) = u(b)$ whenever a_iIb, and proceed with the proof from there. See Roberts (1979, pp. 101–107).
4. See Mehta (1998, pp. 5–9).
5. Cf. Keeney (1996, pp. 147–148).
6. See Jacquet-Lagrèze (1975, p. 91).
7. As usual, transitive and reflexive links are left out.
8. The following paragraph follows the terminology of (Roberts, 1979, Ch. 2).
9. Nothing can be colder than 0 Kelvin. Stevens (1946) takes the existence of an absolute zero (the absence of something) as a criterion for a ratio scale. However, more recent definitions like the one by Roberts (1979) only use the above functional equivalence classes as criterion and allow negative values. For instance, according to the modern definition the money in a bank account may be considered to be on a ratio scale. The 0-point indicates the absence of money and is not arbitrary, but there may also be negative values (debts) in the account.
10. This argument can be more or less convincing, depending on how fundamental one takes the rationality postulates of a chosen model. The

interplay between formalization and intuitive interpretation is always complex in philosophical analysis, and this case is no exception.
11. See Krantz et al. (1990, p. 2).
12. See, for instance, Lassiter (2017, pp. 177–178).
13. This observation is due to A. Soria-Ruiz who uses it, contrary to what I suggest above, to argue that value adjectives have a "round ratio" scale. This is a ratio scale with a certain granularity, which may have only rounded, approximate ratio modifiers like 2, 5, 10, 20, for instance. Granularity requirements can then vary from one type value adjective to another. In my opinion, such examples rather suggest a weaker scale and some operations on ranks like indicated above. However, neither of these arguments is very strong. There could be pragmatic reasons why too much precision is disfavored in ordinary conversations, for example a violation of the Gricean maxim of quantity. A perceived oddness of "1.17 times better than" need not indicate that "better than" is not on a ratio scale or that it is on a more restricted one. Moreover, I must generally caution against taking linguistic behavior as an argument for normative considerations about value structure. When speakers seem to understand what others say (or at least do not object and accommodate), this does not necessarily indicate that the respective statement is meaningful or that it should be understood literally. For example, one might argue that phrases like "ten times better" ought not be understood literally. To put it in general terms, how people commonly talk about the world does not tell us much about the world. How we talk about macrophysical objects and how we talk about values can only ever serve as a weak indicator for the thesis of a physicist or a position in ethics and aesthetics respectively. Domain experts tell the semanticist what certain expressions mean rather than vice versa. This topic will be addressed again in Section 6.4 of Chapter 6.
14. Notice that the scale in Figure 3.2 does not depict in general how these adjectives are related to the comparative. There can be edge cases. For instance, it can be possible that all the best items are bad in a given evaluative situation under some notion of "better than." How one might derive "good" from "better than" is briefly discussed in Section 4.2 of Chapter 4.
15. The situation is complicated from an empirical perspective, since a concave utility function that makes good predictions for some range of input values may yield highly unrealistic results for other input ranges.

According to Wakker et al. (2007) there are also two different mechanisms, intrinsic value and numerical sensitivity, at play in judgments about the utility of money.

Chapter 4 The Complexity of Value

1. Much of the discussion is spelled out in terms of states of affairs. However, substituting one for the other only works under the assumption that states of affairs can be characterized negatively like in "The state of affairs in which there is no tea pot." This is a fairly strong assumption. In this use of "state of affairs" they are equiexpressive with propositions, which are in turn equiexpressive to sets of possible worlds that represent truth-conditionally maximal models of a bivalent, classical, non-modal base language closed under negation.
2. One might think that monotonicity could fail if, for example, a is good and cheap but b is better and also costs more. So b would no longer be good enough, because it is too expensive. This consideration is, however, mixing up different notions of goodness: being good enough in one respect but without costs considered, lower costs as an aspect of goodness, and the mixed aggregative notion of being good as some form of aggregation of being good in the first respect and being "affordable enough." Of course, something can be good enough in one way and not good enough in another way of understanding "good."
3. Scanlon (1998) discusses the value of friendship in more detail and takes it as a typical example of non-instrumental value.
4. "Cost" is meant in the abstract sense; it need not be monetary.
5. A trivial mechanism is to parameterize or reify the context and simply use it to model contextual variations without making any interesting predictions or providing a model of how the context dependence is resolved. Such a model would hardly be of any use without further constraints.

Chapter 5 Multidimensional Value

1. It may seem as if this kind of personal evaluation is not based on abstract value. For example, one might argue that values are interpersonal social structures from the start. However, we clearly use "good" and other value

adjectives for personal evaluation, too, and there is often no clear-cut line between the personal and interpersonal application. Moreover, even a seemingly subjective statement may be meant to convey an objective value judgment. For instance, it is perfectly normal and rational to say "Mary's performance was brilliant, she's clearly the better artist, but I personally prefer Gill's rendition." The fact that in the above example the candidate evaluates his own job prospects is relevant for the example, but a similar example could also be formulated that concerns the value of different jobs in general and for everyone. In the present view, actual evaluations reveal agents' takes on underlying values and their structure no matter whether these are personal or not, subjective or objective, agent-relative or not, morally relevant or not, or supererogatory or not.

2. See Roberts (1979, Ch. 5).

3. The proof that $u(.)$ represents a preorder over the domain of items is trivial. Obviously, if $u(a) \geq u(b)$ and $u(b) \geq u(c)$, then also $u(a) \geq u(c)$, since $u(.)$ is a function into the real numbers and "$\geq$" is transitive. The comparison by "$\geq$" is also reflexive, since $u(a) \geq u(a)$ for any a.

4. Fishburn and Wakker (1995) lay out the history of preferential independence criteria.

5. With a bit of abuse of notation, the vectors are identified with the items. What interests in this condition are the utilities of individual aspects that comprise the vector and represent the underlying ordering relations and not yet their aggregate. In an additive model, this aggregate is their sum, of course, whereas the condition restricts the underlying relations $R_1, \ldots, R_n$ so they comply with this mode of aggregation.

6. See Keeney and Raiffa (1976, pp. 288–292). Notice, however, that in a setting with quantified risk a corresponding conjoint independence condition defined over preferences between items only is a weaker condition than utility independence for lotteries since a condition on preferences between items does not regulate all preferences between lotteries.

7. One case that cannot be captured in the above way is when the parts have no notable value at all and only their ensemble has value. Although this is not a job for value aggregation, it is an important concern of value metaphysics. What makes something a value bearer, and what makes a value bearer distinct from its constituents?

8. These measures are also called normalized monotonic capacities.

9. See Semendyayev et al. (2004, pp. 363–366).

10. For historical reasons social preferences functions are also often called social welfare functions.
11. This is also sometimes called Pareto Principle.
12. Formally, this boils down to invariance of the voting result under permutations of the voters' profiles or their labels.
13. See Moulin (1988, p. 263–267).
14. Since Kendall (1938) studied the corresponding rank correlation coefficient, it is also sometimes called Kendall's Distance or, slightly less accurately, Kendall's Tau. According to Kendall (1938), a rank correlation coefficient is defined between $[-1, 1]$ and he discusses a number of such coefficients. One of them is equivalent to counting the number of inversions needed to get from one combination to another, though.
15. See Deza and Deza (2009, p. 3).
16. Bogart defines the measure for partial orders, where lack of a comparison gives score 0, but the same method can also be used for complete preorders where ties get a positive score that is half of the score of a full preference reversal. How lack of comparability relates to ties is an issue that I want to suppress in this section. We will later use the Borda Count with Averaging Ties, which can be normalized to the size of the domains and will allow us to ignore incomparable items.
17. The number of complete preorders between n items is given by the sequence of Fubini numbers also known as Ordered Bell numbers that can be computed by the the function $f(n) = \sum_{k=0}^{n} k!S(n, k)$, where $S(n, k)$ is the Sterling Number of the Second Kind. The sequence has the number A000670 in The On-Line Encyclopedia of Integer Sequences, published electronically at https://oeis.org, version of May 2017.
18. Note that often there is more than one shortest path.
19. Often the worst method is to sum up direct scores because nobody knows what these scores mean anyway and this method can introduce distortions and cardinal information where there is none. If you ever find yourself in an assessment committee that uses this flawed method, then you can give your voice a good chance to have more weight than those of others by scaling your initial direct scores such that the worst candidate has the lowest and the best candidate has the highest score.
20. There is also some circularity in distinguishing good and bad reasons for explaining choice-guiding decisions that are often spelled out in terms

of various betterness comparisons. However, this might not be a vicious circle since "good" and "bad" mostly seem to serve as aggregates for epistemic criteria when they are applied to reasons. Thus, the strategy to counter this circularity objection would be to distinguish epistemic evaluation of reasons from other aspects of evaluation. Nevertheless, such a conception of practical reasons would fall prey to the same counter-argument mentioned above, that in the end a weighing conception of reasons does not reflect their evaluative components at all but rather tracks personal sentiments about their perceived strength or reliability-based criteria independent of the evaluative component (if there is one).

Chapter 6 Problems of Value Analysis

1. To be precise, Moore acknowledges that there are dictionary characterizations of "good," but these are not based on a proper philosophical analysis. He denies the possibility of a normative definition of uses of "good" and this is the type of analysis we are interested in.
2. Pace Bentham, Mill only defended this view for qualitatively high pleasures and not for the most mundane pleasures, for "[i]t is better to be a human being dissatisfied than a pig satisfied" Mill (1906, Ch. 2); cf. Crisp (1997, p. 28–35).
3. Since the seminal work of Rosch (1975, 1983) and many others on the cross-linguistic variation of color predicates, it is well-known that yellow does not count as a basic color in all languages and that the extensions of color predicates vary from language to language with only partial overlaps and are thus further analyzable, even though the predicates belong to the basic vocabulary of the respective natural language. For the sake of argument we can ignore this line of reasoning and assume, with Moore, that primitive concepts are available and "yellow" denotes one of them.
4. See Moore (1922, §13–14, pp. 16–18).
5. See Feldman (2005, pp. 37–38).
6. See Moore (1942).
7. See also Jacquette (1990) who proposes an explanation based on what Chisholm called "converse intentional properties," without stipulating a full logic of sense and reference. Since I am, for reasons that would go far beyond the scope of this book, a Neo-Fregean and believe that hyperintensional logics like that of Moschovakis (1994, 2006) are nearly unavoidable to

get the semantics of attitude ascriptions and related linguistic phenomena right, I have no quirks with Church's proposal.

8. See my Rast (2020b) for a detailed take on this matter.

9. See for example Väyrynen (2013). Cf. Stojanovic (2015) for the position that multidimensional evaluative content may be semantic.

10. This requirement is not always needed. Kant's notion of freedom does not have much to do with the ordinary use of the word, but this problem is easily circumvented by speaking about "Kant's notion of freedom" or "freedom according to Kant."

11. In this particular use, "normative" does not need to have any moral implications. It merely means that if your beliefs do not conform with the theory or you do not act according to it in practice, then you err and are making a mistake.

12. See McDowell (1985).

13. See Gibbard (1990).

14. See Mackie (1977).

15. See Harman (1975, 1996), Wong (1984, 2006, 2011), Brogaard (2008, 2012).

16. I take "noncontextualism" as a neutral term for value absolutism, the view that the values that underlie value comparisons do not change with the context of their application. Perceived changes are based on differences in the availability of items such as alternatives for action and of other external constraints like the purpose or goal of evaluating items in the first place, but the values always remain the same. See Stigler and Becker (1977) for a defense of this position in economic consumer theory.

17. I do *not* propose that this is the right account of value structure and instead wish to remain agnostic about the question whether value aspects are part of possibly normative meaning, part of possibly normative pragmatic content, part of the justification, or sometimes one and sometimes the other depending on the context of use of the value predicate and for what it may act as a proxy.

Chapter 7 Parity

1. As Erik Carlson points out in private communication, this also follows from Chang's thesis that parity and equal goodness are incompatible with each other. If this assumption is true and in addition every item a is equally

good as itself aIa, then a cannot be on a par with itself because it is already equally good as itself. However, I will not adopt the incompatibility thesis in my own proposal in Chapter 9.

2. My favorite logical account for such cases is Non-Traditional Predication Theory (NTPT) that was developed by Russian logician Sinowjew (1970) and his German scholar Wessel (1989, 1998), cf. Sinowjew and Wessel (1975). In addition to the truth-functional negation, an inner negation is introduced and predication is given an epistemic interpretation. Two predication operations are defined, $a \leftarrow P$ is ascribing P to a ("die Eigenschaft P wird a zugeschrieben"), whereas $a \not\leftarrow P$ is denying P of a ("die Eigenschaft P wird a abgeschrieben"). The first case is then simply abbreviated as $P(a)$ and the second is written $\sim P(a)$, and likewise for relations. The second case acts like a predicate negation but conceptually differs from it in Wessel and Sinowjew's theory. If a vague predicate P is applied to an object a in this theory, this amounts to the statement $\neg P(a) \wedge \neg \sim P(a)$ coming out as true in the corresponding NTPT model, where $\sim$ symbolizes the inner negation. The corresponding first-order logic is bivalent because it only allows $\neg P(a) \wedge \neg \sim P(a)$ to be true whereas $P(a) \wedge \sim P(a)$ is contradictory in this system and $\sim P(a) \rightarrow \neg P(a)$ is a theorem. Wessel (1998) lays out soundness and completeness proofs. Technically, NTPT can also be expressed in a partial logic with a denotational semantics that gives each predicate and relation symbol an extension and an anti-extension, which links up well with 4-valued Belnap-style logics like the ones used by Muskens (1995). However, NTPT is conceptually intriguing precisely because it remains bivalent.

3. See Parfit (1984, p. 451), Griffin (1986, pp. 80–82), Qizilbash (2005, p. 415).

4. Cf. Vincke and Pirlot (1997, pp. 14–16).

5. Chang (2005) discusses other ways in which the intervals that interval orders can represent may be interpreted for modeling parity, but none of these are very promising. The following formalization is also discussed by Rabinowicz (2012, pp. 140–143).

6. Gert (2004) provides a way of associating intervals with items that unfortunately does not lead to the representation suggested here. However, there is no need to provide a translation from items to intervals. We may just as well *choose* a semiorder relation as the basis for Q (and L) and duly note that there are associated intervals, whether these have an intuitively compelling interpretation or not, as long as Q can faithfully represent the

properties attributed to parity and Q and L work convincingly together with the other value relations.

7. If this condition is relaxed, then as additional cases (i) $\max_a = \max_b$ and $\min_a > \min_b$, and (ii) $\max_a > \max_b$ and $\min_b = \min_a$, as well as the nested intervals, need to be considered in the following definition. These should be classified as parity.

8. See Rabinowicz (2010, p. 3) in reply to Gert (2004); cf. Chang (2005, pp. 338–341).

9. He uses "higher than" in order not to presume that degrees of favorings are "numeric" in the sense of cardinal rather than ordinal utility. Presumably, Rabinowicz (2012) uses "=" to denote identity.

10. See Rabinowicz (2012, pp. 156–158).

11. According to Erik Carlson in private communication.

12. This particular decision problem might also call for a lexicographic ranking: First avoid all vacuum cleaners that electrocute you. Then evaluate the remaining vacuum cleaners according to other criteria, maybe using an additive model. These types of models are discussed in Chapter 9.

Chapter 8 Spectrum Cases

1. Temkin in private communication.

2. See the quotation on page 40, Chapter 2.

3. See Handfield (2016).

4. See Rachels (2001, p. 216).

5. Cf. Klocksiem (2016, p. 1319).

6. The definition also works for ordinal utility functions, but, as we shall see, most of the counter-intuitive features of compensatory value aggregation occur when we are talking about quantifiable amounts or intensities of something that contributes value.

7. Saying that "there is an item" in this context just means that it is hypothetically possible, not that it needs to exist in the real world or is a realistic alternative in a decision situation. In the above definitions it is assumed that the domain of items is unrestricted and contains all possible items. In other words, we are *not* interested in cases when there happens not to be an item b' that outweighs a after aggregation by sheer coincidence, because it has not been included in the domain. The conditions are not on items but on aspects and their aggregation.

8. See Bouyssou (2009) for an overview, cf. the practical decision methods ELECTRE I-III described by Roy (1968), Roy and Bertier (1971), Rogers and Bruen (1998).
9. Levi (1986) makes a quite compelling case for using additional criteria to resolve ties.
10. Another, perhaps preferable alternative is to define morality very narrowly in a way that maximizes individual freedom. This might make it reasonable to give the satisfaction of deontic constraints higher value than any other value. Many views in normative ethics are incompatible with such a narrow conception of morality, though, and traded morality and existing social norms are not compatible with it anyway.

Chapter 9 A Theory of Betterness

1. Sometimes in the literature, Borda ranks are reversed, i.e., the best item gets rank 1 and the worst item gets rank n in a strict ordering of n items. The difference is insubstantial, as long as the formulas are adjusted, but for canonical utilities "the better, the higher the utility" is the natural definition.
2. Cf. Eisenführ et al. (2010, pp. 130–134), see also Keeney and Raiffa (1976, pp. 108–112).
3. See Section 2.1 of Chapter 2. I am assuming in the above example that all items are in the respective aspect domains, since otherwise we would get cases of genuine noncomparability.
4. A solution based on relevance has been proposed by Voorhoeve (2013) for some versions of Temkin's puzzles.

Chapter 10 Risk

1. Cf. Hansson (2013, pp. 7-11) who also discusses more colloquial uses of the word.
2. See Section 1.1 of Chapter 1.
3. See Wakker (2010, p. 147) on whose work many of the following points are based.
4. See Kahneman and Tversky (1979, pp. 280–284). Note that they use *another* function for transforming value. Their S-shaped value function

resides on a ratio scale and centers around an anchoring point. Whatever occurs below this point is considered a loss and whatever occurs above it is a gain. The S-shape of this function is a generalization of the Principle of Diminishing Marginal Utility to gains and losses. Differences between small losses are more important than differences between large losses, and, analogously, differences between small gains are more important than differences between large gains (ibid.: 278-280).

5. See Quiggin (1981), Quiggin (1982), who according to Wakker (2010, p. 153) noticed the problem in an article by Handa (1977), together with Fishburn (1978) and others.

6. See Wakker (2010, Ch. 5–6), cf. Wakker (1989).

7. Cf. pages 79–80.

8. Cf. Wakker (2010, p. 160).

9. See Section 3.4 of Chapter 3.

10. See Wakker (2010, pp. 172–181).

11. Of course, money is also a simplification. As I have argued above, monetary value does not work as a general substitute for any value in a noncompensatory account.

Index

Bibliography

Allen, J. F. (1983, November). Maintaining Knowledge about Temporal Intervals. *Communications of the ACM 26*(11), 832–843.

Armstrong, W. (1939). The determinateness of the utility function. *Economics Journal 49*, 453–467.

Arrow, K. J. (1951). *Social Choice and Individual Values.* New Haven, CT: Yale University Press.

Barbera, S. (1980). Pivotal voters: A new proof of Arrow's theorem. *Economics Letters 6*, 13–16.

Bentham, J. (1789). *An Introduction to the Principles of Morals and Legislation.* Oxford: Clarendon Press.

Bernoulli, D. (1738). Specimen theoriae novae de mensura sortis. *Commentarii Academiae Scientiarum Imperialis Petropolitanae, Tomus V V,* 175–192. English translation by L. Sommer published in *Econometrica,* Vol. 22, No. 1 (Jan., 1954), pp. 23–36.

Black, M. (1944). The "Paradox of Analysis." *Mind 53*(211), 263–267.

Bloomfield, L. (1933). *Language.* London: Allen and Unwin.

Bogart, K. P. (1973). Preference structures I: Distances between transitive preference relations. *Journal of Mathematical Sociology 3*(1), 49–67.

Bouyssou, D. (2009). Outranking methods. In C. A. Floudas and P. M. Pardalos (Eds.), *Encyclopedia of Optimization*, pp. 2887–2893. New York: Springer.

Brogaard, B. (2008). Moral contextualism and moral relativism. *The Philosophical Quarterly 58*(232), 385–409.

Brogaard, B. (2012). Moral relativism and moral expressivism. *The Southern Journal of Philosophy 50*(4), 538–556.

Brogan, A. P. (1919). The fundamental value universal. *Journal of Philosophy, Psychology and Scientific Methods 16*(4), 96–104.

Broome, J. (1999). *Ethics out of Economics.* Cambridge, UK: Cambridge University Press.

Broome, J. (2004). *Weighing Lives.* Oxford: Oxford University Press.

Carlson, E. (2010). Parity Demystified. *Theoria 76*, 119–128.

Carlson, E. (2018). Value theory (axiology). In S. O. Hansson and V. F. Hendricks (Eds.), *Introduction to Formal Philosophy*, pp. 523–534. Springer.

Chang, R. (2002, July). The possibility of parity. *Ethics 112*, 669–688.

Chang, R. (2005, January). Parity, Interval Value, and Choice. *Ethics 115*, 331–350.

Chang, R. (2012). Are Hard Choices Cases of Incomparability? *Philosophical Issues 22*(1), 106–126.

Chang, R. (2015). Value incomparability and incommensurability. In I. Hirose and J. Olson (Eds.), *The Oxford Handbook of Value Theory*, pp. 205–224. New York: Oxford University Press.

Chisholm, R. and E. Sosa (1966). On the logic of "intrinsically better." *American Philosophical Quarterly 3*(3), 244–249.

Choquet, G. (1954). Theory of capacities. In *Annals of Institute Fourier, Grenoble*, Volume 5, pp. 131–295. Nundam.

Church, A. (1946, December). Review of "A note on the 'paradox of analysis,'" Morton G. White; "The 'paradox of analysis' again: a reply," Max Black; "Analysis and identity: a rejoinder," Morton G. White; "How can analysis be informative?," Max Black. *The Journal of Symbolic Logic 11*(4), 132–133.

Crisp, R. (1997). *Mill on Utilitarianism*. Routledge.

Critchlow, D. E. (1985). *Metric Methods for Analyzing Partially Ranked Data*. Heidelberg / Berlin: Springer.

Dardanoni, V. (2001). A pedagogical proof of Arrow's impossibility theorem. *Social Choice and Welfare 18*, 107–112.

Davidson, D., J. C. C. McKinsey, and P. Suppes (1955). Outlines of a formal theory of value, I. *Philosophy of Science XXII* (2 [April 1955]), 140–160.

de Finetti, B. (1931). Sul significato soggestivo della probabilità. *Fundamenta Mathematicae XVII*, 298–329.

de Finetti, B. (1937). La prévision: ses lois logiques, ses sources subjectives. *Annales de l'Institut Henri Poincaré 7*, 1–68.

Debreu, G. (1954). Representation of preference ordering by a numerical function. In R. Thrall, C. Coombs, and R. Davies (Eds.), *Decision Processes*, pp. 159–175. New York: Wiley.

Dempster, A. P. (1968). A generalization of Bayesian inference. *Journal of the Royal Statistical Society. Series B (Methodological) 30*, 205–247.

Deza, M. M. and E. Deza (2009). *Encyclopedia of Distances*. Berlin / Heidelberg: Springer.

Diaconis, P. and R. L. Graham (1977). Spearman's footrule as a measure of disarray. *Journal of the Royal Statistical Society. Series B (Methodological) 39*(2), 262–268.

Dubois, D., J.-L. Marichal, H. Prade, M. Roubens, and R. Sabbadin (2001, October). The use of the discrete Sugeno integral in decision-making: A survey. *International Journal of Uncertainty, Fuzziness and Knowledge-Based Systems 9*(5), 539–561. Cit. in online version from 2020-1-24, DOI: 10.1142/S0218488501001058.

Dubois, D. and H. Prade (1988). *Possibility Theory*. New York: Springer.

Dubois, D. and H. Prade (2009). Possibility theory. In R. A. Meyers (Ed.), *Computational Complexity: Theory, Techniques, and Applications*, pp. 2240–2252. Springer.

Dung, P. M. (1995, September). On the acceptability of arguments and its fundamental role in nonmonotonic reasoning, logic programming and n-person games. *Artificial Intelligence 77*(2), 321–357.

Eisenführ, F., M. Weber, and T. Langer (2010). *Rational Decision Making*. Springer.

Feldman, F. (2005). The open question argument: What it isn't; and what it is. *Philosophical Issues 15*, 22–43.

Fey, M. (2014). A straightforward proof of Arrow's theorem. *Economics Bulletin 34*(3), 1792–1797.

Fishburn, P. C. (1967). Interdependence and additivity in multivariate, unidimensional expected utility theory. *International Economic Review 8*, 335–342.

Fishburn, P. C. (1970a). Intransitive indifference in preference theory: A survey. *Operations Research 18*(2), 207–228.

Fishburn, P. C. (1970b). *Utility Theory for Decision Making*. New York, London, Sydney, Toronto: John Wiley and Sons.

Fishburn, P. C. (1978). On Handa's "New Theory of Cardinal Utility" and the maximization of expected returns. *Journal of Political Economy 86*, 321–324.

Fishburn, P. C. (1985). *Interval Orders and Interval Graphs*. New York: Wiley.

Fishburn, P. C. and P. P. Wakker (1995). The invention of the independence condition for preferences. *Management Science 41*(7), 1130–1144.

Frege, G. (1892). Über Sinn und Bedeutung. *Zeitschrift für Philosophie und philosophische Kritik 100*, 25–50.

Geach, P. (1956). Good and evil. *Analysis 17*(2), 33–42.

Geanakoplos, J. (2005). Three brief proofs of Arrow's Impossibility Theorem. Cowles foundation paper no. 1116, Cowles Foundation, New Haven, CT.

Georgescu-Roegen, N. (1936). The pure theory of consumers' behavior. *Quarterly Journal of Economics 50*, 545–593.

Gert, J. (2004, April). Value and parity. *Ethics 114*, 492–510.

Gibbard, A. (1973). Manipulation of voting schemes: a general result. *Econometrica 41*(4), 587–601.

Gibbard, A. (1990). *Wise Choices, Apt Feelings: A Theory of Normative Judgment.* Oxford: Oxford University Press.

Gilboa, I. (2009). *Theory of Decision under Uncertainty.* New York: Cambridge University Press.

Gossen, H. H. (1854). *Entwickelung der Gesetze des menschlichen Verkehrs und der daraus fließenden Regeln für menschliches Handeln.* Braunschweig: Vieweg.

Grabisch, M. (1996). The application of fuzzy integrals in multicriteria decision making. *European Journal of Operational Research 89*, 445–456.

Grabisch, M. and C. Labreuche (2018). Using multiple reference levels in multi-criteria decision aid: The generalized-additive independence model and the Choquet integral approaches. *European Journal of Operational Research 267*(2), 598–611.

Grabisch, M. and M. Roubens (2000). Application of the Choquet integral in multicriteria decision making. In *Fuzzy Measures and Integrals*, pp. 348–374. Physica Verlag.

Griffin, J. (1986). *Well-Being: Its Meaning, Measurement and Moral Importance.* Oxford: Clarendon Press.

Hajek, A. (2009). Dutch book arguments. In P. Anand, P. K. Pattanaik, and C. Puppe (Eds.), *The Handbook of Rational and Social Choice*, pp. 173–195. Oxford University Press.

Halpern, J. Y. (2003). *Reasoning About Uncertainty.* MIT Press.

Hammond, P. J. (1998). Objective expected utility. In S. Barbera, P. J. Hammond, and C. Seidl (Eds.), *Handbook of Utility Theory, Vol. 1*, pp. 143–211. Dordrecht / Boston / London: Kluwer.

Handa, J. (1977). Risk, probabilities, and a new theory of cardinal utility. *Journal of Political Economy 85*, 97–122.

Handfield, T. (2016). Essentially comparative value does not threaten transitivity. *Thought 5*(1), 3–12.

Hansson, S. O. (1990). Defining "good" and "bad" in terms of "better than." *Notre Dame Journal of Formal Logic 31*(1), 136–149.

Hansson, S. O. (2001). *The Structure of Values and Norms.* Cambridge, UK: Cambridge University Press.

Hansson, S. O. (2013). *The Ethics of Risk: Ethical Analysis in an Uncertain World.* Basingstoke: Palgrave Macmillan.

Hansson, S. O. (2018a). Formal investigations of value. In S. O. Hansson and V. F. Hendricks (Eds.), *Introduction to Formal Philosophy*, pp. 499–534. Cham, Switzerland: Springer.

Hansson, S. O. (2018b). Money-pumps. In S. O. Hansson and V. F. Hendricks (Eds.), *Introduction to Formal Philosophy*, pp. 567–576. Cham, Switzerland: Springer.

Hare, R. (1952). *The Language of Morals.* Oxford University Press.

Harman, G. (1975). Moral relativism defended. *Philosophical Review 84*, 3–23.

Harman, G. (1996). Moral relativism. In G. Harman and J. Thomson (Eds.), *Moral Relativism and Moral Objectivity*, pp. 3–64. Cambridge, MA: Blackwell Publishers.

Harsanyi, J. C. (1977). *Rational Behavior and Bargaining Equilibrium in Games and Social Situations.* New York: Cambridge University Press.

Horty, J. F. (2012). *Reasons as Defaults.* Oxford / New York: Cambridge University Press.

Jacquet-Lagrèze, E. (1975). How we can use the notion of semiorders to build outranking relations in multi-criteria decision making. In D. Wendt and C. Vlek (Eds.), *Utility, Probability, and Human Decision Making*, pp. 87–112. D. Reidel.

Jacquette, D. (1990). A Fregean solution to the paradox of analysis. *Grazer Philosophische Studien 37*, 59–73.

Jeffrey, R. (1965). *The Logic of Decision.* McGraw-Hill.

Joyce, J. M. (2008). *The Foundations of Causal Decision Theory.* New York: Cambridge University Press.

Jøsang, A. (2016). *Subjective Logic: A Formalism for Reasoning Under Uncertainty.* Cham, Switzerland: Springer.

Kahneman, D. and A. Tversky (1979). Prospect theory: An analysis of decision under risk. *Econometrica 47*, 263–291.

Kahneman, D. and A. Tversky (1992). Advances in prospect theory: Cumulative representation of uncertainty. *Journal of Risk and Uncertainty 5*(4), 297–323.

Keeney, R. L. (1974, February). Multiplicative utility functions. *Operations Research 22*(1), 22–34.

Keeney, R. L. (1996). *Value-Focused Thinking.* Cambridge, MA: Harvard University Press.

Keeney, R. L. and H. Raiffa (1976). *Decisions with Multiple Objectives: Preferences and Value Tradeoffs.* New York: John Wiley & Sons.

Keeney, R. L. and H. Raiffa (1993). *Decisions with Multiple Objectives: Preferences and Value Tradeoffs.* Cambridge / New York: Cambridge University Press. First. publ. 1976 by Wiley & Sons, Inc.

Kemeny, J. (1959). Mathematics without Numbers. *Daedalus 88*(4), 577–591.

Kemeny, J. and J. L. Snell (1972). *Mathematical Models in the Social Sciences.* MIT Press.

Kendall, M. G. (1938). A new measure of rank correlation. *Biometrika 30*(1-2), 81–93.

Kennedy, C. and L. McNally (2005). Scale structure, degree modification, and the semantics of scalable predicates. *Language 81*(2), 345–381.

Klocksiem, J. (2016). How to accept the transitivity of better than. *Philosophical Studies 173*, 1309–1334.

Krantz, D. H., R. D. Luce, P. Suppes, and A. Tversky (1971, 1989, 1990). *Foundations of Measurement, Volumes I–III.* New York: Academic Press.

Langford, C. H. (1968). Moore's notion of analysis. In P. A. Schilpp (Ed.), *The Philosophy of G. E. Moore.* La Salle, IL: Open Court.

Langford, C. H. and P. A. Schilpp (1943). The notion of analysis in Moore's philosophy. *Journal of Symbolic Logic 8*(4), 149–151.

Lassiter, D. (2017). *Graded Modality : Qualitative and Quantitative Perspectives.* Oxford: Oxford University Press.

Levi, I. (1986). *Hard Choices.* Cambridge / New York: Cambridge University Press.

Luce, D. R. (1956). Semiorders and a theory of utility discrimination. *Econometrica 24*(2), 178–191.

Mackie, J. L. (1977). *Ethics: Inventing Right and Wrong.* London: Penguin.

Marshall, A. (1890). *Principles of Economics.* London: Macmillan & Co.

McDowell, J. (1985). Values and secondary qualities. In T. Honderich (Ed.), *Morality and Objectivity*, pp. 110–129. London: Routledge.

Mehta, G. B. (1998). Preference and utility. In S. Barbera, P. J. Hammond, and C. Seidl (Eds.), *Handbook of Utility Theory, Volume 1: Principles*, Volume 1, pp. 1–47. Boston: Kluwer.

Mill, J. S. (1906). *Utilitarianism.* Chicago, IL: University of Chicago Press.

Moore, G. E. (1903). *Principia Ethica.* Cambridge: Cambridge University Press.

Moore, G. E. (1922). *Principia Ethica* (2nd [reprinted] ed.). Cambridge: Cambridge University Press.

Moore, G. E. (1942). *A Reply to My Critics*, pp. 533–677. Evanston and Chicago: Open Court.

Moschovakis, Y. N. (1994). Sense and denotation as algorithm and value. In J. Väänänen and J. Oikkonen (Eds.), *Logic Colloquium '90*, Volume 2, pp. 210–249. Association for Symbolic Logic.

Moschovakis, Y. N. (2006). A logical calculus of meaning and synonymy. *Linguistics and Philosophy 29*(1), 27–89.

Moulin, H. (1988). *Axioms of Cooperative Decision Making*. New York: Cambridge University Press.

Muskens, R. (1995). *Meaning and Partiality.* Stanford: CSLI Publications.

Nebel, J. M. (2017). The good, the bad, and the transitivity of better than. *Nous 52*(4), 874–899.

Orsi, F. (2015). *Value Theory.* London: Bloomsbury.

Pareto, V. (1900). Sunto di alcuni capitoli di un nuovo trattato di economia pura. *Giornale degli Economisti 10*(20), 216–35; 511–49.

Pareto, V. (1906). *Manuale di Economia Politica.* Milan: Societa Editrice Libraria.

Parfit, D. (1984). *Reasons and Persons.* Oxford UP.

Pollak, R. A. (1967). Additive von Neumann-Morgenstern utility functions. *Econometrica 35*, 485–495.

Qizilbash, M. (2005). The mere addition paradox, parity and critical-level utilitarianism. *Social Choice and Welfare 24*(3), 413–431.

Quiggin, J. (1981). Risk perception and the analysis of risk attitudes. *Australian Journal of Agricultural Economics 25*(2), 160–169.

Quiggin, J. (1982). A theory of anticipated utility. *Journal of Economic Behavior and Organization 3*, 323–343.

Quine, W. V. O. (1951, January). Two dogmas of empiricism. *The Philosophical Review 60*(1), 20–43.

Rabinowicz, W. (2008). Value Relations. *Theoria 74*, 18–49.

Rabinowicz, W. (2010). Value relations: Old wine in new barrels. In A. Reboul (Ed.), *Philosophical papers dedicated to Kevin Mulligan.* Genève: Université de Genève.

Rabinowicz, W. (2012, July). Value Relations Revisited. *Economics and Philosophy 28*(2), 133–164.

Rachels, S. (1998). Counterexamples to the transitivity of better than. *Australasian Journal of Philosophy 76*(1), 71–83.

Rachels, S. (2001). A set of solutions to Parfit's problems. *Nous 35*(2), 214–238.

Ramsey, F. P. (1931). Truth and probability. In *The Foundations of Mathematics and Other Logical Essays*, pp. 156–198. London: Kegan, Paul, Trench, Trubner & Co. Written 1926, cit. in 1999 electronic edition.

Rast, E. (2020a). The multidimensional structure of "better than." *Axiomathes*, 1–29. Publ. online first, https://doi.org/10.1007/s10516-020-09525-4.

Rast, E. (2020b). The theory theory of metalinguistic disputes. *Mind & Language*, 1–19. Publ. online first, https://doi.org/10.1111/mila.12355.

Raz, J. (1986). *The Morality of Freedom.* Oxford: Clarendon Press.

Recanati, F. (2004). Deixis and Anaphora. In Z. G. Szabó (Ed.), *Semantics vs. Pragmatics.* Oxford: Oxford University Press.

Recanati, F. (2010). *Truth-Conditional Pragmatics.* Oxford: Oxford UP.

Roberts, F. S. (1979). *Measurement Theory.* Reading, MA: Addison-Wesley.

Rogers, M. and M. Bruen (1998). A new system for weighting environmental criteria for use within electre iii. *European Journal of Operations Research 107*(3), 552–563.

Rosch, E. (1975). Cognitive representations of semantic categories. *Journal of Experimental Psychology: General 104*(3), 192–233.

Rosch, E. (1983). Prototype classification and logical classification: The two systems. In E. Scholnick (Ed.), *New Trends in Conceptual Representation: Challenges to Piaget's Theory?*, pp. 73–86. Hillsdale: Lawrence Erlbaum Associates.

Roubens, M. and P. Vincke (1985). *Preference Modelling.* Heidelberg / New York / Tokyo: Springer Verlag.

Roy, B. (1968). Classement et choix en presence de points de vue multiples (la methode Electre). *Revue Francaise d'Informatique et de Recherche Operationnelle 8*, 57–75.

Roy, B. and B. Bertier (1971, April). La méthode electre ii: Use méthode de classement en présence de critères multiples.

Samuelson, P. A. (1938). A note on the pure theory of consumers' behaviour. *Economica 5*(17), 61–71.

Samuelson, P. A. (1947). *Foundations of Economic Analysis.* Cambridge, MA: Harvard University Press.

Sartre, J.-P. (1946). *L'existentialisme est un humanisme.* Paris: Éditions Nagel.

Satterthwaite, M. A. (1975, April). Strategy-proofness and Arrow's conditions: Existence and correspondence theorems for voting procedures and social welfare functions. *Journal of Economic Theory 10*, 187–217.

Savage, L. J. (1951). The theory of statistical decision. *Journal of the American Statistical Association 46*, 55–67.

Savage, L. J. (1954). *The Foundations of Statistics.* New York: Wiley.

Scanlon, T. M. (1998). *What We Owe to Each Other.* Harvard, MA: Belknap Press of Harvard University Press.

Schick, F. (1986). Dutch bookies and money pumps. *Journal of Philosophy 83*(2), 112–119.

Schmeidler, D. (1986). Integral representation without additivity. *Proceedings of the American Mathematical Society 97*(2), 255–261.

Schmeidler, D. (1989). Subjective probability and expected utility without additivity. *Econometrica 57*, 571–587.

Schumm, G. F. (1987). Transitivity, preference and indifference. *Philosophical Studies 52*, 435–437.

Scott, D. and P. Suppes (1958). Foundational aspects of theories of measurement. *The Journal of Symbolic Logic 23*(2), 113–128.

Semendyayev, K. A., G. Musiol, H. Muehlig, and I. N. Bronshtein (2004). *Handbook of Mathematics* (Fourth English Edition ed.). Berlin / Heidelberg / New York: Springer.

Shafer, G. (1972). *A Mathematical Theory of Evidence.* Princeton, NJ: Princeton University Press.

Simon, H. A. (1956). Rational choice and the structure of the environment. *Psychological Review 62*(2), 129–138.

Sinowjew, A. A. (1970). *Komplexe Logik.* Berlin / Braunschweig / Berlin: VEB Deutscher Verlag der Wissenschaften / Vieweg Verlag / C. F. Winter'sche Verlagshandlung Berlin.

Sinowjew, A. A. and H. Wessel (1975). *Logische Sprachregeln.* Berlin, Braunschweig, Basel: Deutscher Verlag der Wissenschaften.

Smith, B. C. (2007). The objectivity of taste and tasting. In B. C. Smith (Ed.), *Questions of Taste: The Philosophy of Wine*, pp. 41–77. Oxford University Press.

Spohn, W. (1988). Ordinal conditional functions. In W. L. Harper and B. Skyrms (Eds.), *Causation in Decision, Belief Change, and Statistics,* Volume II, pp. 105–134. D. Reidel Publishing Co.

Stevens, S. S. (1946). On the theory of scales of measurement. *Science 103*(2684), 677–680.

Stigler, G. J. and G. S. Becker (1977, March). De gustibus non est disputandum. *The American Economic Review 67*(2), 76–90.

Stojanovic, I. (2015). Evaluative adjectives and evaluative uses of ordinary adjectives. In D. Bekki and E. McCready (Eds.), *Proceedings of LENLS12: Language Engineering and Natural Language Semantics*. The Japan Society for Artificial Intelligence.

Sugeno, M. (1974). *Theory of Fuzzy Integrals and Its Applications*. PhD thesis, Tokyo Institute of Technology, Tokyo.

Sugeno, M. (1977). Fuzzy measures and fuzzy integrals: A survey. In *Fuzzy Automata and Decision Process*. New York: North Holland.

Temkin, L. S. (1987). Intransitivity and the mere addition paradox. *Philosophy & Public Affairs 16*(2), 138–187.

Temkin, L. S. (2012). *Rethinking the Good: Moral Ideals and the Nature of Practical Reasoning*. New York: Oxford University Press.

Tversky, A. (1969, Jan). Intransitivity of preferences. *Psychological Review 76*(1), 31–48.

van Benthem, J. (1991). *The Logic of Time*. Kluwer. (2nd ed.; first ed. publ. 1983).

van Dalen, D. (1974). Variants of Rescher's semantics for preference logic and some completeness theorems. *Studia Logica 33*(2), 163–181.

Vincke, P. and M. Pirlot (1997). *Semiorders: Properties, Representations, Applications*. Dordrecht: Springer.

von Neumann, J. and O. Morgenstern (1944). *Theory of Games and Economic Behavior* (Second Edition ed.). Princeton, NJ: Princeton University Press.

von Wright, G. H. (1963). *The Varieties of Goodness*. London: Routledge & K. Paul.

Voorhoeve, A. (2013). Vaulting intuitions: Temkin's critique of transitivity. *Economics and Philosophy 29*(3), 409–423.

Väyrynen, P. (2013). *The Lewd, the Rude and the Nasty: A Study of Thick Concepts in Ethics*. New York: Oxford University Press.

Wakker, P. P. (1989). *Transforming Probabilities without Violating Stochastic Dominance*, pp. 29–47. Berlin: Springer.

Wakker, P. P. (2010). *Prospect Theory for Risk and Ambiguity.* Cambridge / New York: Cambridge University Press.

Wakker, P. P., V. Köbberling, and C. Schwieren (2007, Nov). Prospect-theory's Diminishing Sensitivity Versus Economics' Intrinsic Utility of Money: How the Introduction of the Euro can be Used to Disentangle the Two Empirically. *Theory and Decision 63*(3), 205–231.

Wessel, H. (1989). *Logik.* Berlin: Logos Verlag.

Wessel, H. (1998). *Logik.* Berlin: Logos Verlag.

Williamson, T. (1994). *Vagueness.* London: Routledge.

Wong, D. B. (1984). *Moral Relativity.* Berkeley: University of California Press.

Wong, D. B. (2006). *Natural Moralities: A Defense of Pluralistic Relativism.* New York: Oxford University Press.

Wong, D. B. (2011). Relativist explanations of interpersonal and group disagreement. In S. D. Hales (Ed.), *A Companion to Relativism*, pp. 411–430. Blackwell Publishing.

About the Author

Erich H. Rast, PhD, is a senior researcher at Nova Institute of Philosophy of the Universidade Nova de Lisboa in Lisbon, Portugal. He has contributed to research projects on contextualism and the pragmatics and semantics of evaluative language and as the P.I. of a national research project on values in argumentative discourse funded by the Portuguese Foundation for Science and Technology. His current research focuses on the (meta-)semantics and pragmatics of evaluative terms such as "good," on theories of value structure and their relation to decision-making, and on the nature of value-based disagreement.

Rast has also published on indexicality, linguistic context-dependence, type-driven semantics for quantifier domain restriction, abductive reasoning in higher-order logics, concept theory, philosophical and formal aspects of value disagreement, and other topics in metaethics, philosophical aspects of de se attitudes, and the role of computationalism in the philosophy of mind.

www.ingramcontent.com/pod-product-compliance
Ingram Content Group UK Ltd.
Pitfield, Milton Keynes, MK11 3LW, UK
UKHW040618091026
476324UK00010B/180

9 781793 616944